RAP AND RELIGION

RAP AND RELIGION

Understanding the Gangsta's God

Ebony A. Utley

 PRAEGER

AN IMPRINT OF ABC-CLIO, LLC
Santa Barbara, California • Denver, Colorado • Oxford, England

Library of Congress Cataloging-in-Publication Data

Utley, Ebony A.
    Rap and religion : understanding the gangsta's god / Ebony A. Utley.
        p. cm.
    Includes bibliographical references and index.
    ISBN 978-0-313-37668-9 (pbk. : alk. paper) — ISBN 978-0-313-37669-6 (ebook)
1. Rap (Music)—Religious aspects. I. Title.
ML3921.8.R63U75   2012
782.421649—dc23   2012005635

ISBN: 978-0-313-37668-9
EISBN: 978-0-313-37669-6

16 15 14 13 12   2 3 4 5

This book is also available on the World Wide Web as an eBook.
Visit www.abc-clio.com for details.

Praeger
An Imprint of ABC-CLIO, LLC

ABC-CLIO, LLC
130 Cremona Drive, P.O. Box 1911
Santa Barbara, California 93116-1911

This book is printed on acid-free paper ∞

Manufactured in the United States of America

Copyright Acknowledgment

Earlier versions of excerpts from chapter 2, "Doin' It for Daddy" originally appeared in Utley, Ebony A. " 'I Used to Love Him': Exploring the Miseducation about Black Love and Sex." *Critical Studies in Media Communication* 27, no. 3 (2010): 291–308. Copyright Taylor and Francis.

If there is a God, does such an entity reach out to us like the hand that Michelangelo painted on the ceiling of the Sistine Chapel? Or is it the other way around: Does our mind reach out to embrace a God that may or may not be real?

—Andrew Newberg, MD, and Mark Robert Waldman,
How God Changes Your Brain

Contents

Preface

When I was a teenager, I didn't listen to rap on Sunday. Perhaps I felt guilty because, as my mother suggested when I was 15, I hadn't memorized as many verses from the National Baptist Hymnal as I had rap lyrics. Or perhaps the guilt came from my pastor's testimony that when he got saved he discarded all of his secular music, and I still had mine. Either way I was committed to my no secular music on Sunday concession until I heard Snoop Dogg blaring from a car radio in the church parking lot after an 11 a.m. worship service. Hearing his lyrics at church shocked me, but I was secretly excited by my Sunday school peers' blatant resistance to the religious rules.

Experiences like this caused me to reevaluate my understanding of rap music. As diligently as I had tried to separate them, a lifetime of membership in a conservative black church coupled with a lifetime of listening to rap made constant connections in my mind. Although rap emerged from an "unchurched" generation in the mid-1970s, memorizing its lyrics served the same purpose as memorizing the hymnal; both were salves for hard times. I was just as easily comforted by Thomas A. Dorsey's "Precious Lord" as Tupac Shakur's "Keep Ya Head Up." The church and hip hop share a great potential for creating safe spaces where oppressed people can express themselves as well as receive comfort and hope in the face of harsh realities. Of course, I describe an ideal world. Patriarchy and heterosexism compromise the empowering potential of churches and hip hop. Women and members of the gay and transgender community have never been entirely safe in either space. As a progressive-minded woman, there are (hetero)sexist rap lyrics and patriarchal religious practices that infuriate me, but the resistive synthesis of rap and religion also inspires me.

In fact, the more I listen to rap (especially on Sundays), the more aware I become of rap's plethora of religious tropes, the prominence of God, and the ways rappers live religion by incorporating traditional religious practices into hip hop's contradictory conceptual spaces. I am fascinated by

Tupac's crucifixion on the cover of the *The Don Kiluminati*, intrigued by the similarities between Lauryn Hill's description of her lover and her God, encouraged by Jesus walking through the hood with Kanye West, and emboldened by Five Percent Nation claims that the black man is God. Experiencing rap and religion in action inspires me to break even more rules. I am the unlikeliest hip hop head—a black woman reared in a fundamentalist Baptist household on the border of an Indianapolis ghetto. But I first heard the call of the gangsta's God when Snoop Dog blasted from a car radio in that Sunday-service parking lot.

Acknowledgments

I used to read acknowledgments and think, "how many people does it really take to write a book?" Now I know. First, I would like to thank Michael Eric Dyson and Anthony B. Pinn. Even though they have never met me, my work would not be possible without their initial groundbreaking publications on rap and religion. Thanks to my Praeger editor James Sherman for supporting this project, my personal editor Janelle Brunner for catching my random tense shifts, and my cover artist Brian Gallagher for his visual representations of the gangsta's God.

To my assistant Carrie Patterson: Thank you for showing up to my office on time once a week for an entire year. Thank you for brainstorming with me, for responding to the random texts, e-mails, and phone calls, for collecting books from the library and downloading articles in PDF, for creating so many spreadsheets that I've lost count, and for spending long nights with my *Chicago Manual of Style* and not cracking its spine. Thank you for reminding me of deadlines, passwords, and all of those other details that can escape an absent-minded professor. This book would not have been possible with you.

To Marcia Dawkins: Thank you for reading, commenting, rereading, and commenting again on each draft of this manuscript. No one else but the two of us knows what the earliest stages of this book looked like. I am also grateful that you can keep a secret. Thank you for always being down to discuss a new idea and push me in the directions I needed to go. I would never have had the motivation to keep writing without you.

To my hip hop criticism and pop culture students from Northwestern, Marquette, and Long Beach State: This book is for you. Thank you for the great in-class conversations, interesting final papers, and hilarious presentations. Thank you for hipping me to new music, voting on cover art, participating in my survey, and just generally being receptive to seeing the world in new ways. Special thanks go out to my former student assistants: Jocelyn Arana, Kimberly Batino, Sacha Braddock, Keovmorkodh Chhuon,

Hailey Eklund, Christianna Frederick, Caesar Guyot, Shawntelle Latini, Christopher Moore, Lisette Neira, Robert Nelson, Gina Robinson, Lauren Todoroff, Lauren Walton, Elizabeth Wagner, Louis Williams, Carina Windom, Russell Wood, and Robin Yancey.

To the hip hop heads in my life: Thank you for filling in the gaps in my playlists. Reynaldo Anderson, Marcus Armstrong, Tom Atchinson, Adam Bradley, Pirate Lee Bray, James Britt, Leslie Frank Cedeno (aka Emcee Bodega Man), M. G. Hardie, Daniel White Hodge, Laura Garris, Travis Gosa, Andre Johnson, Marion Kendrick, Herbert Kimble, Joel Martinez, Miracle LeRoy, Stevie McBride, Kristi McLaughlin, Monika Alston-Miller, Monica Miller, Mark Anthony Neal, Christopher Peterson, Josef Sorett, Brian Taylor, Nikki Valdez, and Oliver Wang.

Special thanks to my emotional and intellectual support system: Jessica Abrams, Rodney Arnett, Johnel Barron, Christopher "Eclipse" Brown, Emily Corrigan, Lisa Corrigan, Jacquelyn Courtrell-Washington, Bernard Chris Dorsey, Brandon Gamble, Joshua Gunn, Rachel Hastings, Amy Heyse, Travis Lee, Nneka "Ify" Ofuele, Jennifer Reed, Marc Rich, Andrew "Dru" Ryan, Rod Shapiro, Shira Tarrant, Tiffini Travis, Anthony Utley, Chery Utley, O'Shea Utley, Ken Walden, and Khonsura Wilson. Now I finally have something other than the book to talk about.

Last but not least, I'd like to thank Paula Shin and her family—Chuck, Syrah, Charley, and Owen. The five of you are my life/work balance. Paula, thank you for always being available for lunch on what should have been a writing day. Thank you for listening to me complain about various aspects of this process and patiently asking what I was going to do even when you knew the answer. Owen, thank you for being a beautiful baby distraction. Charley, your energy always keeps me on my toes. Syrah, thank you for being my sidekick at all kinds of hip hop events and thanks for that long night of reviewing liner notes. Chuck, thank you for fixing stuff, feeding me, and letting me borrow various members of your family when I needed them.

Finally, to my readers: thank you for your interest in rap and religion.

Introduction

Understanding the Gangsta's God

Hip hop is a form of expression and a response to oppression. Originating in the mid-1970s in the South Bronx with four core elements—MCing, DJing, breaking (dancing), and writing (graffiti)—hip hop has become an integral part of American culture. Despite variations inspired by genre, geography, class status, and gender, at its core, hip hop's elements were a groundswell of creativity where individuals could have a good time, express themselves, find an accepting community, battle their opponents through dance, rhyme, or art, and make some legal money.

The terms *hip hop* and *rap* are not synonymous. Rap is merely one aspect of hip hop. Rhythmic speaking over a beat emerged from the legacy of the MC and became the most portable and the most profitable of the four elements. Many audiences have mixed feelings about rap's crazy admixtures of pleasure and power, pornography and profound public commentary, profanation and numinous obeisance, but rap music's cultural and economic viability has not diminished since the release of its first profitable single, "Rapper's Delight," in 1979. Intervening in the public domain as a sometimes fun-loving and other times angry voice, rap music pushed the boundaries of decorum with its unyieldingly aggressive yet honest in-your-ear depictions of urban American life and urban Americans' desires.

Rap music is indivisible from the distorted, tumultuous, and predominantly African American and Latino environment from which it hails. Specific changes in the urban landscape like urban renewal programs, draconian federal policies, deindustrialization, an expanding prison-industrial complex, and increasing unemployment adversely affected and simultaneously inspired the minority populations that created hip hop culture. For example, urban renewal and highway improvement projects ploughed through working-class neighborhoods and relocated massive numbers of disadvantaged people into public housing projects. The dispossessed were piled on top of each other in what eventually became unkempt, poorly maintained, deteriorating roach-and rodent-infested buildings.

Reaganomics of the 1980s, as described by sociologist William Julius Wilson, further restructured the urban landscape. "The Reagan and [George H. W.] Bush administrations—proponents of the New Federalism—sharply cut spending on direct aid to cities, including general revenue sharing, urban mass transit, public service jobs and job training, compensatory education, social service block grants, local public works, economic development assistance, and urban development action grants."[1] With city pockets emptied, there was no additional federal aid to ameliorate inferior public education, drug, HIV/AIDS, and homelessness problems.

As if these disadvantages were not enough, American industry became globally and technologically driven in the late 1970s and 1980s. Unskilled and semiskilled manufacturers lost their jobs and found themselves unqualified for the new service and technology sector positions. Those who procured employment often lacked job security and benefits while new welfare reform policies neglected to pick up the slack. Rising tuition costs and affronts to affirmative action compromised many people's opportunities to matriculate or return to college. Meanwhile, cheap foreign labor increased competition for remaining jobs.

Because of these social shifts, many impoverished, undereducated, and unemployed youth joined gangs. Individual reasons for gang affiliation vary, but the undisputable result of increased gang formation was severe police repression. Besides a heightened presence in urban neighborhoods, illegal searches, and subduing strategies that advocated beating or shooting first and asking questions later, police departments also increased their technopolicing in the form of massive databases with the names and addresses of "gang members" and electronic surveillance that included aerial helicopters.

The aforementioned conditions resulted in feelings of racial discrimination, victimization, alienation, and eventually the perception that participation in the drug economy was the most viable option for economic mobility. After crack arrived in major cities like New York, Los Angeles, and Miami in 1984–85, individuals addicted to crack and individuals addicted to the money and respect that came with being a prominent player in the crack game exacerbated the already dire situation in urban communities. Families were torn apart. Too many users, dealers, and innocent bystanders were murdered when people gave up opportunities in higher education for the seemingly lucrative appeal of drug distribution.

Increased crack circulation combined with sentence disparities for crack versus cocaine drastically increased the numbers of imprisoned African Americans. By the end of 2007, "more African Americans [were] under correctional control—in prison or jail, on probation or parole—than were enslaved in 1850, a decade before the Civil War began."[2] Three strikes laws that imposed mandatory extended sentences for convicted felons made it increasingly difficult for individuals to exit the revolving door of probation, parole, and prison. Some argue that the disproportionate imprisonment of African Americans within the extremely punitive and increasingly privatized prison-industrial complex has replaced slavery as an institutionalized form of oppression. Urban problems persisted through the 2000s when the percentage of African Americans seeking employment rose as high as 16 percent. By some estimates, the number of unemployed black teenagers no longer looking for work in 2010 was as high as 70 to 80 percent.[3]

These oppressive social conditions took their toll on heterosexual partnerships, which increasingly became relationships of resentment or exchange. Women resented men who were unable to improve their social status or living conditions. Men directed their feelings of powerlessness toward "bitches and hoes," women they considered a stumbling block toward their opportunities for success. Resentment relationships became relationships of exchange when men and women gave up on loving one another and traded money and/or sex to enhance their status. For example, when the money runs out, the gold digger divests herself. When the man no longer desires the gold digger, he cuts off his financial support. As they vie for power, each partner is expendable. Such bartering prohibited the development of sustainable loving relationships.

Not only heterosexual partnerships, but all relationships had the potential to be compromised by these performances of power. In the absence of other forms of social capital, urban youth prioritized respect "loosely defined as being treated 'right' or being granted . . . the deference one deserves."[4] Respect became so essential to many individuals' self-esteem that they imagined themselves as powerful mafia gangsters, drug dealers, and gang members. Although some hip hop gangstas were former drug dealers and others have been affiliated with gangs, a gangsta is primarily a form of posturing. N.W.A. (Niggaz With Attitude) popularized the term with "Gangsta, Gangsta" (1988), a rap single where Ice Cube and Eazy E brag about their physical and sexual prowess. Soon after the song's release, "gangsta rap" became the commercial descriptor for a genre of rap music that profited from its immodestly vulgar and violent braggadocio. Despite claims of reality, the gangsta is not a real person. Instead, the gangsta is an extremely irreverent embodiment of the distorted and tumultuous environment from which it came.

Even removed from its origins, the gangsta is an enduring identity that allows youth to imagine themselves as authoritative figures. Although the gangsta is not real, gangsta images that are marketed as real empower rappers whose aggressive posturing earns not only money but also respect. The gangsta, for the purposes of this study, is any rapper who portrays him or herself to be an impenetrable force of nature—unstoppable and unafraid—in an urban landscape that is wildly out of control. Because of this posturing, many audiences assume that gangstas are unconcerned with God. Cultural theorist Michael Eric Dyson disagrees. "To a remarkable degree, many hardcore rappers, as profane and as vulgar as they can be, are figures who by virtue of their meditations on fate, judgment, death, and God force us to contend with the ultimate truths and proclamations of the gospel."[5] As an ultimate authority, God plays an important role in the maintenance of a gangsta identity. *Rap and Religion: Understanding the Gangsta's God* examines how talk about God is augmented by the presence of religion in urban neighborhoods.

Religion in the Hood

In the earliest rap, which was predominantly party music, there was a paucity of God talk. When hip hop culture initially developed from the decimation of the South Bronx in the mid-1970s, it was such an innovative and expressive cultural celebration of life that hip hop itself figured as the inner city's savior. But when rap began to respond to the deteriorating social conditions exacerbated by the crack cocaine epidemic, celebrations of life gave way to ruminations on death, and God became more prominent. However, when rap embraces religion, the result is a complex incorporation of traditional and nontraditional religious beliefs and practices that respond to the social conditions of the time.

Federal, state, and local government divestment from predominantly African American urban environments in the 1980s and '90s inspired a resistive religious attitude from hip hop heads. Whether rappers self-identified as Muslims or merely appropriated Sunni, Nation of Islam, or Five Percenter discourse, embracing Islam, commonly described in hip hop as "the black man's religion," was an opportunity to position oneself in opposition to white Christian American values. After the terrorist attacks on the World Trade Center in New York City on September 11, 2001, mainstream media outlets portrayed Islam as the face of terror. As a result, the religion's resistive nature became less of a badge of honor and more of a liability for hip hop heads with mainstream audiences. Muslim rappers continued to rap about their religious beliefs, but the numbers of rappers who were not Muslim but incorporated Islamic themes declined significantly.

Christianity, on the other hand, has consistently played a prominent role in the African American neighborhoods that nurtured hip hop. From the imposition of Christianity on stolen African slaves through the Christian impetus that inspired Reverend Martin Luther King Jr. and the Civil Rights Movement, church and Christianity have been staples in African American communities. Seventy-five percent of African Americans who identify as religious are affiliated with Protestant churches. Theories of oscillation can be appropriated to help explain the various connections an African American might maintain with the church even if he or she never attends one. Personal oscillation identifies an individual who regularly attends church. Representative oscillation identifies a close friend or family member who regularly attends church while the individual in question infrequently attends. Vicarious oscillation implies there is a church in the neighborhood but neither the individual in question nor a close friend or family member has ever attended. Finally, nonoscillation is the denial of the importance of church.[6] With churches and liquor stores on too many urban corners, the majority of African Americans oscillate between their communities and the church in one form or another. An individual does not have to attend church in order to be familiar with Christianity. Christian beliefs and practices can be unintentionally inherited from one's environment. Scholars Monica R. Miller and Ezekiel J. Dixon-Roman describe the process of being socialized into religion as the development of a religious habitus wherein someone can encounter religious beliefs and practices from family, friends, and community without ever having to join a religious institution.[7] Furthermore, a Christian habitus is functional insofar as it helps the hip hop generation cope with death and their desires for financial success.

When murder rates reached their apex in the mid-1990s, gangsta rappers in particular reconciled the death of their friends and family by portraying themselves praying and grieving in Christian churches. Gangsta rappers inscribed their bodies with Christian themes as tattoos, wore crucifixes and crosses, appropriated Bible verses with greater frequency, incorporated gospel music into their samples, and mimicked Jesus's death and resurrection. Unanticipated violent deaths created conditions for rappers to return home for funerals as well as to return to dominant Christian religious practices.

Tragedy draws individuals to Christianity, but the fervor with which rappers have returned to church is unmatched by the love of money. Hip hop academics Marc Lamont Hill and Josef Sorett have accounted for the simultaneous rise of the bling era of hip hop with the bling era of the new black mega church. Hill writes, "Hip-hop's obsession with 'flossing' and 'stunting' is matched only by the New Black Church's flair for the ostentatious. Many of today's superstar preachers are similarly lavish in their public appearances."[8] The largess and excess symbolized in visual depictions of physical churches in hip hop videos suggest that the church is no longer a place just for God; it is a place where money resides. Prosperity gospel is not limited to Sunday sermons. The acquisition of wealth as a signifier of success has been interpreted as a blessing from God by both preachers and rappers. Sorett argues, "To invoke Christianity, whether or not one expresses an exclusive allegiance to its theological tenets, has been to avail oneself of rhetorical, cultural and financial capital."[9] Cultural Christianity, the experience of being surrounded by a Christian habitus without necessarily embracing Christianity as a ritualized practice, reasserted itself in hip hop when rappers realized that Christianity could be used to justify their capitalist aspirations.

There is an additional profit incentive for incorporating Christianity. In a community where attending church is a high cultural priority, performing church in terms of praying, dancing holy, incorporating a gospel singing style, imitating preacher cadences, pretending to be a leader of the lost, and/or acknowledging God are signs of a communal connection. An artist with church roots is more acceptable to Christians than someone who is admittedly irreligious or atheistic. Hip hop community members who do not attend church regularly but recognize its cultural viability will readily consume familiar performances of church. Outsiders may also consume the performance of church because it represents that which is foreign and augments the voyeuristic experience at the heart of much rap music.

Performances of church are pervasive, but some gangstas use them to critique Christianity. They mock Christian capitalism with talk of expensive blessings and tithes. They critique church complicity and ineffectivity during slavery, colonialism, the Holocaust, and urban decay. They castigate

Catholic priests for sodomy and call out congregations for their hypocrisy. For better or for worse, Christianity, as the dominant religion in the neighborhood, reigns in contemporary religious rap repertoire.

The Gangsta's God

Rap and Religion: Understanding the Gangsta's God asks: why do rappers include God in their raps about murder, misogyny, and mayhem? The book answers the question by emphasizing the relationship between God talk and a gangsta's quest for meaning and power. Rap's intimacy with social ills provides the primary context for a gangsta's God talk, which includes the questions: Why am I here? Who is God? What is God's relationship to me? And how could a good God allow evil? Gangstas express frustration with those who misunderstand them ("only God can judge me"), desperation ("dear God, please don't let me die tonight"), uncertainty about God's power ("dear God, I wonder can you save me"), and invincibility ("I was born a God"). Rappers seek God to understand senseless deaths, dysfunctional relationships, and the sundry social ills of the world they inherited. At the same time, they seek God to empower them to be respectable murders, misogynists, and agents of mayhem in the hyperbolic rap worlds of their lyrics and videos.

Throughout this book, I provide evidence for what rappers are saying about God and what they are saying about themselves and their communities when they rap about God. I focus on two central monotheistic God figures—a Supreme God "out there" who exists in the universe and God "down here" that walks the earth with human beings. Although inspired by Christianity and Islam, these figures do not adhere to a particular faith. Their primary purpose is to fulfill quests for meaning, power, and respect.

God is "out there" when the gangsta perceives a vast distance between humanity and God. God is "out there" and not "up there" because looking up to God suggests a reverence that many gangstas are not sure God has earned. While God "out there" may be all-knowing, as long as God remains silent on certain pressing issues, like how could a good God allow evil to befall innocent people, the chasm between God and God's creation remains. Theodicy questions like these comprise the central quest for meaning. However, God "out there" also represents a desire for intimacy. The ubiquity implied in "out there" (surrounding us everywhere at once) conveys hope that God will one day make it all make sense and help humans understand the meaning of life. If God were "up there," God would be too far away, too inaccessible.

Unlike God "out there," God "down here" is intimately involved with the gangsta. God "out there" is petitioned for meaning—questions gangstas cannot answer on their own—but God "down here" is a reservoir for power that gangstas can access to empower themselves. God "down here" is wily, unpredictable, provocative, and a staple in the lyrics of gangstas who perceive themselves the same way. God "down here" blurs the lines between God and humanity so much so that God "down here" and the gangsta are frequently the same person.

Jesus is the transitional God figure because, according to the Bible, God "out there" sent Jesus "down here" to sacrifice himself via a death, burial, and resurrection to redeem humanity. The physical experience of walking the earth anchors Jesus to the human experience. Many theologians argue that this is the point of Jesus—only a God who walked among humans could truly redeem them. This perspective is not lost on gangstas who connect with Jesus's experience with haters (persecutors), murder (crucifixion), and resurrection (redemption). Jesus is familiar with suffering because he suffered. Jesus is familiar with victory because his resurrection conquered death. Literally, Jesus's battered body embodies power and resistance. Oppressed people who appropriate Jesus become invincible. There is no evidence, however, that the historical Jesus was either the Son of God or resurrected from the dead. The historical Jesus was an ordinary man who lived an extraordinary life dedicated to speaking the truth and agitating for justice even when his message was unpopular. From the Christian and the historical perspective, Jesus remains an icon of perseverance.

Quests for meaning, power, and respect can reach their pinnacle through a combination of God "out there" and God "down here." An immense amount of comfort can be gained from a God who provides answers to life's looming questions. It is empowering to imagine oneself as "set apart" because of a personal relationship with God "out there." To be down with the divine—the Ultimate Supreme Being—is to ooze an aura of invincibility. This invincibility is encapsulated by the phase "only God can judge me," which is most often bantered about in response to questionable life choices narrated by artists who believe that God understands a survival by any means necessary mentality. A similar invincibility can also be accrued by describing oneself as a powerful God. Although it is easy to interpret this type of God talk as disingenuous, imagining God as one's "ride or die" companion or envisioning oneself as God is a very necessary fantasy for constitutors whose real world is too often too bleak to promise personal advancement or empowerment.

This book describes God "out there" and God "down here" examples that are neither a full representation nor a comprehensive collection of every rap song that references God. My sample is limited to mainstream rappers that quite truthfully are skewed toward the personal favorites in my private collection. My strategy is to look closely at God talk within rap lyrics, videos, and liner notes in order to determine who God is, what God does, where God resides, and how God functions in a genre that is largely committed to conversations about murder, misogyny, and mayhem. I am not interested in passing moral judgments or evaluating rappers' spiritual journeys. Within these pages you will not find lengthy discussions about the mere presence of religious symbols, rappers who became religious, or hip hop's impact on the church. The crossover is certainly there but not the focus of this project.

Chapter 1, "Communing with God," explores how invoking God "out there" through public acknowledgments, prayers, and pilgrimages creates a community for God "down here." Chapter 2, "Doin' It for Daddy," considers how women rappers lyrically construct God "out there" as a father and their lovers as Gods "down here." As the Christian God who was sent from "out there" to "down here," chapter 3, "The Jesus Piece," analyzes how rappers identify with Jesus as a companion, a crucified martyr, and a commodity. Chapter 4, "Dealing with the Devil," discusses the adversarial role of the devil "out there" and the trickster/badman characteristics of men who describe themselves as the devil "down here." Chapter 5, "Godly Power," recognizes how rappers appropriate the power of God "out there" and self-deify as Gods "down here" to resist oppression, establish hierarchies, and regulate intimate relationships. Finally, chapter 6, "The Rap on Rap and Religion," surveys hip hop fans about their personal religious beliefs and their interpretations of gangsta's beliefs about Jesus, the devil, and God.

Whether characterized as "out there" or "down here," the gangsta's God emerges from the gangsta's lived experiences. Because gangsta is a moniker adopted by disempowered hip hop heads seeking empowerment, the gangsta's God is more closely aligned with a set of social circumstances than a particular religion. Although the terms *rapper*, *artist*, and *gangsta* are used interchangeably throughout the book, the gangsta's God is a significant phrase. It alludes to a socially constructed deity whose purpose is to provide meaning and power in a world of chaos and disenfranchisement.

Chapter 1

Communing with God

Invocation is central to rap music and religious practice. During hip hop's early days when the DJ was busy with his ones and twos, MCs (masters of ceremony, microphone controllers, or movers of the crowd) spoke over the records by invoking the spirit of the party gods. With phrases like "Rock on my mellow" or "That's the joint" or "Ho, everybody get your hands up," the MC's responsibility was to call forth a mood of revelry with his words. Today the MC's responsibility has expanded to include spitting 16 bars over a beat, but when rappers perform they invoke their own names, the names of their affiliates, as well as the names of their neighborhoods, cities, states, and geographical regions. Rap invocations appeal to familiar people and places for inspiration and guidance.

Rap music also contains traditional invocations in the form of public acknowledgments of God and prayers to God. Because it is customary for a rapper to thank his or her mentors (see any award show involving Lil Wayne and Baby), it is also relatively commonplace for them to shout out what God has done for them. Like anyone else under distress, rappers frequently invoke God for assistance and answers. The power of the spoken word for either praise or supplication is as essential to rap music as it is to traditional religious practices.

Paying attention to pilgrimages or the physical places where rappers go to invoke the presence of God provides additional insight to the parallels between rap music and religious practice. Rap videos depict spiritual communities, unpretentious churches, and grandiose cathedrals as the places rappers go in order to feel close to God. This chapter considers how rappers' public acknowledgments, prayers, and pilgrimages invoke the presence of God "out there." Through acceptance speeches, liner notes, lyrics, and videos, the chapter describes who God is, what God does, and how rappers' characterizations of God reflect hip hop communities "down here."

Public Acknowledgments

Two prominent examples of rappers who publicly acknowledge God come from award acceptance speeches and liner notes. Throughout the years, various artists have taken the opportunity to thank God in one or both of these venues. The pressing questions are: (1) Who is the God they are thanking? And (2) what does this God do for them? A random sample of over 60 liner notes yields the following results. God is always a monotheistic omnipotent male most frequently called God but also acknowledged as Lord, Creator, Jesus (Christ), Savior, Allah, Almighty, Father, and Jah. There were no acknowledgments of gods plural.

Rapper Mase expresses the sentiment of hip hop's Christian critics when he challenges rappers' vague references to God in his 2001 autobiography *Revelations*. Mase writes: "But I just ask, which God? Your God is whatever you worship. Money can be your God. You can say 'God' as much as you want. You can say you're spiritual. Which spirit? There is the spirit of lust. There is the spirit of deceit. You can say you're religious. But you put your pants on religiously."[1] Of course, an individual's spiritual or religious walk is between that person and his or her God. There is no way to determine whether rappers reference "the God of this world" identified as Satan in II Corinthians 4:4, the benevolent Christian Creator of the heavens and earth, or some other Divine Being.

The only claim that can be proven is the regular recurrence of God acknowledgments. Rappers address God by using multiple names that represent a variety of potential relationships. More humility is expressed through the moniker Lord than the more generic call to God. The name Creator endows one's deity with the power to create life and by extension the power to sanction death. As will be discussed in chapter 3, Jesus's resurrection/victory over death makes him the Christian Savior. Allah aligns with Islamic beliefs. Jah rules in the Rastafarian faith. Almighty is dominant whereas Father is intimate. Oftentimes, the above names are used in conjunction with each other, but each of the names specifies a level of intimacy between the rapper and his or her higher power.

God's identity is only partially defined by what God is called. God's identity is also premised on what God does. In both acceptance speeches and liner notes, rappers are more inclined to either say "first and foremost I would like to thank God" or simply thank God first before family, friends, and other affiliates. God's activity in their lives warrants a primary acknowledgment. Despite varying names for God, rapper references to a divine power can be summed as follows: God is responsible for blessing, bestowing talent, and creating opportunities especially for African Americans.

For example, during the 1994 MTV Video Music Awards (VMAs), Snoop, then known as Snoop Doggy Dogg, began his best rap video acceptance speech with the following: "First of all I wanna um thank God for giving me the opportunity to be a rapper and to do this thang called rap and to move something positive in this world as a black man." Of all the controversial things for which Snoop is known, publicly advocating for positive black masculinity is not one of them. After presenting at the previous year's (1993) MTV Video Music Awards, Snoop turned himself in to the police. He was an accused accessory to the murder of Phillip Woldermarian. Snoop claimed that his bodyguard shot Woldermarian (from the car he was driving) in self-defense. Despite the fact that he maintained his innocence, Snoop had not yet been cleared of any charges when he accepted his 1994 award. Snoop's gratitude to God for the opportunity to use his rap talent to positively represent black men is significant because it presented an opportunity for him to prove to a primarily white audience that he was not a criminal.

The MTV VMAs are a mainstream event. Because a diverse group of artists are regularly honored, there has never been a predominantly African American VMA celebration. When Snoop moved toward the stage, he was surrounded by a bevy of white fans clamoring for his attention. Some white fans in the front row were formally dressed. Snoop, on the other hand, was dressed in the West Coast rapper uniform—a long-sleeve T-shirt partially covered by a large casual shirt and Dickies. Snoop awkwardly moved through the crowd, touching the hand of a fan here and there. The only clearly identifiable camera shot of other African Americans was Snoop's family (who looked surprisingly sedated). Snoop accepted the Moonman award then placed it on the stage. After a few false starts, he turned his back to the crowd, gripped a towel around his neck, and paced a bit before beginning his speech.

When Snoop thanked God for the opportunity to be a rapper, he thanked God for the opportunity to (a) be alive, (b) be out of prison, and (c) be able to profit from his talent and experiences.[2] Snoop was visibly uncomfortable in front of his audience. He used God to distance himself from his white audience's stereotypes of black men and to suggest how he believed God saw him. Snoop's God was a barrier against the white audience in the room and the predominantly white legal system that was prosecuting him. Three years after the murder, a jury cleared Snoop of all charges, which could be interpreted as evidence that Snoop was being unfairly targeted. Irrespective of others' impressions, God blessed Snoop with the ability to do something positive. Because God sustained him, Snoop was unconcerned with white fans that may support him one day and demonize him the next. His affiliation with God helped him create an aura of invincibility necessary to sustain a career where one is simultaneously loved and despised by fickle fans. Public acknowledgments of God provide black rappers facing majority-white audiences the opportunity to inform outsiders that they are more than their art. The invocation gives props to God and says "I am a sentient spiritual being even if my rap and my lifestyle do not reflect it." For this reason alone, the acknowledgment of God is important even when it seems insignificant.

When Common received the first televised award of his career at the 2007 BET Awards, he, like Snoop, referred to the relationship between God and black people. He began his acceptance speech for Hip Hop CD of the Year with, "I just wanna thank the most high God for allowing me to use my voice to represent God as much as I can, and when I talk about God you know I talk about having fun, I talk about who we are as black people and what we wanna do to progress." Instead of using God as a buffer against white stereotypes of blacks, Common used God to encourage identification among blacks.

Unlike the MTV VMAs, the BET Awards is a predominantly African American event. However, the BET Awards audience differs from the BET Hip Hop Awards audience. The hip hop crowd is usually limited to a younger and rowdier hip hop audience whereas the general awards crowd includes hip hop artists but also "celebrates African Americans and other minorities in music, acting, sports, and other fields of entertainment over the past year." A BET Awards crowd is as likely to include black billionaires, bastions of the Civil Rights Movement, and upcoming rappers wearing rented jewelry sitting side by side in the same auditorium. Common's comments about God's relationship to fun and progress were particularly tailored to this diverse African American crowd.

Common appealed to hip hop youth that might perceive the God of their parents' generation as boring and irrelevant by clarifying that talking about God is talking about having fun. For those audience members frustrated with their perception of hip hop's perpetual playfulness, Common positively represented his generation by talking about God's relationship to black progress. To further bridge the age, class, and lyrical content gaps among this diverse black audience, Common went on to say that he does not differentiate himself from other rappers who are expressing themselves as young black men. This acknowledgment was important from Common who is generally considered a socially conscious rapper who is more intellectually and lyrically mature than his peers. Again, a public acknowledgment of God is situated between a rapper and his audience. For Snoop and his white audience, God was his bastion. For Common and his black audience, God was his bridge. Both Snoop's and Common's messages can be translated into common Christian argot. Snoop stated "only God can judge me"; Common conveyed that "with God all things are possible."

Rappers frequently acknowledge God for making "this" or "it" or "everything" possible. The ambiguity may be partially attributable to the expansive and profitable opportunities God has created for them. Other opportunities have been described as turning dreams into a reality or providing guidance during difficult times. Rappers specify gratefulness for their talents variously described as my mind, creativity, vision, and inspiration. Overall, acceptance speeches and liner notes most frequently acknowledge God for His blessings—life, health, strength, wisdom, and support in the form of family and other human allies.

Even though acknowledgments of thanksgiving are commonplace, rappers depict themselves working in partnership with God. When Nicki Minaj accepted her 2010 Rookie of the Year Award at the BET Awards she said, "I wanna thank God for this opportunity because I feel like whether the album does well or not I'm still paving the way for so many girls and I'm putting a lot of hard work into it." God is not using Nicki to pave the way; Nicki is doing that on her own. She summed up many rappers' perspectives when she acknowledged God for the opportunity and herself for the hard work. God merely opened the door; Nicki walked through it. It would appear that faith without works is indeed dead. Additionally, Nicki reminded audiences that rapping is difficult work. The overglamorization of the genre could easily give the impression that anyone with an excellent PR team could become an award-winning rapper, but for those who acknowledge God, the feat is best achieved with God on one's side. Admittedly, rappers are not known for their humility. In line with the individualism of hip hop, God may bless, bestow talent, and create opportunity but it is a rapper's responsibility to do the rest.

Prayers

Rappers' God acknowledgments are a unique form of invocation because they occur during the best of times. The euphoria surrounding an album that has finally been released or an award that has finally been received is a celebratory moment that lends itself to expressions of gratitude. While many rappers also thank God in their rap prayers, the overwhelming majority of rapper prayers are responses to hard times—dealing with detractors, depression, and death. Because ideas about God develop from personal experiences, it is no surprise that the God to whom rappers pray primarily provides assistance during these hard times. Faith in God's pending assistance is premised on His omnipotence. There is nothing God cannot do. Despite an unwavering belief in God's power, the God to whom rappers pray is ironically often silent—refusing to provide explanations for the prevalence of hard times in the first place.

There are hundreds of prayers in the rap music canon. Some are actual prayers where rappers pray on a track without musical accompaniment. Others are rap prayers where the prayer is rapped over a beat. There are raps about praying, conversational prayers that include a voice of God responding to the rapper's queries, and traditional prayers that are variations of the Hail Mary, the Lord's Prayer, the child's prayer, the 23rd Psalm, and the Arabic invocation of the *Basmala*. There are no geographical or generational distinctions among these prayer categories. There are also few gendered distinctions. Men and women both pray for God's assistance during hard times.

Prayers may differ in presentation, but the common purpose of prayers—especially a public prayer in a hip hop forum—is decreasing the distance between God and humanity. Stereotypically, God is often thought of as "out there" whereas humans are "down here" on earth. Prayer creates intimacy with God. Beleaguered rappers who perceive themselves facing one obstacle after another frequently go to God for assistance and answers.

Rappers speak to God concerning a variety of distressing situations. Sometimes the petitions are nonspecific like the catchy hook of MC Hammer's "Pray" (1990), which states, "We got to pray/Just to make it today." This call for communion with God only implicitly acknowledges hard times. T. I.'s "Prayin' for Help" (2004) is also nonspecific in its petition. T. I. seeks divine support to change his life and reach his goals. Nas and the Bravehearts' "Pray" (1999) conveys a greater sense of urgency. The second chorus states, "I only pray when shit is fucked up . . . I only pray when

I need His help the most, what." These generic prayers are not religious in the ritual sense, but practical in the sense that a bout of bad luck would encourage the religious and irreligious alike to begin bargaining with God. More specific prayers define distressing situations such as negotiating relationships and coping with death.

Andre 3000 hopes to ameliorate his loneliness by petitioning God for "a sweet bitch" in "God (Interlude)" (2003). The track opens with Andre repeating "come in God" as if he were on a walkie-talkie. Andre responds to God as if they were having a conversation, but listeners never hear God's voice. He is shocked to discover that God is a "girl." He honestly admits his faults to Her and expresses his desire for a partner who will stand by him because "life ain't easy." At the end of the prayer, God grants his request for a supportive woman with a nice ass. Andre's loneliness is only partially resolved by female companionship. The prayer also confirms his desire for a nurturing and accessible God who is intimately invested in human affairs. The God of "God (Interlude)" is idiosyncratic because She is a woman invoked through technology. Whereas technology may increase social isolation by reducing physical interaction among humans, it can make it easier to access God. Realizing that God is a girl assures Andre that he is not alone. God, similar to the partner he requests, understands life's difficulties and wants to stand by him.

Although he is vulnerable with God, Andre is still irreverent. God is first referenced as a girl child. Then he expects Her to understand that oral sex with someone other than his girlfriend is not cheating. He objectifies the woman of his dreams by focusing on the size of her ass. God is made in the image of his ideal woman—one who understands and acquiesces to his desires. His female God services him and, like a madam, brings suitable women to him. God helps Andre through his distressing situation, but his characterization of women is also distressing. Because communing with God welcomes human imperfection, even progressive ideas about God can still be regressive.

For other rappers, the problem is not the absence of a significant other, but the presence of too many unscrupulous people. A Tribe Called Quest describes myriad problems in "8 Million Stories" (1993). Phife Dawg has problems with thieves, a temper-tantrum-throwing little brother, the police, and his coach. But mostly his problems are with the women in his life. As his problems multiply and intensify, A Tribe Called Quest beseeches God to help. Eve thanks God for her support system in "Life Is So Hard" (2001) but she asks for His protection from her enemies including people who pretend to be friends. Lil' Kim also laments the friends who betrayed her. In "Heavenly Father" (2003) she prays for love, joy, peace, and happiness—characteristics that are missing from her life. Nicki Minaj raps about her haters in "Can Anybody Hear Me?" (2010). Verse 2 is a prayer where she thanks God for her talent, but confesses that her adversaries' constant disrespect is stressful. She admits to doing the best she can but ponders giving up. Nicki does not directly ask God for assistance, but by addressing the verse to God, she hopes that even if no one else can hear her, God will.

Negotiating relationships is an essential part of the human experience, but coping with death is the primary distressing impetus for God invocations. Since the 1990s death has permeated rap music so much so that the phrase "requiem rap" was coined to describe the ubiquitous mourning music.[3] Within the hip hop community, prospects for longevity are disproportionately compromised by homicide, suicide, police brutality, substance abuse, and disease. Unexpected encounters with violent death frequently increase a mourner's desire to commune with God. Upon seeing a friend in a casket, Joe Budden raps in "Ventilation" (2008), "So I figured I'd say a prayer for him, got on my knees quick/And realized I don't ever pray until I need shit." As Jean Grae contemplates suicide in "Take Me" (2003), she samples Psalm 23:4 and prays that God will take her "through the shadows of valleys of death." The double entendre of Jean Grae's prayer is that she wants God to take her life and she wants God to take away her desire to end her life.

Many rap prayers ask for God's protection after death. Variations of the following child's prayer are most popular:

Now I lay me down to sleep
I pray the Lord my soul to keep
If I should die before I wake
I pray the Lord my soul to take.

Common, Joe Budden, Kid Cudi, Lil Wayne, Master P., Noreaga, Snoop, and Tupac have all incorporated versions of the child's prayer. When one is unfamiliar with the ritual of prayer, praying something that sounds familiar is a common response. It is even more common to rely on tropes from one's childhood. Sampling the child's prayer requires no spiritual maturation or religious affiliation. This particular child's prayer has no religious foundation. Its significance lies not in its religiosity but in its vulnerability. Death is the quintessential hard time that forces rappers to deal with the limits of their humanity. The circulation of the child's prayer among these very grown men, several of whom have gone to great lengths to create hard-core personas for themselves, suggests that despite their posturing, even rappers fear death and desire God's protection. Some rappers humble themselves before God to deal with distressing situations. Others are emboldened to demand answers.

Rappers frequently ask God: "where are you?" and "why is life so hard?" Consider the following examples. Ja Rule asks why God is never there when people in pain call on Him in "Father Forgive Me" (2007). In "Dear God 2.0" (2010), Black Thought of The Roots queries, "Why is the world ugly when you made it in your image?/And why is living life such a fight to the finish?" The Lady of Rage wonders in "Confessions" (1997), "They tell me not to question God, but the question is/Will I make it to live another day cause times get hard." Rage concludes "Confessions" asking if God can hear and see her. Tupac also hopes God is listening in "Hail Mary" (1996), "Nothing to Lose" (1997), and "Letter 2 My Unborn" (2001), but he cannot be sure. In "Blood on the Wall" (2009) Joe Budden prays to God but laments the crisis in communication when he realizes he could be hearing God wrong, or maybe God has abandoned him.

Accustomed to the silence that other rappers lament, 50 Cent takes matters into his own hands in "Many Men" (2003). "Every night I talk to God, but he don't say nothing back/I know he protecting me, but I still stay with my gat." In the chorus, 50 notes that he no longer cries or looks to the sky, but still desires God's mercy when he does what he has to do to survive. God's silence also goads Ja Rule to action in "One of Us" (2000). In a powerful twist of lyrical fate, Ja Rule inverts hierarchy and imagines that he is God. Ja Rule demands that God pray to him: "Now you call on me every night bended knee until you start to realize I ain't answerin'." He wonders whether God would resort to violence to protect and provide for his family. He wonders whether God would love his wife and still lust for other women. Ja Rule concludes that life is hard, and if he judges God unfairly, God should aim a slug up to the sky. Because God has not yet become one of us, Ja Rule decides to become God. He fills God's silence with the sound of his own voice. The commonality in each of these queries is that despite the silence, God has not yet outlived God's usefulness. Rapping about being caught up in an environment not of their own making and acting disreputably with the sole comfort that God understands and will have mercy on them is a popular sentiment among rappers who feel trapped—physically, emotionally, socially, and economically. Even when silent, the potential existence of a merciful God who sympathizes with oppression remains a psychologically sustaining force.

Some rappers, however, deal with God's silence by speaking for Him in their conversational prayers.[4] God's primary role is a father in the conversational prayers within Ras Kass's "Interview with a Vampire" (1998); DMX's "Covo" (1998), "Ready to Meet Him" (1998), and "Angel" (1999); and Joe Budden's "Pray for Me" (2009). God never speaks a monologue. Instead, He responds to His rapper son's life queries. The recurring theme across conversations is boldness. DMX consistently calls God out on His absence. In "Ready to Meet Him," he wonders, "What'd I do so bad that it sent you away from me?" Ras Kass directly asks God, "Did God create man, or did man need to create God?" After a near-death experience, two men drop Joe Budden off in front of a gate to meet a man with no face. Joe Budden's first response to God is "Who the fuck is you?" Joe Budden proceeds to blame God for his personal misfortunes and a host of other social ills including drugs, guns, and AIDS. No matter how confrontational the rappers, God never retaliates. God never admonishes them for being disrespectful. This open and honest freedom of expression empowers the rappers and their audiences to go to God with their concerns. For a generation of youth raised without their biological fathers, the accessibility of a father God in these lyrics fills an essential lack.

The father-child relationship cultivated during these conversations is one of tough love. God reminds them that He is the omniscient and omnipotent Creator. When rappers complain about His absence, He declares that He has always been present. His will is divine and hard times are part of life, but God still wants to parent, nurture, and help them as long as they are willing to help themselves. He provides an unlimited number of opportunities to turn one's life around. God is the model man. God is accountable, forgiving, patient, and loving. The conversational prayers encourage audiences to believe that God is observing, listening to, and caring about humans despite their hard times. When living a life that frequently changes for the worst, going to a God that is constant, resolute, and absolute is comforting.

No other rapper has dedicated as many tracks to his struggle to become the man God wants him be than Dark Man X. The darkness that inspired his moniker has plagued DMX his entire life. Growing up in foster care, group homes, youth camps, and jail, DMX felt abandoned by his family, especially after the death of his grandmother. He developed a hard-core persona and a penchant for self-medicating that ensured survival on the streets. Even after DMX turned his life around and became a multi-platinum-selling rap artist, he was haunted by his past. The pit bull defied one too many laws. Self-medication became drug addiction, and recidivism plagued his fledgling career.

DMX's very public life obstacles endeared him to his audiences. Rap fans struggling to move from where they were to where they wanted to be could identify with DMX. DMX acknowledged the responsibility that he felt toward these audiences in his prayers. In a total of six actual prayers, DMX goes to God not just for himself, but on behalf of his fans. DMX consistently includes substantive prayers to God on his overtly secular albums. DMX is very rarely publicly accused of hypocrisy because of his honesty. His music and prayers confess his sins and discuss his struggle between good and evil. He thanks God for his blessings and asks for God's forgiveness. He admits the difficulty of maintaining faith because he is unfamiliar with the concept of unconditional love.

Journalist Heidi Siegmund Cuda describes DMX's prayers as sermons. DMX has described himself as a preacher of rap.[5] He recognizes God's call on his life to minister to God's people. Whereas other rappers ask God to assist or answer questions for them, the majority of DMX's prayers praise God for what God has done for him. His prayers further differ from other rappers because DMX addresses God with the honorific titles of Lord, Father God, or Jesus. There is no confusion about the Christian God to whom DMX is speaking. Furthermore, when the prayers are spoken without musical accompaniment, there are no distractions between the man's word and God's ears.

Despite the purity of the prayer, God is not DMX's only audience. Public prayers encourage community and collective consciousness. With the exception of the first prayer, each of the others begins with "Let *us* pray." DMX intercedes on behalf of his "brothers and sisters in the hood." During "The Prayer VI" (2006) DMX invokes God and a congregation by praying entirely in the plural sense. DMX's public prayers build a relationship with God and with community. Prayer is more than just invoking God's name. Prayer builds a bridge to God so that the rapper can go to God or God can go to the rapper. This survey of several rap prayers has shown that the impetus for that desire and the approach individuals take when they speak to God will vary, but the desire to commune with God remains constant.

Pilgrimage

Public acknowledgments of God and private prayers to God can be done anywhere at any time by anyone. No special circumstances or sacrifices are required. A pilgrimage, on the other hand, demands a locational shift from where one is to another distinct geographical position. Pilgrimages are invocation rituals that require intentionally visiting a physical place that represents God. The hajj, for example, is an annual pilgrimage to Mecca observed by millions of Muslims each year. Obligated by the fifth pillar of Islam, Muslims who are physically and financially able are required to make the pilgrimage at least once in a lifetime. Other faiths inspire similar albeit voluntary pilgrimages—Jews to the Western Wall in Jerusalem, Christians to the Holy Land, Hindus and Buddhists to Nepal. Each of these physical places becomes a sacred space because of the spiritual and sometimes supernatural histories attributed to them.

Individuals physically go to sacred spaces to seek solace and answers to life's pressing questions. A pilgrimage to a sacred space is a prayer in motion. Both prayers and pilgrimages are integral to hip hop. Since hip hop's sacred spaces are also physical places, its pilgrimages are best identified via rap music videos. The videos depict pilgrimages of enlightenment, pilgrimages of personal transformation, and pilgrimages of proximity to God.

The paradigmatic pilgrimage of enlightenment is Arrested Development's "Tennessee" (1992). Speech's rap prayer asks God for guidance. God guides him back home to Tennessee. Tennessee's significance lies in its characterization as a wilderness "outta the country and into more country." Entering the wilderness is an unconventional pilgrimage because pilgrimages are usually directed toward a predetermined destination. However, the biblical significance of the wilderness alludes to how God led the Israelites through the wilderness for 40 years before delivering them to the Promised Land (Deuteronomy 8:2–10). Similarly, the Holy Spirit guided Jesus through the wilderness for his 40-day temptation (Luke 4: 1–2). Wilderness pilgrimages are painful—filled with trials and loss. Their success is entirely contingent upon faith in God. Characteristic of a wilderness pilgrimage, Speech lyrically admits that he does not understand God's plan. The wilderness journey focuses more on character building than arriving at the destination.

Furthermore, the video's images invite the viewer to embark on a pilgrimage through black history. The entire video appears in black-and-white, representing the South's segregationist history as well as the simplicity of rural southern life. Arrested Development dress in Afrocentric gear. Other African Americans engage in everyday activities in a small rural community. No whites appear in the video. There are many shots of the Tennessee landscape. Toward the video's conclusion, viewers see an artist drafting a charcoal image of two lynched men that transitions into the infamous photograph of the Marion, Indiana, 1930 lynching of Thomas Shipp and Abram Smith. The video fades to black on that death scene. The pilgrimage through ancestral history traffics in pain, loss, and enlightenment. Through his pilgrimage, Speech learns that God is guiding him to enlighten others by revisiting the wilderness moments of black history.

"Tennessee" is a unique pilgrimage because of its emphasis on journeying through a rural wilderness in search of historical enlightenment. The more traditional rap pilgrimages depict individuals journeying through the concrete jungles of the urban United States (which are wildernesses in their own right) in order to arrive at a church, which symbolically represents a personal transformation. For example, "Jesus Walks: The Church Version" (2004) depicts an alcoholic, a gang member, and a prostitute pilgrimaging through Chicago's inner-city streets to the church where they can repent for their sins. Plagued by external violence as well as their internal vices, the characters need the help of angels to arrive unscathed. Riot footage is interspersed within the video's depiction of their journeys to augment the difficulty of arriving at one's destination. When they arrive, pastor Kanye West preaches that he hopes Jesus will walk with those that need his help through their individually harrowing odysseys. The significance of physically walking adds extra emphasis to the importance of pilgrimaging from one set of life circumstances to another. Similarly, the young man in E-40's "Things'll Never Change" (1996) is uneducated, unemployed, unloved, and destitute. When E-40 appears and drops a cross into the cup of the character that is playing himself, the young man physically gets up and walks to church to change his life.

The lyrics of both "Jesus Walks" and "Things'll Never Change" depict persistent contemporary social issues that disproportionately affect poor African Americans—racism, crime, police harassment, drug dealing, parental abuse, homelessness, teenage pregnancy, domestic abuse, etc. Each song also samples an original track that acknowledges the continuity of similar trials and tribulations. "Jesus Walks" is based on a Negro spiritual that asks God to walk with an individual through the trials, sorrows, and troubles that he or she encounters along a "pilgrim journey." West sampled directly from the A.R.C. (Addicts Rehabilitation Center) Choir's recording of "Walk with Me." Every member of the choir is a former addict who has experienced a personal transformation. "Things'll Never Change" samples Bruce Hornsby's "The Way It Is" (1986), a song that describes poverty and institutional racism, as well as Tupac's "Changes" (1998) where Tupac implores individuals to change, but laments the persistence of racism, hatred, poverty, the prison-industrial complex, and violence to the extent that he contemplates suicide.

The videos' characters seek personal transformation because they cannot change these persistently oppressive social environments. The church as the pilgrimage destination is an oasis where such transformation is possible. As physical structures, the churches include religious symbols that would have been familiar even to the irreligious. The videos' incorporation of stained glass windows, a pulpit, preachers, Bibles, and women in church hats reaffirms religious ritual in ways that confirm the destination for the pilgrims within the video and those audiences seeking similar personal transformations from their television or computer screens.

The pews of both churches are filled with worshippers who have already completed their pilgrimages. They welcome the newcomers. No one inside the church passes judgment on the characters. Some parishioners are relieved that the newest pilgrims have decided to seek God's presence. Another distinct characteristic of pilgrimages is their communal nature. In part, a pilgrimage becomes special because other people have completed it. Furthermore, when individuals arrive at the destination, they are greeted by other journeyers—all of whom have made the commitment and the sacrifices necessary to achieve a personal transformation, which is more possible when surrounded by a supportive community.

The aforementioned pilgrimages were inspired by external forces, but pilgrimages of personal transformation can also be necessitated by mental instability. The Geto Boys' "Mind Playing Tricks on Me" (1991) is a song about paranoia. Scarface's schizophrenic and suicidal thoughts compel him to church. In the third verse, Scarface enters a modest southern church. The pews and floor are carpeted in red. A Bible rests on a small lectern; an empty offering tray sits on the front pew. A banner on the wall quotes Hebrews 13:13—"Remember them that are in prison as bound with them." Scarface's pilgrimage differs from the previous examples because his fellow pilgrims are implied. The scripture urges him to recognize that being imprisoned by his dark thoughts is just as constraining as physical incarceration. It also reminds him that there are fellow sufferers.

The church is empty except for a young boy who hands him a Bible as he prays for forgiveness. The boy simply appears. Perhaps he is a younger version of Scarface, or perhaps he is an angel. Scarface accepts the Bible, opens it, and raps, "I know the Lord is lookin' at me/But yet and still it's hard for me to feel happy." Scarface knows that a modicum of solace can be found in his pilgrimage destination to the church, but transformation requires more than visiting the building; pilgrimages of transformation require community. Without the physical presence of community, Scarface remains unfulfilled. The remainder of his verse depicts him distancing himself from those who would love him. Going to God is more than acknowledging God or going to church. Going to God requires community.

The final type of pilgrimage—a pilgrimage of proximity to God—is prompted by death. Communion with others and God is essential during and after life. The most significant visual indicator of a pilgrimage of proximity to God continues to be the church. In addition to being sites of personal transformation, rappers pilgrimage to church for funerals, processionals, and confessionals. Funeral pilgrimages are circumstantial because of the unanticipated death of a loved one or an unexpected personal encounter with one's own mortality. Depictions of funeral pilgrimages provide opportunities for rappers to surrender either a loved one or themselves to God. Processionals, on the other hand, are resolute, intentional processions into church sanctuary. This entrance into the sacred space where God resides is designed to empower the rapper to resist death not surrender to it. The final pilgrimage of proximity to God is entering church to cleanse one's soul through confession. During these confessions, a rapper can unburden himself by speaking freely to God about deaths that he has witnessed, has caused, or desires to occur in the future.

In both Bone Thugs-N-Harmony's "Tha Crossroads" (1995) and T. I.'s "Live in the Sky" (2006), the videos' characters must surrender to the angel of death. Although the angel of death's arrival is always unanticipated, the characters acquiesce and the choruses iterate the rappers' prayers to God for an afterlife either meeting at the crossroads or living in the sky. "Tha Crossroads" opens with a funeral in progress. Women sing an a capella version of the chorus from the spiritual "Mary Don't You Weep" as the angel of death walks to the casket to carry the deceased away. When the music begins, the introductory shots of the group's four members depict them rapping in a church. The remainder of the video alternates from urban death scenes to shots of the rappers in church.

A stained glass rose window figures prominently in the background of the church scenes. Traditionally, the patterns of light filtered through the colored glass of rose windows, like the one in the video, represent the warmth and comfort of God's watchful eye. Bone Thugs-N-Harmony's pilgrimage to God's presence provides the comfort they need to surrender to the reality of death. The group's members are angst-ridden when family and friends are taken from them in the death scenes, but they are at peace when rapping about God's judgment in the church.

T. I.'s "Live in the Sky" describes and depicts the death of T. I.'s closest friends. When he enters a church for a funeral near the end of the video, he walks past the mourners directly to the casket, and is surprised to realize that the funeral is his own. T. I. then surrenders to the angel of death, played by Forrest Whittaker. Even though the song is about death, the emphasis on living in the sky (as opposed to dying and going to heaven) resists death's finality. The funeral is the only church scene. On the whole, the video is not overtly religious, but the church as a physical building does the symbolic spiritual work in this requiem rap. The church is the space where T. I. is finally able to accept the reality of his mortality. Walking the aisle of the church upon his entrance and exit is T. I.'s pilgrimage of proximity to God—finally surrendering to living in the sky.

Sean "Diddy" Combs's videos "Victory" (1997) and "Angels" (2010), both of which feature posthumous verses from the Notorious B.I.G., are excellent examples of proximity to God for self-empowerment in the midst of death. The presence of Biggie's voice reminds audiences of death's ability to rob us of those we love all too soon. "Victory" is an action-packed high-drama video that depicts Diddy running for his life. Approximately five minutes into the nearly eight-minute video, Diddy's enemies promise to eliminate him, and he enters a darkened church where he kneels, crosses himself, and raps the first line of verse 3, "Put your money on the table and get your math on." Doves fly out of his hands; a live Jesus moves on the cross. Diddy continues to rap about money for less than a minute before the scene changes. Diddy's church entrance is a demonstration of his invincibility. He has the supernatural ability to make doves materialize from his fingertips. He mocks the crucified Jesus with his freedom of mobility. Additionally, the lyrics confirm his economic prowess. Proximity to God equals power.

The role of the cathedral in "Angels" is similar, although the camera's attention to the details on both the outer carvings and the stained glass windows is awe inspiring. Because the video is shot in black-and-white, the light filtered from the stained glass windows is the only light inside the church. The effect is a larger-than-life shadow of Diddy as he enters. As Diddy looks up, he further draws our attention to the verticality of the church and its high ceilings, which were originally designed to encourage visitors to look up, think up, and be spiritually lifted up closer to God. Diddy kneels on the marble altar floors in front of a crucifix as the lyrics explain that if Diddy is with his lover when the angels call, he will ignore them. Despite the kneeling moment of humility, the song contrasts the spiritual context inspired by the structure of the church. The cathedral is simply the place where Diddy goes for exactly one minute to feel empowered enough to resist the call of the angels.

In both processionals, the pilgrimage to the church is simply one stop on Diddy's path to victory. The awe-inspiring churches would be out of place in most urban neighborhoods (and one would surmise, expensive to rent for a video shoot). When Diddy enters, the church is big, and he is small, but his journey to the altar is still the central focus (of worship). Instead of cutting to the church with the principal already inside, both videos emphasize his larger-than-life entrance into the church. The camera captures Diddy walking toward the altar to represent agency—a conscious decision to go to the recognizable places where God resides in order to buffer his own invincibility. The grand cathedrals represent permanence, power, wealth, reverence, and respect—all of which are qualities that Diddy wishes to embody. When enemies threaten to kill him, when angels threaten to take his loved one, Diddy goes to church to be closer to God to resist the hostile forces of violent and unexpected death.

Nas's pilgrimage of proximity in "Got U'r Self A . . . " (2001), titled after the refrain "I hope you got yo'self a gun," also centers on death. Nas reenacts the moments before Tupac's and Biggie's deaths by placing himself in their positions. The final verse takes place in a cemetery where Nas and his boys pour out a little liquor for their "fallen brothers and soldiers." The rest of the video's visuals depict Nas rapping from the sanctuary and a confessional booth within a Catholic church. The inherent incongruity is that Nas praises the gun instead of God as the great equalizer.

In the opening scene, Nas walks up the steps of the church as if his body were weighted by the unconfessed sins of his soul. His legs drag; his head hangs. Upon entering, he removes his hat, the camera angle shifts behind him, and we see the prevalence of red on the carpet, chairs, curtains, candles, and banners that Nas sees. Red most likely symbolizes blood. The first Passover required Israelites to smear their doorposts with the blood of a lamb so that God would pass over those homes when the plague destroyed Egypt. Red also acknowledges redemption via Jesus Christ's blood sacrifice on the cross. Red doors on churches throughout Christian history have indicated sanctuary from the outside world. Visual themes of redemption and safety can help explain why Nas readily enters the church and confesses his sins to the priest.

During the confession, audiences realize that "Got U'r Self A . . . " is an ode to Nas's lyrical prowess. The double entendre of shots from his barrel includes bullets and words. On the surface, this message seems to have little to do with God, but rapping is often compared to the divine process of creation because the rapper's power over the word creates new rhythms and meanings in the same way that God's words created the heavens and the earth (Genesis 1:3–26). Nas's presence inside the church within the first two verses of the song aligns him with the power of God's word. Because the video depicts death's imminence, Nas's church appearance is an opportunity to cleanse his soul before it is too late. The priest looks none too happy with Nas's more violent turns of phrase, but he welcomes him into the church, listens to the confession, and blesses Nas. Nas's proximity to God provides him with the opportunity to deal with the death of his companions and reenter a world where death surrounds him and his words are his most vicious weapon.

Eminem's "Cleanin' Out My Closet" (2002) is the final pilgrimage of proximity to God example. Unlike Diddy or Nas, Eminem infrequently makes religious references. On the whole, his music fails to reveal a consistent religious or spiritual belief, and yet this video begins and ends in a church. Eminem also wears a suit and tie, which is further uncharacteristic of his rapper persona. At no point in the song does he rap about God, church, or religion. Instead, the track is addressed to his mother. It is about the early death of his childhood due to her abuse, about the irrevocable death of his relationship with his mother, and figuratively about his desire for her actual death as he fills in a grave in the rain during the chorus.

The closet is the explicit motif in the rap, but the introductory shot of a closet door opens into a sanctuary. Cleaning out one's closet is a confessional exercise that Eminem like Nas saw fit to complete in an empty church. Eminem's church is large but less opulent than the previous examples. There are four rectangular stained glass windows in the back of the church—two flank both sides of the door, which emits the most light. Eminem kneels in a position to pray at the altar before the rap begins. The sanctuary is shown three more times before Eminem finishes his confession, leaves, and the closet door closes behind him.

Eminem's choice to don a suit and go to church appears be an intentional pilgrimage of proximity to God. Being in church, however, does not temper anything he has to say. It simply provides an opportunity for him to be in the presence of God and feel free to rap about his mother, "You selfish bitch, I hope you fuckin' burn in hell for this shit." Both Nas and Eminem pilgrimage to church to confess but not to repent. The vulnerability within each of their confessions is made possible by proximity to God. Their empowerment occurs when they feel safe enough in the presence of God to express exactly how they feel.

The gangsta's God is approachable. Rappers can go to God with their appreciation, concerns, fears, and even anger. The braggadocio characteristic of rap music encourages rappers to approach God boldly in order to demand assistance and answers. There are no prescriptions for an appropriate presentation. Rappers go to God exactly as they are, wherever they are, in whatever forum they choose—award shows, liner notes, rap prayers, conversational prayers, and/or music videos. Furthermore, God's perpetual silence aids in God's accessibility. Because, as 50 Cent raps in "Many Men," God "don't say nothing back," God remains nonjudgmental. God's silence is a safe space in which gangstas can be vulnerable. As they lament the desire for companionship, the stressors of success, and the sudden, oftentimes violent death of loved ones, they contradict the stereotypical nature of hip hop as callous and individualistic. Communing with God is an opportunity for honest reflection. God's silence forces them to be accountable for their own quests for meaning. As they pose their pressing questions, they establish a community of individuals searching for similar answers. Communing with God is only partially about a God "out there." Public acknowledgments, prayers, and pilgrimages create a community for God "down here."

Chapter 2

Doin' It for Daddy

Women rap about God as a father and a lover. Because the father often represents a girl's first introduction to heterosexuality, he is, in essence, her first man-love. Women who mature without biological or surrogate father love often spend their adult lives trying to fill their fatherlack—an intense desire for a physically and/or emotionally absent father. Several rappers fulfill this desire through lyrical creations of daddy God, lover God, and daddy-lover God.

In the absence of human fatherly support, daddy God "out there" becomes the ideal protector. Daughters of God seek His guidance especially when it comes to navigating their interpersonal relationships. When women rappers encounter an ideal man who satisfies all of their physical, emotional, and sexual needs, he is considered so much of a blessing that he lyrically becomes a lover God "down here." And other times, God is a daddy-lover—a divine protector/provider patriarch. Daddy-lover God exists "out there" but his identity is modeled after imperfect men "down here." His problematic characteristics are based in the dominant-submissive relational hierarchy of a woman who is dependent upon one authoritarian man to be both father and lover.

Women rappers' relationships to father and lover Gods adhere to gendered expectations for men to be protectors and providers and for their women to worship them. These expectations emerge from society in general and also from within hip hop in particular. In the hip hop world, women are underrepresented as executives, producers, and artists. *Hip Hop Divas*, the most comprehensive history of mainstream women in hip hop, was published in 2001 and featured only 12 rappers. The Recording Academy presented a Grammy Award to Missy Elliott for the best female rap solo performance in 2003 and 2004. The category was nixed every other year because of nominal contenders. Da Brat, Eve, Foxy Brown, Lauryn Hill, Lil' Kim, Missy Elliott, Salt 'n' Pepa, and Nicki Minaj are the only female rappers to have gone platinum or sold over one million copies of an album. Furthermore, women are dependent upon men for their success. No female rapper has successfully entered the rap game without a man's assistance. Jermaine Dupri introduced Da Brat. DMX and the Ruff Ryders presented us with Eve. Jay-Z announced Foxy Brown's arrival. Wyclef Jean and the Fugees spurred Lauryn Hill's solo career. The Notorious B.I.G. mentored Lil' Kim. Timbaland initially produced for Missy Elliott. Hurby "Luv Bug" Azor created Salt 'n' Pepa's image and sound. Nicki Minaj is first lady of Lil Wayne's Young Money roster of artists.

Throughout hip hop history, women appear to be dependent upon men. Male privilege permeates the careers of even the most successful female rappers. Neither rap nor religion will ever eradicate gendered expectations, but examining the relationship between women rappers and God provides unique insight as to how women interact with this male privilege. Daddy God helps women gain independence. Lover God creates relational reciprocity. And the combination of the two, daddy-lover God, perpetuates patriarchy. Although I have limited this chapter to a select few female rappers, examining how these women rap about God problematizes hip hop's stereotypical depictions of women's dependency upon men.

Daddy God

As authority figures, fathers socialize their daughters' relationships to patriarchal power. God is frequently imagined as a father not simply because this perspective follows religious tradition, but also because many female rappers desire a father love that will mature them into empowered, autonomous women. The Lady of Rage, Lil' Kim, and Foxy Brown seek daddy God's assistance in negotiating patriarchal power within hip hop and religion in order to create acceptable identities for themselves. Hip hop demands that its women be sexually available. Traditional Abrahamic religions demand that women be virginal and pure. These women seek a father who can help them resist the irreconcilable gendered expectations for women and mature into the women they want to be.

The expectations for women in hip hop are largely influenced by the ubiquity of video models. Audiences anticipate seeing male rappers surround themselves with silent, sexy women. Female rappers violate the expectations for silence by using their voices, but it is nearly impossible for them to escape a male presence or the demand to be sexy. There are innumerable female rappers whose names we may never know because they were not physically attractive enough to appeal to rap audiences.

Unconventionally beautiful and skilled lyricists like Mia X and Lady of Rage were unmarketable as "big girls." Missy Elliot's career took off with her creative visual self-packaging as an action figure in "Sock It 2 Me" (1997) and a cyborg in "The Rain (Supa Dupa Fly)" (1997). In order to sustain her success, Missy could not remain a plus-sized female rapper. Instead of hiding her body in clever costuming, Missy Elliott had to reveal herself. As she lost weight, her raps became increasingly sexually explicit. Da Brat and Lauryn Hill went from around the way girls to sexy women wearing revealing outfits as they became more popular. Lil' Kim and Foxy Brown's prominent marketing feature was always sex. They emphasized their sexual prowess as part of a power play that allowed them to usurp temporary power from men smitten by their sexual skills and to exert power over other women who lacked said skills.

Outside of rapping about sex and exuding sexiness, there is very little room for women in hip hop. The Lady of Rage, however, simultaneously resists and participates in this narrow worldview. By most mainstream beauty standards, The Lady of Rage would not be considered physically attractive. Instead of being celebrated as the only female rapper on Death Row Records, she was marketed as one of the boys. During a time where other female rappers were dolling up by wearing weaves and wigs, Rage's first single celebrated the nontraditional beauty of natural hair in afropuffs. She is also known for portraying the emasculating, man-hating bully who could never get a date on *The Steve Harvey Show* and *Next Friday*. Additionally, her moniker is oxymoronic because it implies that she is a lady who adheres to hegemonic femininities, and yet she embodies rage— a masculine characteristic perceived as stereotypically unbecoming of women. In his study of female gangsta rappers, Josh Haugen analyzes Rage's flow and lyrical assertiveness and concludes that the rapper who refers to herself as "the lyrical murderer" and "fatally feminine" is acutely aware of her "lack of fit into the hegemonic expectations of lady-ness."[1]

Neither Rage's appearance nor her persona adheres to gendered expectations for women in hip hop. "Confessions" (1997) is the first hip hop track performed by a woman who publicly and explicitly confesses her sexual activity to God. The five minute and thirty-four second rap consists of one verse. There is no chorus. There is no bridge. Rage prays/raps an interrupted monologue to God. She begins by asking forgiveness for forsaking God and yielding to sexual temptation. She describes death all around her, queries whether she will be punished by the virus "that breaks down your nervous system," and considers whether hell is the hot consequence for acting on sexual desire. Rage is paranoid and suicidal when she invokes daddy God to help guide her through a minefield of contradictory sets of expectations. Patriarchal hip hop expects Rage to love sex, and she does. Patriarchal hip hop expects Rage to be sexy, but she is not. Patriarchal Christianity expects Rage to love God, and she does, but patriarchal Christianity expects her to be virginal, and she is not. Rage loves God and she loves sex. Her introspective and tension-filled confession describes the pleasures of sex within a religious context that strictly prohibits fornication. She is a conflicted daughter of God who receives clarity the more she talks with God. Her relational intimacy with God empowers her to talk *to* Him as opposed to talk *about* Him. Her familiarity with her Father reflects an intimacy that mediates blasphemy.

Throughout the song, Rage begs God for forgiveness. She begs God to clear the confusion perpetuated by "false prophets and religions" and to help her find her way to Him. The song's outro is a chorus of amens. Rage's ad-lib demands sample the Negro spiritual, "I Want Jesus to Walk with Me," as she asks God to come walk and talk with her. Rage's demands for daddy God's presence mark the process of her self-discovery. With Him by her side, she embraces her sexuality as the full realization of her womanhood and a meaningful connection to God. Addressing desire and sex acknowledges that the divine being created Rage to be a sexual being. Rage's divine daddy's presence is necessary for her to feel secure and confident about her (hetero)sexual relationships. Daddy God helps Rage grow into a mature woman who is not just following the rules but realizing that she does not have to be a sexy minx or a chaste Christian.

Although the song is about sex, Rage rejects the norms of patriarchal hip hop culture that relegate most heterosexual exchanges to pornographic and titillating sex acts. Rage refuses to depict consequence-free sex in "Confessions." She disrupts hip hop's normalization of female objectification. Her honest conversation about sex, HIV/AIDS, and Christian prohibitions against fornication does not minimize the importance of pleasure and desire. Additionally, in an era of video vixens and gangstresses, Rage combats sexism by exercising control over her representation so that her discussion of sex will not confirm others' notions of a sexually licentious black woman. By discussing her (sexual) sins on her own terms, Rage achieves a level of empowerment that is especially important for a black woman who wishes to speak seriously and innovatively about her sexuality. Daddy God is a masculine figure, but most importantly for Rage, He is a nurturer. He encourages her violation of these gendered expectations and grants her the courage to discover herself.

In their heyday, Lil' Kim and Foxy Brown were readily considered sexy by male and female fans. Unlike Rage, they built their careers by bragging about their sexual prowess. They never appeared to be morally convicted by their sexual desires, so their relationship with daddy God does not require learning to embrace their sexuality. Instead, their relationship with daddy God helps them resist the stereotype that they are only sex objects. Daddy God helps them confront their enemies and in the process demonstrates to their audiences that there is more to these women than meets the eye.

Lil' Kim and Foxy Brown appropriate the 27th Psalm to describe how their relationship with daddy God helps them deal with their adversaries. Verses 1 through 6 read as follows according to the New King James Version of the Bible:

> The Lord is my light and my salvation. Whom shall I fear? The Lord is the strength of my life. Of whom shall I be afraid? When the wicked came against me to eat up my flesh, my enemies and foes, they stumbled and fell. Though an army may encamp against me, my heart shall not fear. Though war may rise against me, in this I will be confident.

Lil' Kim focuses on verses 1 and 2 in "Single Black Female" (2000). Foxy Brown recites 1 through 3 in "Broken Silence" (2001). The initial verses focus on defeating one's enemies. Considering the long-standing antagonism between Kim and Foxy, their focus on enemies is eerily pertinent.

Kim and Foxy used to be friends. In fact, Kim helped jump-start Foxy's career, but as their fame escalated so did the enmity between two young women trying to occupy the same sex symbol, gangstress, baddest female MC space. Their rivalry climaxed in a February 25, 2001, shootout between Kim's entourage and that of the rap group Capone-N-Noreaga. Ostensibly, the exchange of gunfire that injured one man was exacerbated by Foxy's insults toward Kim on the 2000 Capone-N-Noreaga cut "Bang, Bang." Both *Notorious K.I.M.* (2000) and Foxy's *Broken Silence* (2001) include subtle barbs directed at each other. When these women rap about God's power to defeat their enemies, they take it very seriously.

"Single Black Female" consistently criticizes inferior female rappers (possibly Foxy) and reiterates Kim's ability to sustain herself as a single black female. After the murder of her lover and mentor, Notorious B.I.G., Kim dismisses claims that he was writing her rhymes and brags not only about her lyrical self-sufficiency but also about how she established the standards for female rappers. The album, *Notorious K.I.M.*, is simultaneously a tribute to him and a declaration of her independence.

Kim's appropriation is less loyal to the biblical 27th Psalm. Instead of following the psalmist's example and speaking *about* his enemies, Kim speaks *to* her enemies: "So when you MCs come to eat up my flesh and blood/Ya'll all will stumble and fall (ha ha!)." The New King James Version reads, "The Lord is my light [guidance] and my salvation [security]." Alternately, Kim's Lord is the light *of* her salvation, which emphasizes her steadfast security and not her desire for guidance. Kim's faith in her salvation/security implies that she does not fear her enemies. Instead, she warns her enemies to fear her Lord. As the psalm continues, the psalmist expresses his desire to commune with God in the house of God. True to the self-sufficient theme of "Single Black Female," Kim omits this portion of the passage and concludes with a daddy God whose primary role as her protector is to cause her enemies to stumble and fall.

Foxy's use of the same biblical passage one year after Kim is most likely not a coincidence. "Broken Silence," the title track, is a song about personal and professional pain. Foxy raps about broken relationships, a broken spirit, and broken wings. Many verses on *Broken Silence* are dedicated to Foxy's ex-fiancé, Kurupt. Considering the album as a whole, one might assume that her brokenness is partially attributable to the failure of this relationship. Foxy seeks a daddy God who will supplant that dysfunctional relationship with guidance, security, and the promise of peace. In "Broken Silence" Foxy challenges Kim's appropriation by remaining faithful to the biblical text and presenting herself as introspective rather than vengeful.

The track opens with Foxy speaking Psalm 27, verses 1 through 3:

> The Lord is my light and my salvation; whom shall I fear?
> The Lord is the strength of my life; of whom shall I be afraid?
> When the wicked came against me to eat up my flesh
> My enemies and foes, they stumbled and fell
> Though an army may encamp against me
> My heart shall not fear
> Though war may rise against me
> In this I will be confident.

An instrumental beat precedes Foxy's male background vocalist singing, "I will survive."

In addition to a recitation that is more faithful to the original biblical text, another important difference between Foxy and Kim is that Foxy's enemies have already been defeated. Note the past tense: "they stumbled and fell." Because the defeat of Kim's enemies has not yet happened there is no guarantee. Foxy differentiates herself from Kim by demonstrating more of a personal dependency upon God. She trusts her God to do in the future what He has done in the past. The inclusion of "Though an army may encamp against me/My heart shall not fear/Though war may rise against me" suggests that Foxy is confident that despite the presence of armies and the horrors of war, her faith in God will conquer additional adversity. Foxy figures daddy God as the protector she needs to guide her in all aspects of her life. The defeat of Foxy's enemies and victory in war are by-products of her confidence that with daddy God on her side, she will survive and be made whole.

Kim and Foxy depict themselves in need of a protector God because they are besieged by enemies. The articulated assault on black femininity is familiar in and outside of hip hop. Black women who have historically been unprotected create a daddy God who assumes that role. The protection, however, works differently for each rapper. Kim's provision of protection makes her even more independent. She uses God to amass more power over her enemies and upends the hierarchies until she is literally the Queen Bee–sitting on top of the world. Daddy God's presence helps her achieve power. In contrast to Kim's inverted hierarchy, Foxy's God protection is less about power and more about nurturing. The security she desired from the man who left her heartbroken is re-created in the arms of her daddy God. God's articulated role in Psalm 27 allows Kim and Foxy to create a daddy God whose unconditional love defeats enemies and heals a broken heart.

Rage, Kim, and Foxy create a daddy God who helps them negotiate the tension between sex and salvation. Daddy God elucidates options for how women can exist in a world where there are so many prescriptions for womanhood that simply do not fit how many women see themselves. Daddy God's presence also suggests to audiences that women rappers are more complex than hip hop's representations generally allow. Women rappers' introspections reveal frequently overlooked aspects of their identities.

Lover God

Because of hip hop's stereotypical investment in black women's sexual availability, black women are rarely depicted in affirming heterosexual relationships. Popular culture in general (especially Tyler Perry) often depicts black women as rancorous and unlovable individuals. In real life, marriage rates for African Americans are declining faster than rates for other ethnic groups. An imbalanced sex ratio exacerbated by higher mortality and incarceration rates for black men makes approximately 77 unmarried black men available for every 100 unmarried black women under age 40.[2] The shortage of marriageable black men increases the likelihood of man sharing as well as proclivities to commit infidelity. Research reports that African Americans have high infidelity rates and that infidelity is one of the leading causes of divorce second only to physical abuse. The ideal man who is 100 percent committed to his woman and willing to provide for her in every way is so rare that when he does exist, black women deify him. Consistent with popular culture presentations of black relationships, Khia and Salt 'n' Pepa (SNP) speak from a position of lack as they imagine their ideal lover God. Trina and Tiye Phoenix, however, debunk the stereotypes as they describe being blessed by a lover God.

In "When I Meet My King" (2002) Khia imagines that meeting her king will be "like walking through the gates of heaven." She describes his hair blowing in the wind, his pride, his strength, and the lion within. Although she never raps the word *God* in the track, her description is reminiscent of the Rastafari Conquering Lion of the Tribe of Judah, another name for Ethiopian Emperor Haile Selassie I who some Rastas believe was the incarnation of God on earth. Others believe that true Rastas strive to be human Gods. Khia awaits one of these proud dreadlocked brothers who thinks of himself as a king and will treat his woman like a queen. Khia's lover God provides for her sexually, emotionally, and financially. He is willing to physically protect his family from harm. He takes her places, buys her things, feeds their children. Their heavenly relationship will last forever because her king will neither play games nor commit infidelity. Their love for each other will sustain them during hard times. Although awaiting a king sounds like the stuff of fairytales, Khia's desires are consistent with other women's criteria.

SNP search for a lover God who provides sexual pleasure and commitment in "Do Me Right" (1997). Spinderella describes a man who drowns her in passion, romances the cat, and wants marriage and the baby carriage. Pepa is unimpressed by a man with money. She wants a man who will perform for her and is attracted to the God in her. Salt concludes the song praising her lover for taking her to the next level, making her heart skip beats, and raising her temperature with his skills. She wants him to give her "that God kinda love/That work it out through the hard times kinda love." Although the women's pleasure is paramount, each rapper also describes how she would reciprocate this love.

The song is significant because sex and commitment are integral characteristics of each woman's lover God desires. One without the other is insufficient. Even a man who can provide for a woman's material needs cannot become a lover God until he can sexually please the woman to whom he is committed. SNP are famous for vanguarding hip hop's conversations about women's sexual pleasures, safe sex, and AIDS. This song's use of "God kinda love" further affirms that for women to be sexually and spiritually whole, sexual pleasure must be an essential part of their committed relationships. The track's progressiveness is diminished only by the fact that they have yet to find this lover God.

Trina, on the other hand, tells the world about her lover God in the liner notes to *Da Baddest Bitch* (2000). Like Kim and Foxy, Trina appropriates Psalm 27. The note reads as follows:

> The Lord is my light and my salvation; whom shall I fear? The Lord is the strength of my life; of whom shall I be afraid? When the wicked, even mine enemies and my flesh [sic], they stumbled and fell. Though an [sic] host should encamp against me, my heart shall not fear; though war may rise against me, in this I will be confident. One thing have I desired of the Lord that will I seek after; that I may dwell in the house of the Lord all the days of my life, to behold the beauty of the Lord and to inquire in his temple. For in the time of trouble, he shall hide me in his pavilion; in the secret of his tabernacle shall he hide me; he shall set me high upon a rock and now mine head shall be lifted up above mine enemies round about me; therefore I will offer in his tabernacle sacrifice of joy; I will sing and praise unto the Lord.

The inclusion of verses 1 through 6 in their entirety is significant because liner notes are always pressed for space. Peppered with photos of the artist, advertisements for upcoming records, order forms for artist paraphernalia, and acknowledgment lines like "If I forgot anyone please don't curse me out" or "There are too many people to thank individually," Trina made a conscious choice to reprint verses 1 through 6. Trina is as faithful to the original as an adult repeating a verse from memory that she learned in childhood. The interesting part of Trina's reference is not the verses themselves but the dedication that follows: "I would like to dedicate this album to my significant other, my better half, my love, my strength, my life, I couldn't have done it without you no way no how together we've built something so strong so special. Thanks for 'everything.' For always being by my side and most of all for being my best friend 'I Love You, Josh.' "[3]

Trina attributes the same qualities to Josh as she does to God. Both of them are described as the strength of her life. Her choice of the words "built something so strong" connotes a sturdy and lasting foundation not unlike the house, temple, pavilion, or tabernacle of God. Trina links her love and appreciation for God to her man. Either Josh's love is so good it must be divine or Trina's love for the Divine is so strong that she looks for it reflected in her men. The dedication can be read as Trina praising and worshipping Josh as her lover God.

Tiye Phoenix describes an "unconceivable, indescribable, indestructible" relationship in "Bless Me" (2009). She visits heaven when she has sex with a partner who unlocks her inner goddess. Her lover God's provisions are sexual and emotional. There is no mention of money or any other material exchange in her description of the relationship. In the chorus she asks her lover to "keep blessing me with your love and I'll be yours tonight." Tiye's time with her lover God sounds egalitarian and idyllic. She addresses her lover as "you" or "babe" throughout the song. The direct address creates intimacy as well as the opportunity for audiences to imagine the lover as a woman. Other than the singular instance where she refers to the lover as "him" and when she clarifies that the lover is not a misogynist, the song creates space for the possibility of nonheterosexual intimacy.

For religious conservatives, it is probably no more blasphemous to make room for the lover God's femininity than it is to associate the lover God with sex. Sex shaming is a common practice used to maintain power "over a people through careful regulation of their bodies, their perceptions of their bodies, and their reproductive capacities."[4] Marvin Ellison explains: "Religious communities, by communicating explicitly negative, often shaming messages about sexuality, attempt to control people and coerce them into compliance with moral convention."[5]

Religious sex shaming commonly demonizes women as weaker vessels and temptresses to evil. Women who were not virginal madonnas became licentious whores. The whore stereotype was virulently directed toward black women as their historical role as sexually available breeders followed them off of the plantation. Black women responded by developing a politics of respectability that "black women throughout the twentieth century have used . . . to enhance their reputation, ensure social mobility, and create a positive image for their communities."[6] Unfortunately, the moralistic politics of respectability prohibited sex to the extent that black women were encouraged to appear asexual in public. Respectable women did not have sex outside of marriage, and when they did have sex it was for procreation and not pleasure.

The emergence of black female rappers who demanded that audiences listen to their explicit descriptions of sexual pleasure was a significant shift because they rejected religious and cultural sex-shaming practices. Because of foremothers like Lil' Kim and Foxy Brown, black women who would otherwise have been stifled by the politics of respectability or stigmatized for rejecting them now had models for publicly articulating their sexual desires.

Some critics argue that these women were simply selling sex in the same capitalist tradition that slave masters justified breeding as a form of sex work that reproduced labor and wealth for the plantation. These artists certainly created products expecting to garner a profit, but conversations about sex and God are about more than revenue. These examples revalue women's bodies, the perceptions of their bodies, and their reproductive capacities. Kelly Brown Douglas believes human sexuality is "a gift from God" and that "human sexuality makes human relationships possible—including the relationship to the divine. The quality of a person's relationship to God, therefore, hinges in many ways on her or his awareness and appreciation of her or his own sexuality. To be estranged from one's sexuality in all of its dimensions portends a diminished relationship with God."[7]

By associating sex with God and describing sex as god-like, these women take their power back from religious sex shaming, the politics of respectability, and gendered expectations for women in hip hop. After having been the chaste Christian, the sexy minx, the bad bitch, the brokenhearted, and the damsel in distress, there are few other roles for female rappers to play until they construct a God who allows them to realize their full potential as women. This significant realization, of course, is entirely attributable to the presence of a masculine God. The patriarch remains the locus of power. Consistent with the vicissitudes of patriarchy, women benefit from patriarchal privilege until they no longer benefit from patriarchal privilege.

Daddy-Lover God

When Lauryn Hill found herself at the familiar crossroads where Christian prohibitions against sex met with hip hop's expectations for its women to be sexually available, she turned to a daddy-lover God. Like the previous figures, Hill's daddy-lover God is a protector and a provider, but unlike the previous figures, His love is conditional. Hill's lyrics describe a woman struggling to stay in relationship with an authoritarian daddy-lover God whose demands for absolute loyalty and obsequiousness mirror the controlling ultimatums of a jealous lover. In an interview, Hill describes God's significance to her personal life. "And what I did was one of the biggest sins you can do when you have such a tight relationship with God—I put someone before Him. I fell deeply in love and put a man before God."[8] The regret that she expresses for disobeying daddy-lover God, falling in love, and replacing Him with a mere mortal is epitomized in "I Used to Love Him" (1998).

"I Used to Love Him" is a tension-filled narrative about a relationship with a young man whose negative influence is replaced by God. The five minute and thirty-nine second track is often perceived as a celebratory song of empowerment written and arranged by Hill and performed by Hill and Mary J. Blige—the Queen of Rhythm and Blues. "I Used to Love Him" is one of a few sung tracks on *The Miseducation of Lauryn Hill*, yet Hill's superb lyrical dexterity, crisp enunciation, staccato sounds, driving bass line, and frequent line-by-line exchange with Blige makes it the paradigmatic example of hip hop music with roots in both rap and rhythm and blues.

To audiences familiar with the artists' personal stories, Hill and Blige are sister friends who understand the pain of love. It is rumored that *Miseducation* was inspired by Hill's own dysfunctional love relationship with a married Wyclef Jean, the front man for the Fugees trio of which Hill and Prakazrel Michel were a part. Hill described an anonymous relationship that may have been with Jean. "I'm a lot hurt and I'm a lot disappointed. Half of these niggas that I meet, they don't know about relationships. And when they hurt you, they don't know it. Or if they do know, they don't really give a f—— because they've been so bruised, battered and scarred themselves."[9] A source close to Hill said she never healed from her broken heart.[10]

Blige's fans knew how much she used to love lead singer K-Ci from the R&B group Jodeci despite their very public and abusive relationship. Blige's struggles with addiction were also very public. The presence of these two women singing the same story as a single protagonist affirms the recurring experiences of black women who must also disassociate themselves and their love from an unhealthy relationship. Not only do Hill and Blige support each other but the camaraderie and shared experience suggest they support their audiences as well.

On the surface, "I Used to Love Him" is a quintessential breakup song. Hill describes a tenuous relationship with a young man in the first verse.

She asks the Father to forgive her indiscretions. In the second verse, Blige admits to choosing "a road of passion and pain," and likens her love to an unhealthy addiction. The pain of the relationship intensifies as the women alternate singing lines that describe themselves as torn, confused, wasted, used, stuck, and frustrated at "the crossroad." By the third verse, Hill and Blige testify to the joy they felt in finally abandoning the young men and indulging in true love with their Creator. Each verse is separated by a chorus of "I used to love him but now I don't." In this extremely woman-identified song, Hill and Blige depict themselves as survivors of an oppressive love. However, the song's redemptive suffering theme and its metaphors reveal a dominant-submissive abusive relationship not only between the women and their hetero love but also between the women and their daddy-lover God.

Redemptive suffering is the belief that suffering is an essential part of the spiritual maturation process. Redemptive suffering has its roots in the Christian tradition of Jesus Christ's ultimate sacrifice of his life in order to bring salvation to humankind. Many black Christian women emulate this surrogacy when they perceive suffering as something that brings them closer to God. Hill and Blige take full responsibility for the relationship with their respective young men and portray themselves as deserving of punishment. In the beginning of the song, Hill prays (present tense) that the Father will forgive her indiscretions with the young man. Although she describes the relationship in the past tense, Hill prays in the present, which suggests she still seeks forgiveness. Even after the relationship's demise, Hill has not forgiven herself. Thematically, the song reaffirms guilt and shame rather than forgiveness and redemption.

Furthermore, the song's natural metaphors belie a healthy intimate relationship. For example, in the first verse, Hill describes the young man as the ocean and herself as the sand. The ocean is a meandering, expansive, dynamic, tumultuous, powerful, and occasionally violent life force. The sand is a barrier that limits the ocean and redirects the wind, but erosion is inevitable as the ocean beats the sand into submission. As the ocean ebbs and flows, it sometimes wrenches and other times gently carries pieces of the sand away with it. In either case, the ocean and wind shape the sand. This is the natural metaphor of domination and submission chosen to describe not only the relationship with the young man but also the relationship with their Father/Creator.

Their daddy-lover God love, which is "greater than planets and deeper than any oceans," supposedly supersedes the superficial love for the young man, but the encompassing nature of this oceanic love seems suspiciously like exchanging one dominating force for another. The song begins and ends with oceanic metaphors for love. Because the ocean's essential characteristics remain unchanged in each metaphor, it is eerily ironic that the same ocean is oppressive as a young man and liberating as the Creator. Hill's man and her God are all-encompassing beings who swallow her up leaving little room for her to love herself.

If the Creator's love is "deeper than any oceans," Hill and Blige still desire the masculine and all-encompassing properties of the ocean. Perhaps, now that they are deeper in the water, they are in more danger than they were before. As daughters dominated by a patriarchal father God, Hill and Blige remain susceptible to masculine oppression. Furthermore, the Creator metaphor equates God with the aforementioned unpredictable, uncontrollable, ubiquitous power of nature. The Creator becomes synonymous with nature and masculinity as dominating forces.

In addition to its natural metaphors of domination, the song also includes recurring journey metaphors. Hill and Blige depict themselves as travelers on "a road of passion and pain" journeying away from their sin and toward the Father's forgiveness. By the end of the song, Hill and Blige completely let the Creator control their lives. Their dependency, however, first on the young man and then on the Creator has left little room for a progressive journey toward healing themselves. The song's climax occurs when the women encounter the crossroads. The crossroads stall their journey by presenting them with choices—continue on the current path, return from whence they came, or abandon the road of passion and pain for two unknown potentially salvific alternatives. Individuals facing crossroads are forced to choose between the blurred boundaries of oppositional dichotomies like dark and light, past and present, evil and good, and wrong and right. Hill and Blige signify on these various intersections when they describe their sin intersecting with their repentance. Ironically, their ultimate choice is to retreat as opposed to progress forward. They return to the familiar.

The chorus seems to propel the travelers toward redemption but the movement into a new future is compromised in this instance as well. The chorus, "I used to love him but now I don't," implies their pain has not been replaced with anything. The conjunction *but* implies a disruption and a change of direction—perhaps moving forward then turning around. And implies a continuation. "And now I don't" would represent memory, continuity, and progress toward a healing place as opposed to a retreat to an insecure place that led to the initial suffering. An emphasis on self-love would demand an interpretation along the lines of "I used to love him and now I love *me*." Self-love would require Hill and Blige to seek healing for their hurt selves after the relationship with the young man. The crossroad retreat and the lack of continuity in the chorus belie the empowering breakup message. By the end, Hill and Blige return to the "safe space" of the Creator, the same tenuous position that led them to embark upon their journey of passion and pain.

Many of the song's metaphors perpetuate passivity. Hill describes the young man stealing her heart like a thief in the night. Several New Testament Bible verses (Matthew 24:42–44, 1 Thessalonians 5:2–4, and 2 Peter 3:10) encourage vigilance by describing the day of the Lord approaching as a thief in the night. The "thief in the night" metaphor implies that Hill is victimized because of her negligence. She allows herself to be vulnerable with the wrong savior. In addition to perpetuating guilt for her indiscretion, the phrase conveys how easily the young man and her daddy-lover God can stand in for one another. Furthermore, Hill's stolen heart represents her emotions and desires. When the young man steals her heart under the cover of darkness, he surreptitiously destabilizes her emotional epicenter. In the absence of her heart, Hill depends on the young man for her emotional stability, like a transplant patient depends on a pacemaker. This state of dependency is rendered undesirable when Hill references her dulled senses and blurred sight, both of which are symptoms of the unhealthy addiction to artificial love that Blige describes in the second verse. Hill and Blige recount an unhealthy addiction to artificial love, and yet neither woman sings about resisting these effects or attempting to rescue themselves or each other. Instead, they wait to be saved by a Creator who showed them the true meaning of love in exchange for control over their lives.

"I Used to Love Him" appears to be an empowering breakup song, but its theme of redemptive suffering and its metaphors reveal oppressive patriarchal dominating forces, regressive movements, and perpetual passivity. Despite the emphasis on movement there is no movement away from constraining forces or toward a healthy embrace of self-love. Hill and Blige were and still are incapacitated by love. Instead of taking the time to heal, they pass the stolen heart from the young man to the Creator—from one masculine-identified being to another. We are left with no indication that Hill's and Blige's next heterosexual courtship will not reaffirm the same notions of personal responsibility without personal forgiveness. Hill and Blige have not healed sufficiently to maintain a relationship whether the lover is a foolish young man or the Creator. Hill refers to her God as a Father; but instead of nurturing her and helping her heal, He is also a surrogate lover—a destructive oceanic force who inhibits her ability to move forward. Hill brings the distant daddy God closer by giving Him the characteristics of a lover. As God fills the role that Hill desires, lyrically He becomes more like the young man she was trying to escape. The result is a woman rapper's relationship with a daddy-lover God that is as problematic and complicated as her real-life relationships with men.

Implications

The aforementioned female rappers' relationships with God reflect their intimate relationships with men. Daddy God is a nurturing protector who aids His daughters in finding their identity in relationship to patriarchal power. The gift of unconditional father love establishes a daughter's self-esteem and empowers her to renegotiate gendered expectations for her behavior. Lover God provides for His woman. The expression of His love is not limited to sex but always includes it. Reciprocity and mutual sexual pleasure are essential criteria for lover God relationships. Ironically, Rage, Kim, Foxy, Khia, SNP, Trina, and Tiye re-create gendered expectations for women by adhering to the social expectations for men to be protector/providers. God's overtly masculine characteristics, however, reflect traditional Christianity as well as the male-dominated hip hop industry. God is so completely male identified in these examples that there is very little room for a feminine Mother God or goddess to protect, provide, or befriend the women. In fact, no mainstream female rapper has released an entire track explicitly dedicated to a woman God.[11]

Women rappers' dependency on men is certainly traditional, but not entirely problematic. All three God figures are rooted in human desire. These desires dictate the need for different God figures at different times. Girls and women need fathers, and women desire lovers. Daddy God "out there" is the paradigmatic model of the perfect father. Lover God "down here" embodies the consummate manifestation of a loving partner. In their idealized representations, daddy God and lover God are both created in the benevolent image of a God "out there." However, when girls, immature women, and/or women who are wounded experience a fatherlack so profound that they conflate the father and the lover, the relationship may mirror the dominant-submissive pattern articulated in "I Used to Love Him."

Even adult women who refer to their lovers as daddy, big daddy, or big papa are conveying a power differential in their relationship. Male rappers often self-identify in this way as a means to convey their sexual prowess over women. bell hooks affirms this kind of response when she observes that "patriarchy invites us all to learn how to 'do it for daddy,' and to find ultimate pleasure, satisfaction, and fulfillment in that act of performance and submission."[12] Doin' it for daddy is problematic because it demands domination and submission. Doin' it for daddy-lover God is even more problematic because God's ultimacy confirms that domination and submission are the way things ought to be. Even though Hill perceives her daddy-lover God as "out there," her God's oppressive characteristics essentially convey a larger-than-life Man. God becomes who humans need God to be. Daddy-lover God exists because too many of us are used to doing it for daddy.

Chapter 3

The Jesus Piece

Jesus was gangsta. Jesus fraternized with sexually licentious women, cavorted with sinners, worked on the Sabbath, had a temper, used profane language with religious people, praised faithfulness over stilted forms of religious piety, and honored God more than the government. Gangstas respect Jesus because they see the parallels between his life and theirs. Consider Jesus's life story. His mother was homeless at the time of his birth. He was reared by a stepfather whose family tree was filled with some unscrupulous characters guilty of murder, incest, and rape. Jesus grew up as a poor minority terrorized by state-sanctioned oppression. As a single male in his late 20s/early 30s, Jesus and his posse of disciples made public appearances at parties where he appreciated his people's affinity for wine. Jesus was self-taught and unemployed, but went about the business of dropping knowledge wherever he could get an audience. Because of his penchant for speaking against what was popular, Jesus had haters. He was betrayed by one of his boys and couldn't get a fair trial before he was executed.

The Jesus story is the gangsta's story. The average rapper grows up in poverty without a biological father figure. The average rapper is also a minority who experiences discrimination while trying to access a comprehensive education from underfunded and overcrowded public schools. Gainful employment eludes the average rapper who lacks basic skills or who has a felonious past because of his or her attempts to counter the effects of poverty. Despite these challenges, the average rapper raps unceasingly—engaging street battles, releasing mixtapes, dropping knowledge wherever there is an audience. Once the rapper is discovered, he or she becomes rich, famous, and increasingly under surveillance. Inevitably, critics will try to censor, imprison, and crucify his or her reputation.

Both Jesus and the average rapper experienced state-sanctioned surveillance and subjugation. As the God "out there" sent "down here," Jesus is the crucial piece that bridges God and humanity. Jesus's physical experience of walking the earth and his psychological experience of being persecuted intimately entangles him with human beings. Although the Jesus of Christianity is a God that resides in heaven, the gangsta's Jesus is anchored to earth. Jesus "down here" serves multiple purposes for the gangsta. Jesus is sometimes a companion. Other times gangstas appropriate Jesus's crucifixion to visually depict suffering. Furthermore, when rappers wear the iconic "Jesus piece," lavish jewelry emblazoned with an image of Jesus's face, Jesus becomes the puzzle piece that connects Christianity and capitalism. Rappers acknowledge these pieces of Jesus by focusing on the God "down here" as a companion, a crucified figure, and a commodity.

Companion Jesus

The companion Jesus who walks and rides with rappers is usually African American. Jesus's race is important because it corroborates Jesus's identity as a fellow oppressed person. If Jesus's skin color is akin to African Americans', then not only is Jesus subject to systematic oppression, but Jesus also embodies resistance to these forms of oppression. Slave intimacy with Jesus initially created a space for racial affinity with Jesus. Enslaved Christians described Jesus as a comforter and friend who empathized with their physical oppression. Jesus was, after all, a poor Jew born in a lowly manger to a teenage mother unwed at the time of conception. Furthermore, he was betrayed by one of his own and beaten before he was crucified. Jesus was a liberator for the enslaved—a divine warrior who would eventually overwhelm the South's slavocracy. Despite these similarities, the slaves' Jesus was not yet black in pigmentation.

In the 1920s and 1930s African American leaders began to emphasize pigmentation. Marcus Garvey, Langston Hughes, and Countee Cullen among others argued for the literal and symbolic blackness of Jesus in an attempt to buffer the self-esteem of African Americans who were finally considered fully human but were far from being considered fully equal to their white counterparts. Black Jesus embodied the beauty of blackness, challenged the seemingly naturalized privileges of whiteness, destabilized Eurocentric Christian norms, and affirmed black people's struggle against racism—intentional acts and/or collusion with violent, hateful, or discriminatory practices based on skin color. Alternately, other black freedom fighters completely rejected black Jesus because they saw the hypocrisy of Christianity as a hindrance to black liberation. Black Jesus's characteristics are socially constructed and contingent upon one's perspective.

Contemporary gangstas, like Clipse, Kanye West, and Lil Wayne for example, confirm Jesus's blackness in order to construct an empathetic companion. Snoop and The Coup, on the other hand, offer an antagonistic black Jesus companion who represents the limits of Christianity for African Americans.

Clipse (Pusha T and Malice) depict black Jesus riding in the backseat of their Cadillac on the cover of their first commercial album about peddling drugs. The image of a black Jesus on a drug run with Clipse was appealing and not offensive to many fans who bought *Lord Willin'* (2002) because it represented Jesus as a ride or die companion for the gangstas and the hustlas who were trying to make enough money to leave the hood. Jesus literally rides in the backseat. His head is slightly titled and he gazes directly at the audience. Blood seeps from under the crown of thorns, and there is a bloody hole in the elongated hand that extends toward Clipse. Clipse appears in the sky above Jesus's head in broken, blood-red block letters that further symbolize the broken, bloodied body of Jesus. Clipse's Jesus looks like them. His racial marking celebrates the beauty and the burden of blackness.

The cover conveys the consequences of living within a postindustrial condition. The unkempt, boarded-up factory in the distance reflects the disturbing reality of deindustrialization's effects on working-class communities. Many unskilled and semiskilled workers were left without jobs when U.S. factories were systematically dismantled and relocated abroad where foreign labor was cheaper. The barren tree, the discarded furniture, and the thin, stray dog all represent social decay. Clipse's Jesus understands that their potential involvement in unscrupulous activities results from a perceived lack of opportunity for young black males in Virginia or anywhere for that matter. His presence is not so much of a contradiction as it is an acknowledgment of their desire for protection, sympathy, and hope in the midst of an untenable situation. The bloodied black Jesus rides in the backseat; Malice is driving. Jesus does not interfere with free will, but he is a welcome companion who neither condones nor condemns their crack involvement.

And yet Lord willin' Clipse are moving out of these conditions. The car represents mobility. Whether they are making a drug run, driving to the studio to record a track, or leaving Virginia Beach for good (the welcome to Virginia Beach sign is behind them), they've decided to take Jesus with them on their quest for upward mobility. Jesus represents possibility. As Jesus extends his hand, not only does he point toward a better future, but he also reaches out to protect them. They could literally turn around in their seats and Lord willin' pursue a different direction as long as Jesus is riding for and with them. The fact that Clipse are both looking to the sides and not straight ahead implies that they are open to possibilities. Although they are leaving, they are surveying the environment in an attempt to remember their community and stay connected to their past. The graffiti artist who paints their names on the side of a building solidifies their presence in communal memory. Clipse desire to be remembered in the same way that Jesus is memorialized.

Jesus's memory is kept alive when he rides with Clipse and when he walks with Kanye West. Jesus walked with West all over the world. In addition to the original 2004 "Jesus Walks" track, West released a radio remix, performed the song at the 47th Grammy Awards, and produced three videos. The Church Version, the Chris Milk Version, and the Street Version are all featured on the *The College Dropout Video Anthology*. "Jesus Walks" presents the incongruity of walking with Jesus in a corrupt world. West opens the song with the lament: "We are at war with terrorism, racism, but most of all we at war with ourselves." He geographically situates the song in his hometown of Chicago, a city that has and still is suffering the repercussions of losing its industries, and describes it as a war-torn locale filled with death and systemic oppression. West's recourse from postindustrial Chicago is selling drugs to make economic ends.

Despite the postindustrial backdrop, "Jesus Walks" is an uplifting street anthem that reminds killers, murderers, drug dealers, strippers, victims of welfare, and your average club goer that Jesus walks with them. During an interview, West intentionally locates Jesus in the hood. "When I ride through the hood right now, or if I go back to Chicago. If I'm in areas where there's abandoned buildings, or where there's poverty, or where they tore down the projects where there's still a lot of gang activity, or any place like that you can hear, you can hear, you can hear the hummin' from 'Jesus Walks' as you walk down, it's like a theme song for where you're at."[1] Of the three videos, "Jesus Walks: The Street Version" is the only one that visually represents Jesus walking through the hood with West.

The black-and-white video opens with West taking a phone call from the mattress in his sparsely furnished bedroom. The spiritual "I'll Fly Away" plays and iconic images of Jesus are cut in as West gets ready for his day. West tries to slip past Jesus on his way out of the house, but Jesus wakes up, grabs his crown of thorns, and rushes after him. Jesus walks behind West but cautiously steers him away from trouble. An empty refrigerator becomes full after Jesus's touch. A disabled family member can dance after Jesus touches him. The video shows Jesus imagery from churches around Chicago until West and Jesus find themselves in a church. After West preaches his second verse from the church's pulpit, the video portrays other Jesus figures interacting with the people outside the church.

Neither Clipse nor West purposely present black Jesus to make a political statement about racism. In his lyrics and interviews, West consistently claims he is uninterested in Jesus's facial features, but each Jesus in his video is African American. Companion Jesus is black because he understands how poverty affects African Americans, and he passes no judgment about the decisions made by impoverished people. Jesus rides and walks with the gangstas and not vice versa. Black Jesus has no ego. He does not demand to be followed; he willing follows the gangstas to places only their comrades would be willing to go. Like a true homie, black Jesus offers unconditional acceptance. Furthermore, black Jesus offers assistance not systemic change.

This Jesus of personal responsibility is further embodied by Lil Wayne's cartoon character Trap Jesus, the biggest dope dealer in the south. *Trap* is both a noun and a verb defined as an urban area where drugs are sold or the activity of hustling to make money usually via selling drugs. Trap Jesus is an urban appropriation of Jesus from the animated special *Freaknik: The Musical* (2010).[2] The plot revolves around four friends who comprise a rap group called Sweet Tea Mobsters. They travel from Sweet Tea, Florida, to Atlanta to compete in a rap battle for the chance to win "a lifetime supply of money, clothes, and hos." They encounter obstacles and distractions along the way and are ultimately encouraged by Trap Jesus.

Trap Jesus demands respect from the Sweet Tea Mobsters. He reminds their leader Virgil not to casually call him "dawg." Trap Jesus makes it clear that he deserves to be addressed by his referential title. His disciples are instigators who would like to kill the Sweet Tea Mobsters but they can act only with Trap Jesus's authorization. In addition to the cross tattoo on his forehead, Trap Jesus has two tears tattooed under his right eye to represent people who are no longer alive. Fear Me is tattooed over his eyelids.[3] Trap Jesus wears a gold chain as he pours wine from a jug of water and as powder cocaine materializes into a rock of crack when pressed between his fingers. He has put in work (participated in the drug economy) since he was nine years old. Trap Jesus is the man other men admire.

It is from this position of respect that Trap Jesus provides solid guidance to the Sweet Tea Mobsters. They are frustrated, lost, and bickering among themselves when they arrive on his block. Virgil is ready to give up on attending the battle but Trap Jesus, despite his many contradictions, is inspirational. Virgil whines that "it's like God himself don't want us to make it." Trap Jesus retorts, "Y'all act like you know His mutherfuckin' plan. You thought you'd be able to just walk up and win the battle, huh? It ain't supposed to be easy. He's testing your faith. Your commitment to the game." Then he proceeds to explain how God showed him favor in the crack game because of his work ethic.

The Sweet Tea Mobsters are ready to quit and die until Trap Jesus reminds them that "the path we choose is ripe with trials and tribulations." His message is one of faith and perseverance. His model as a dope man is questionable but Trap Jesus does not advocate for the Mobsters to sell drugs or to be violent. Instead, he encourages them to use their natural (God-given) talents. He generously lends the crew his Lamborghini because "lambos are just material possessions. They mean nothing to me." Trap Jesus's supportiveness mediates his interpretation as an entirely blasphemous character. He is the voice of reason and perseverance embodied in a character the aspiring rappers could relate to. His recurring ghetto commandment is, "If you want somethin' bad enough, you gotta man up and earn it, but if you a bitch, you don't need to breathe." Even though his reference to bitches communicates intolerance for masculine displays of femininity, Trap Jesus and the Mobsters are trafficking in male homosocial spaces where their survival is contingent upon their ability to be the best.

Trap Jesus is a sympathetic companion because he is subject to the same forms of persecution as those who look up to him. When Virgil once again finds himself in a desperate situation, he cries out, "Tell me what to do," and Trap Jesus appears in the heavens on the phone from prison. Virgil notes his confinement and Trap Jesus replies, "That nigga Judas straight snitched on me." The hilarity of the moment shows how even Trap Jesus is subject to betrayal and that confinement does not curtail his ability to provide assistance. Virgil cried out for help and Trap Jesus appeared. Even though he is imprisoned, Trap Jesus is still accessible. He encourages Virgil by reminding him to "man up or bitch out." In one more ironic twist, Trap Jesus's prison guard reminds him that it's time to go and he makes a final request of Virgil. "I'm gonna need you to come bail me out, ya heard." Trap Jesus has so empowered Virgil that he is now confident that Virgil can save him too. Virgil does not buckle under the pressure. He prepares to use his God-given talent—not violence, not illegal activity—to help himself and those around him.

Virgil is not discouraged by Trap Jesus's condition. If nothing else, Trap Jesus understands him better because they are living the same life as black men facing obstacles while on their daily grind. His confinement is not a hindrance as much as it is a reality that black men can help each other overcome. Trap Jesus is trapped in the prison system because he was caught trapping (selling drugs) in the trap (hood). Both "traps" represent a cycle of impoverishment and imprisonment. Because Trap Jesus embodies this predicament, he is an accessible companion who looks and acts like his followers.

Thus far, black Jesus has been an ally, but sometimes the similarities between black men and black Jesus create an antagonistic companionship. Snoop Dogg includes a black Jesus in his mini-movie music video, *Murder Was the Case* (1994). In the 18-minute video, Snoop is initially gunned down by an African American rival named Jay Cee in a jealousy-fueled drive-by shooting. While near death in the hospital, Snoop makes a Faustian pact with a white devil who helps him secure earthly redemption and resurrects him as an original gangsta.[4] When Snoop proves ungrateful for this intervention, the devil punishes him by forcing him to relive the shoot-out as an aggressor instead of a victim. Unsurprisingly, this behavior lands Snoop in prison where Snoop murders Jay Cee. While in prison, Snoop and his ally are killed by white prison guards. In the final scene, the white devil stands next to Snoop's headstone ready to claim his soul.

Companion Jesus's role in this narrative is small but significant. When the white devil makes his pact with Snoop, for approximately three seconds the white devil transmogrifies into a black Jesus replete with a white loincloth, dreadlocks, a crown of thorns, blood dripping down his temple, and bloodied hands. The radical intimacy of a white devil's conflation with a bloody black Jesus creates a historically accurate space of death that mimics the white physical and spiritual oppression of vulnerable black bodies. The distinctively black Jesus's naked, bloody, and battered body foreshadows the inevitability (violent) death for black men in general and Snoop in particular.

Snoop's companion Jesus shows the limited potential of a bloody black Jesus not just for black men but also for black people who adhere to Christianity. Black Jesus, in this instance, is not a liberator. Instead, he embodies the limitations of a Christianity used to oppress black people by sanctioning slavery, promoting gradualism in racial equality, or encouraging retributive redemptive suffering—suffering that should be welcomed because it results from wrongdoing and will be eventually rewarded in a heavenly afterlife. This battered black Jesus is inextricability bound to a white devil to show how he has been has been victimized by Christianity.

Although black Jesus's appearance is brief, his link to oppression, victimization, and, more specifically, murder is further apparent in the experiences of his alter ego, Jay Cee. Emphasis on the initials of his name makes J. C. a ready foil for Jesus Christ.[5] As *Murder*'s antagonist, Jay Cee is a walking space of death. He initiates the hunt for Snoop. He represents a threat to Snoop's life. As black Jesus's alter ego, Jay Cee goads Snoop into killing him. Snoop's affinity for black Jesus is premised on a shared death-bound subjectivity. By murdering Jay Cee, Snoop transcends this subjectivity. He rejects the (white, Western) Christian ideal of (black) bodies as a site of suffering.

Boots of The Coup also finds himself rejecting Christianity by murdering his black Jesus companion. In the video "Me and Jesus the Pimp in a '79 Granada Last Night" (1998), Boots drives the streets of Oakland with a pimp named Jesus. In Jesus's heyday, he violently murdered one of his prostitutes who also happened to be Boots's mother. The night that they are cruising together is Jesus's first day of freedom after serving 15 years for an unrelated murder charge. Boots feigns friendliness as he eventually drives Jesus to a secluded area and executes him.

Like Jay Cee, Jesus the pimp has a sinister side and is allegorically used to critique Christianity. If Jesus represents the central focus of Christian worship, and Boots's mother in her complete reliance on Jesus represents a devoted and subservient worshipper, then their relationship could be interpreted as a black church woman being pimped by Jesus. Young, single black mothers who are struggling financially can become dependent on church leadership when they transfer their devotion to Jesus to a male pastor. The male pastor/female worshipper hierarchal manipulation is compared to a prostitute's relationship with her pimp in "Me and Jesus the Pimp."

Boots hints at the parallels when in the rap, his mother asks six-year-old Boots's opinion of "Jesus when he broke off some bread." Subtly referencing the biblical account of Jesus feeding the multitudes, and overtly suggesting that Jesus the pimp sometimes allowed his mother to keep some of her money for food, the shared message is that Jesus provides only when it suits him. Additionally, Boots inherited Jesus from his mother. The pimp may or may not have been his biological father, but he was certainly his only father figure. After Jesus went to prison, 12-year-old Boots wrote him letters and received advice on how to be a man. Boots religiously followed Jesus's counsel on how to be steadfast, calculating, and in control. Ironically, following Jesus's advice gave Boots the strength to exact revenge. Boots learned from Jesus, but had to kill him in order to become his own man.

Boots's satirical perspective on God and religion are apparent in other aspects of the song. At the beginning of verse 3, Boots describes the rain as God's piss or vomit. In the chorus he samples Parliament's live Oakland performance of "Swing Down, Sweet Chariot" (1977). Besides the fact that Jesus the pimp looks ridiculously full of himself mouthing "Oakland, do you wanna ride?" the sample references Parliament's infamously secular mothership, not the sacred chariot of Christianity. "Me and Jesus the Pimp in a '79 Granada Last Night" critiques individuals' intimacy with an exploitative Jesus companion.

Companion Jesus represents black masculine resistance. Riding, walking, or trapping with Jesus empowers black men to do what needs to be done to avoid being trapped in undesirable circumstances. Companion Jesus mirrors the experiences of black men so well that sometimes they wrestle with him to rid themselves of constraining beliefs. Murdering the antagonistic Jesus companion empowers Snoop and Boots to grow out of their inherited racist and patriarchal beliefs about Christianity and live independently as free men.

Crucified Jesus

The aforementioned companion Jesus and the crucified Jesus resonate with gangstas because of their shared experiences. Tupac and the Outlawz, for example, describe their search for a not-too-perfect saint who hurts, smokes, drinks, understands their pain, and carries them through hard times in "Black Jesuz" (1999). As a companion, Jesus is only slightly more influential than humans. Jesus remains subject to drug runs, urban drama, imprisonment, and death. Companion Jesus is consistently embroiled in the power struggles of persecuted black males. Jesus involves himself in the human experience, but cannot miraculously alter it even to save his own life. His behavior is governed by the rules on earth. The crucified Jesus, however, has greater power because he embodies the potential to resist death.

The cross represents Jesus's victory over death. Cheating death makes Jesus the gangsta's hero. The cross as a symbol of death visually resurrects memories of unjust persecution from Jesus to ancestors who hung from lynching trees. Beginning with the physical and psychological violence enacted to perpetuate slavery, impoverished African American communities are disproportionately threatened by death via inadequate sanitation, expensive or unavailable preventative health and rehabilitation treatments, the presence of toxic waste sites, police use of excessive force, and intercommunity violence. Prospects for longevity are further compromised by economic instability and increasingly punitive criminal justice policies. Gangstas who depict death as a way of life are drawn to crucified Jesus not because they want to die, but because staring down death makes them feel most alive. According to cultural critic and minister Michael Eric Dyson, gangstas see a crucified black Jesus as "the God who literally got beat down and hung up, the God who died a painful, shameful death, subject to capital punishment under political authority and attack, but who came back, and keeps coming back, in the form and flesh we least expect."[6] Gangstas often portray themselves as those forms who keep coming back. When gangstas represent themselves as Jesus, they are usually not healing the sick, feeding the multitudes, teaching in the temple, or loving women and children. Gangstas represent themselves as a crucified Jesus who is resisting authority. Crucified Jesus is the prototype for visual depictions of death as well as life after death for rappers crucified by media and malcontent competitors.

Kanye West carefully orchestrated his public appearance as Jesus. A bearded West appears on the February 2006 cover of *Rolling Stone* in a crown of thorns with bloody scars crisscrossing his face. In case the antiquated image of West in a burlap cloth did not immediately signal an appropriation of Jesus, the caption reads: The Passion of Kanye West. Even those unfamiliar with Christian passion plays that dramatized the trial, suffering, and crucifixion of Jesus would have been familiar with the 2004 Mel Gibson film, *The Passion of the Christ*, which graphically reenacted the brutality of the final hours of Jesus's life.

If there were ever a rapper who believed he could turn water into wine, it is Kanye West. West's hubris is legendary. In the *Rolling Stone* interview, his strong sense of self is substantiated by the quote, "If I was more complacent and I let things slide, my life would be easier, but you all wouldn't be as entertained. My misery is your pleasure."[7] West has been severely criticized as an egotistical megalomaniac who erroneously believes the government administered AIDS and that President George W. Bush does not care about black people. Critics of the cover argued that West was "morally and mentally challenged." West is used to being crucified by media. While promoting his third studio album, *Graduation* (2007), West spoke directly to the press: "Print what you want. Try to make it seem like I'm some like type of lunatic 'cause you only make me hotter. You only raise my prestige. Thank you very much." Then he responded directly to the self-divination critiques:

> They feel like, "Yo, he's got a God complex because he said if they wrote the Bible again he would be in it." Duh, yeah I would be in it. I feel like I'm one of the more important people in pop culture right now, one of the only people with an opinion. The Bible had 20, 30, 40, 50 characters in it. You don't think I would be one of the characters of today's modern Bible?[8]

The key to interpreting West is understanding the biblical importance of the word.

In the biblical book of John, chapter 1, verses 1 and 14, Jesus is introduced as the Word who became flesh. West appropriates Jesus as the living Word of God in order to empower his own words. The cover is striking not because it is blasphemous, but because it exposes the hypocrisy of those who are quick to cast blame yet unwilling to suffer for justice or to speak the truth. As Jesus, West has a right to say what he wants. More importantly, West has a right to say whatever he feels God needs him to say because he is willing to bear the burden of the cross.

Surprisingly, West's self-representation of Jesus is temperate compared to rappers who actually position themselves on a cross. Remy Ma is the first female rapper to do so, on the mixtape *Shesus Khryst* (2007). The cover depicts a topless Remy on a cross. Long hair conveniently covers her nipples. She wears cloth panties, but the contours of her breasts, stomach, and hips reveal a curvaceous body. Her arms are bound with ropes. Blood streams from the nails in each hand. There is graffiti on the cross; a skull is etched above her head. To her right is a cemetery, to her left a cityscape. Bright sunlight streams from the heavens giving the dark cover a sepia-toned glow.

Remy further emphasizes her femininity in the "Shesus Khryst" video. It opens with Remy on her back. The camera pans her body; her arms are raised above her head and bound to a horizontal cross resting on the ground. Occasionally, there are shots of Remy standing without the cross. She wears a crown of thorns; a white cloth covers her breasts like a halter top and a similar cloth is wound around her waist as a skirt. In her opening lines she raps Jay-Z is Jay-Hova, Nas is God's son, and Remy is the Bronx's savior, Shesus Khryst. In her single verse, Remy brags about her lyrical prowess. It culminates in the line, "these old chicks genesis, this is revelations and I'm the New Testament."

If Kanye is crucified by media, Remy is crucified by the male and female malcontents who underestimate her resilience. She vehemently calls out former boss, Fat Joe, for a bogus contract. She dis(mis)ses him, describes her independence, and declares that she cannot be controlled. She acknowledges the women who are responsible for the female rapper genesis, but reveals to them that their time has come and gone. She respects Jay-Z and Nas's self-deification by limiting her reign to the Bronx so as not to impose on their respective boroughs, but Remy's most important announcement is that it is time for a woman savior.

Her crucifixion is feminized and sexualized to draw attention to her body. Remy extends the traditional spectacle of crucifixion to include sexualizing death. She encourages audiences to enjoy looking at an attractive, partially clothed, bound, and vulnerable woman. However, Remy also resists these patriarchal expectations for femininity by refusing to remain on the cross. The cross is merely a temporary setback that inspires her determination and increases her redemptive potential. Audiences are encouraged to read her crucifixion on the cover art as a transition from the death in the cemetery to life in the cityscape. The video appropriately concludes with a shot of an empty cross to visually imply that Remy has been resurrected. Her representation's significance lies in the affirmation that a woman can feminize and sexualize Jesus's death and resurrection in order to draw attention to the power of a living woman savior. Femininity is not a liability; it is an asset that sets her apart from Jay-Hova and God's son. Shesus Khryst offers her beauty and her talents to the world. Remy may have been the first female rapper to self-crucify, but she was not the first rapper depicted on a cross. The male rappers who paved the way for Shesus Khryst are Nas and Tupac Shakur.

Queensbridge rapper Nas drew controversy when he hanged himself from a cross in "Hate Me Now" (1999). The visual narrative opens with a stormy sky as a backdrop for the credits. A shadowed Nas stands in front of pillars of fire. Then the scene cuts to him dragging his cross through an angry mob who heckle him and throw stones. The scenes alternate between Nas walking away from the fire and Nas walking through the mob. Mob members are dressed in long robes and turbans. Nas's body is scarred. He wears a crown of thorns and a cross around his neck. The reenactment is reminiscent of Good Friday—the day Jesus walked the *via dolorosa* (way of grief) to his crucifixion.

In this introduction and in the last scenes of the video that revisit Nas hanging from a cross, Nas draws parallels between his persecution and that faced by Jesus. In "Hate Me Now" the appeal of Jesus is not his death, but his refusal to die. Nas draws strength from the resurrection of Jesus. He and featured artist Sean "Diddy" Combs's recurrent ad-libs of "I won't stop, I can't stop, It ain't never gonna stop" suggest that acquiescing to death is merely the first step to overcoming death and living in perpetuity. Nas becomes more powerful with every attempt to eliminate him. Additionally, Nas walks with a forward movement away from the fire, an allusion to hell, and also away from the haters who represent hell on earth. Nas as Jesus is powerful enough to move out of those situations. Being persecuted is a badge of honor because it means an individual is notable enough to be hated on. In an interview with *Rolling Stone*, Nas explains, "I wanted to be crucified like Jesus in the video, to get back at all those people that don't want to see a black man doing his thing."[9]

Nas is certainly inspired by Jesus, but his appropriation of resurrection power emboldens "Hate Me Now" to diverge from the biblical narrative. "Hate Me Now" impugns the haters. Diddy declares that he wants the "weak, jealous motherfuckers" to die. Nas draws hatred for his material possessions—money, clothes, cars, jewelry, and women. The video's contemporary drinking and partying scenes are a constant reminder of how Nas differs from Jesus. Nas's encouragement of hatred, displays of crass materialism, hedonism, and arrogance directly contrast Jesus's life on earth. At the exact moment that we first see Nas hanging from a cross, we hear Diddy say, "I like this . . . I like the way this feels." Whereas Jesus prayed in Matthew 27:46 "My God why have you forsaken me," Nas says, "Do it now! Get this shit over with."

Nas's reenactment is consistent with the video's initial disclaimer:

Since the first recorded crucifixion in 600 B.C. many thousands upon thousands of men and women have been crucified for their beliefs, their convictions, their love and their crimes . . . some have been guilty, some have been innocent. Some were nailed to a cross, others tortured in life. Nas believes in the Lord Jesus Christ and this video is in no way a depiction or portrayal of his life or death.

There is little biblical accuracy within the video, and yet Nas is eager to be crucified because being persecuted is a badge of honor. It means God has shown him so much favor that envious detractors want to kill him. Nas is grateful that God has given him enough conviction and material possessions to incite envy. It is important to note that the cross that appears in Nas's reenactment and the multiple platinum crosses that Diddy wears in the video's contemporary scenes are not crucifixes. They memorialize the resurrected Jesus. Taking comfort in how Jesus's story ends allows Nas to prepare for an attack. He consciously makes a video that he knew many individuals could perceive as blasphemous. Otherwise, he would have omitted the disclaimer, but he also anticipates being resurrected. Because he follows his beliefs, he has faith that he will regain success in his career. The same power that brought Jesus, the ultimate conqueror, back to life will do the same for Nas's reputation.

Before there was Kanye, Remy, or Nas, Tupac Shakur aka Makaveli crucified himself on a cross on the 1996 cover art for *The Don Killuminati: The 7 Day Theory*. No other rap crucifixion has more fully encompassed the tropes of death and resurrection than this image. The cover depicts a black man who resembles Tupac, including the characteristic head wrap and the THUG LIFE tattoo across his abdomen, which is an acronym for The Hate U Give Little Infants Fucks Everyone. The cross is imposed over a worn Bible that rests on a light brown crinkled background that resembles paper. Blood streams down his body past the THUG LIFE. There are nails in his hands and feet, barbed wire around his wrists and ankles. A larger crown of thorns is weaved into his head wrap. The cross is an urban map including: Hollywood, South Central, Los Angeles, Watts, Compton, Long Beach, Detroit, Chicago, Manhattan, Queens, Bronx, East Orange, Brooklyn, New Orleans, Atlanta, and Houston. The cities are labeled in their approximate geographical regions. A compass rests on top of the cross, and West, which represents Makeveli's home in California, is visibly marked with a W. The caption reads: "In no way is this portrait an expression of disrespect for Jesus Christ.—Makaveli."

Many fans interpreted this cover as evidence that Tupac faked his own death. *The Don Killuminati: The 7 Day Theory* was released two months after the 1996 Las Vegas drive-by shooting that ultimately led to Tupac's untimely murder. Two years earlier, Tupac survived a near-death experience after he had been shot five times in what appeared to be a robbery in New York. Fans believed that if Tupac could cheat death once, he certainly could do it again. Besides, Tupac lived death. His artistic corpus is filled with narratives about his experiences with death from the murder of comrades to descriptions of prison as a confinement like death to visions of death and the afterlife in his videos. Numerologist fans have interpreted the seven in the seven-day theory to mean that Tupac is still alive. The number seven signifies perfection and completeness because the Lord rested on the seventh day (Genesis 2:2). Alive theories highlight the facts that Tupac was shot on September 7th at 4:03 a.m. $(4 + 0 + 3 = 7)$ at the age of 25 $(2 + 5 = 7)$ and died seven days later on the 13th.

Finally, alive theories are fueled by Tupac's Makaveli moniker. Tupac was an avid reader of Italian political theorist Niccolò Machiavelli who was infamous for his work, *The Prince*, which advises political leaders to undertake innovative and unscrupulous actions to usurp and sustain power. Machiavelli is said to have faked his own death to fool his enemies. Tupac adopted Makaveli as his alias just before he died. In this context Makaveli is sometimes read by ardent fans as mak-alive, make alive, mock-a-veli, which suggests he is mocking those who believe him to be dead, or mack-a-veli because he pimped not only death but the music industry into succumbing to the belief that he is dead while maintaining multiplatinum album sales. The Machiavellian correlation only adds fodder to the conspiracy/divination theories alluded to by the album's title and cover art.

A superficial interpretation of the aforementioned resurrection themes makes the cover look like an excellent marketing ploy. And it was. But it also communicates an important message to the urban United States (especially the thugs living in those cities noted on the cross) about the necessity of resisting death. Dyson explains that if facing death is normal for "the nobodies of American life—poor, black, desperate, hopeless, urban citizens," then cheating death is the ultimate act of resistance and the ultimate manifestation of power over one's social situation.[10] Life after death is psychologically empowering because resurrection communicates invincibility. Audiences need to believe that Tupac conquered death in order to accept their own potential for greatness. Otherwise Tupac's untimely death is evidence that they too could die at any time. Even after accepting Tupac's death, normalizing the potential for resurrection resists any attempts to erase his memory. Since 1996, over 10 posthumous CDs have been released including *Resurrection*, the 2003 soundtrack to the movie about Tupac's life told in his own words. Tupac's posthumous success is proof positive of Dyson's claim that "early death and unfulfilled potential mean the possibility of achieving after life what could not be achieved in life."[11] Therefore Tupac's crucifixion acknowledges the familiarity of death and alludes to the possibility of resurrection and infinite life through one's art.

Other rappers have similarly appropriated resurrection themes. The Notorious B.I.G.'s album titles reflect how death was a primary force behind his music. His first studio album was titled *Ready to Die* in 1994. *Life after Death* was released only 16 days after his untimely murder in March 1997. The posthumous album *Born Again* (1999) perpetuates similar themes. 50 Cent resurrected Tupac's and B.I.G.'s gangsta ethos in 2003 not with his album *Get Rich or Die Tryin'*, but with a promotional campaign about surviving multiple gunshot wounds. Resurrection is a theme that can mark the end, the beginning, or the middle of one's career. Album titles with key words like *return, resurrection,* and *rebirth* as well as music videos with death and resurrection scenarios are a staple for rappers reinventing themselves mid-career.

Tupac was the first to take the place of the crucified Jesus in mainstream hip hop, not to celebrate death but to encourage resurrection as a form of resistance. Although it appears blasphemous, these artists push the boundaries of religion until they arrive at Jesus—an accessible model—for surviving ostracism, patriarchal expectations for women, jealousy, and death. Jesus is a cultural icon for resisting the rules, especially those for life and death. By imitating a Jesus who suffered and yet emerged victorious over death, gangstas boldly appropriate Jesus's resistance as their own.

Commodified Jesus

The added benefit of appropriating Jesus is that it sells well. Gangstas incite controversy every time they imagine themselves as God "down here." Some gangstas welcome this criticism of their use of Jesus as proof that they are under attack like Jesus. Feelings of personal, social, and economic inferiority have been consistently countered by the declaration of a personal relationship with Jesus. Gangstas celebrate capitalism and consumption through the commodification of Jesus on album covers, in videos, and also around their necks. The Jesus piece is extravagant jewelry emblazoned with an image of Jesus's face.

Notorious B.I.G. rocked the first Jesus piece, a diamond-studded pendant of Jesus's face that cost no less than $10,000. He bragged about it in "I Love the Dough" (1997): "You seen the Jesus, dipped in H-classes . . . even got rocks in the beards and mustaches." Biggie's Jesus piece, designed by his jeweler, Tito, consisted of blinding H-color diamonds in Jesus's beard and mustache. Unlike an ornate cross or crucifix, which serves as a reminder of Jesus's death, the blinged out serene face of Jesus celebrates life and living it to the fullest. Throughout "I Love the Dough," Biggie and Jay-Z rap about their wealth. It is no accident that Jesus is a prominent exemplar of conspicuous consumption. The Jesus piece symbolizes a non-judgmental, compassionate figure who promises a better (fiscal) future in the midst of poverty.

An MTV News tribute to Biggie acknowledges the Jesus piece as one of his most influential signature accessories. Kanye West's Jacob the Jeweler Jesus pieces receive the most attention today, but other rappers wear and rap about their unique Jesus pieces. Whether made of wood, metal plates, gold, platinum, diamonds, or other gemstones, the Jesus piece must always appear excessively lavish because the Jesus piece represents God's favor. Wearing Jesus so close to the heart is not unlike wearing the image of any patron saint endowed with the powers of protection. When faced with conflict in "Hypnotize" (1997), Biggie responds, "So I just speak my piece, keep my peace/Cubans with the Jesus piece (thank you God), with my peeps." Wearing his Jesus piece on a Cuban link chain allows him to speak his mind and keep his cool (by refraining from using his piece, which is slang for gun). Purchasing a Jesus piece provides peace of mind. Whereas Biggie's favor manifests as peace, other rappers find favor in gemstones. In "Not Give a Fuck" (2003), Fabolous describes "lemon gems" in one of his Jesus pieces. The Game acknowledges his solvency in "The Documentary" (2005) when he raps, "I'm far from religious, but I got beliefs/so I put canary yellow diamonds in my Jesus piece." Fabolous covets respect from others by bragging about his extravagant Jesus piece. The Game shows respect to Jesus by blinging out his Jesus piece. The two perspectives coalesce around financial favor.

Jesus is an icon of prosperity. Purchasing a blinged out Jesus piece is akin to consuming one's salvation while erasing any contradictions between one's ideas about Christianity and one's desire for capital. This practice is firmly situated within Christian prosperity gospel messages that urge believers who tithe to expect affluence in return. Jesus is partially responsible for these interpretations. His John 14:2 allusions to preparing mansions in his Father's house led followers to believe that heaven would be opulent. These expectations are enhanced by Revelations 21 descriptions of the new heaven as a city of pure gold adorned with precious stones. The Jesus piece is merely a material item that bridges God's riches "out there" in the new heaven with conspicuous consumption "down here." The Jesus piece is a little bit of heaven on earth.

Even though the rapper penchant for a capitalist Jesus is commonplace, the practice seems disingenuous to some critics. Journalist Elizabeth Mendez Berry challenged Jay-Z for wearing a Che Guevara T-shirt and Biggie's platinum Jesus piece. She was distracted by the contradictory nature of a hustler simultaneously celebrating a socialist revolutionary, capitalism, and Jesus. Jay-Z responded with the "Public Service Announcement" (2003) line "I'm like Che Guevara with bling on, I'm complex." Jay-Z is correct. The relationship among rappers, their Jesus pieces, and capitalism is indeed complex because it is inextricably linked to slavery.

One of the reasons African slaves were introduced to Christianity was to ensure their complicity. Slaves who could be convinced that God sanctioned slavery would be more content to remain slaves. Slaves who believed that slavery was punishment for ancestral hedonism would not revolt. Underground railroad conductor Harriet Tubman once said, "I freed a thousand slaves. I could have freed a thousand more if only they knew they were slaves." Christianity and its perpetuation of retributive redemptive suffering contributed to some slaves' complacency. Ironically, more than a century after slavery's eradication in the United States, rappers wear chains with images of a white Jesus around their necks. Even when his face is metal, Jesus is never shown with non-Anglo features, dreadlocks, or Afros. A black man wearing a white Jesus around his neck suggests that he may still be mentally, emotionally, and spiritually shackled by the oppressor's chains. Not only is he potentially wearing blood diamonds, which represent the Christianity-sanctioned colonization of Africa and the raping of the continent for its natural resources, but a black man wearing the lavish Jesus piece also represents slaves from the African Diaspora whose spirits were terrorized by Western notions of sin, evil, and hell until they accepted the white Jesus. The whiteness of the Jesus piece epitomizes the power of whiteness to oppress people of color around the globe. The Jesus piece's celebration of capitalism succumbs to a racial hierarchy where whiteness represents power.

Kanye West interrogates complicity in the conflict diamond industry in "Diamonds from Sierra Leone" (2005). The video opens with a first-person narrative: "We work in the diamond rivers from sunrise to sunset under the watchful eyes of soldiers. Every day we fear for our lives. Some of us were enslaved by rebels and forced to kill our own families for diamonds. We are the children of the blood diamonds." The black-and-white video is an exercise in contrast—the beauty of Prague versus the intolerable conditions of the diamond mines, indigent black child soldiers handing diamonds to rich white adult customers, blood streaming from conflict diamonds and crucifixes representing the blood of Jesus. In the first verse of his remix, West concedes, "I thought my Jesus piece was so harmless."

While a Jesus piece represents God's favor for some, if it is filled with conflict diamonds, it also represents the absence of that favor for others. Whether it resurrects memories of slavery in the United States or draws attention to modern slavery in Africa, the splendor of a Jesus piece made with blood diamonds maintains hierarchies between the rich and the poor. And in part, that is why rappers wear it. West explains in the "Diamonds from Sierra Leone Remix" (2005), "Spend your whole life trying to get that ice . . . how can something so wrong make me feel so right?" African Americans who have historically been impoverished desire displays of affluence. Jesus is the piece that fits between poverty and prosperity. The Jesus piece can be interpreted as reparations—an opportunity for African Americans to receive something in return from the unpaid labor of their slave ancestors. In these instances, the Jesus piece is a reminder that African descendants are no longer in chains. Being able to afford such a lavish emblem partially levels the playing field between whites whose privilege rests in their racial status and blacks who acquire privilege through a newfound class status.

Consuming the Jesus piece as a route to class privilege, however, is reminiscent of selling black bodies as routes to capital. The United States is a consumer culture. Its citizens have been socialized to think of themselves as consumers and products to be consumed. At no place is this more apparent than hip hop—the epitome of American capitalist enterprise. Ironically, the black face of hip hop underscores the historical moment when black bodies were considered products before they were considered human. As long as the Jesus piece is sold without diminishing the power of Jesus, wearing the Jesus piece as an icon reminds rappers that they can sell themselves as gangstas, niggas, and bitches without selling their souls. Jesus, once again, is redemptive.

Jesus is the gangsta's crucified consumable companion—the missing piece between life or death, affluence or poverty, and independence or imprisonment. As the God "out there" sent "down here" to experience oppression, be crucified by his haters, and be resurrected, gangstas feel an affinity for Jesus. This kinship makes it natural for them to depict themselves hanging out with Jesus, hanging from a cross as Jesus, and hanging Jesus pieces around their necks. Their displays of affection are complex but not blasphemous because gangstas see themselves in Jesus. Hip hop's visual representations of Jesus mirror gangstas who have finagled oppression into a consumable product that communicates the potential for an indestructible self.

Chapter 4

Dealing with the Devil

The devil is no stranger to black people. There's an old-school African American quip that goes a little something like this: "There wasn't no devil in Africa till the white folks took him with them in the first empty slave ships. White folks ended up with us, and we ended up with the devil."[1] Before colonialism and slavery, most African cultures did not have a devil. Instead, the African Diaspora embraced a Janus-faced ambiguous trickster figure known as Exú in Brazil, Echu-Elegua in Cuba, Papa Legba in Haiti, Esu-Elegbara in Nigeria, and Legba in Benin.[2] This trickster mediates the liminal spaces between heaven and hell, divinity and humanity. The trickster is both disruptive and reconciliatory, profane and sacred, good and evil and thus neither. Dichotomous religious worldviews were accustomed to strictly good versus evil, black versus white, and wrong versus right polarizations. Their malevolent devil was the antithesis of the benevolent Christian God. Conceptually, Eurocentric Christians were perplexed by the trickster's integrative characteristics and conveniently conflated the enigmatic qualities of the African trickster with their macabre devil in order to terrorize slaves into obedience.[3]

Both dichotomous and integrative traditions inform rapper discourse about the devil. Many rappers characterize the devil as an evil antagonist somewhere "out there" who threatens their spiritual and physical well-being. In this sense, the devil "out there" operates within a spiritual realm in direct opposition to God "out there." Other rappers embrace the trickster "down here" when they describe themselves and their peers as devils—equal parts good and evil, good people who can be goaded into evil, or bad-men with just enough evil in them to defeat the devil. Badman tales are infamous for describing human tricksters either bold enough to best the devil or blasphemous enough to brag about being in relationship with the devil. Popularized during the 1890s as an oral narrative tradition, the bad-man was a folklore hero because he did whatever the hell he wanted. Sometimes that included going to hell and telling the devil that he was "too bad to stay." A badman was so bad (i.e., powerful) that even the devil could not tell him what to do. The inherent braggadocio of rap music originates with the trickster/badman and is naturally suited for devil talk.

In hip hop culture the devil "out there" is mostly nefarious—a legacy of the good-versus-evil dichotomy. However, trickster/badman "down here" legacies empower more rappers to appropriate devil characteristics or confront the devil rather than cower before him. Moreover, the devils in rappers' lives are not always spiritual but also social. African Americans oppressed by slavery, the end of Reconstruction, Jim and Jane Crow, police brutality, urban blight, and other forms of white supremacy clearly see the devil as a social ill that often manifests as whiteness—an omnipotent power with which African Americans must learn to bargain. Overall, the devil appears in rap music as an antagonist—namely an adversary, a tempter, and a trickster/badman.

The Adversary

Hip hop has its haters. In the early 1990s, critics like C. Delores Tucker, Tipper Gore, and Reverend Calvin O. Butts III publicly condemned rap music and advocated for censorship. In fact, when 2 Live Crew's *As Nasty as They Wanna Be* (1989) was deemed obscene by a circuit court ruling, a store clerk was arrested for selling the album and group members were arrested for performing songs from the album. In 1990, a U.S. Court of Appeals overturned the ruling and recognized 2 Live Crew's First Amendment rights. Ice T, on the other hand, acquiesced to his critics and pulled "Cop Killer" from his 1992 *Body Count* album because its controversial lyrics attracted national attention, including disdain from then president George H. W. Bush.

Hip hop faced major public criticism again in 2007. During his radio program, *Imus in the Morning*, Don Imus referred to the women on the Rutgers basketball team as "nappy-headed hos." Imus was fired for his remarks, but he publicly defended himself by claiming freedom of speech and identifying similar misogyny in rap music. The controversy spurred a congressional hearing on hip hop titled "From Imus to Industry: The Business of Stereotypes and Degrading Images." The two controversies were almost 20 years apart, but both demonstrate how hip hop can be unduly targeted as the cause of misogyny in U.S. culture as opposed to merely one of its manifestations.

Haters are not always hip hop outsiders. The infamous battles between hip hop crews are legendary. One of the first hip hop beefs in the late

1980s was the bridge war between Boogie Down Productions led by KRS-One and Marley Marl's The Juice Crew. The battles were over the original birthplace of hip hop—BDP's Bronx or the Juice Crew's Queensbridge. Ten years later, internal hip hop conflicts had not diminished. The media-fueled beef between Tupac Shakur and the Notorious B.I.G. resulted in their untimely murders in September 1996 and March 1997 respectively. In the twenty-first century, hip hop beefs are more likely to be marketing strategies than reflections of true antagonism between crews.

In addition to outsiders and contemporaries, hip hop haters also include the conflicting parts of a rapper's self. Scarface of Geto Boys chases a figment of his imagination who appears a lot like him in "Mind Playing Tricks on Me" (1991). Marshall Mathers exists in tension with Slim Shady and Eminem. *T.I. vs. T.I.P.* describes T.I.'s battles with himself. Nicki Minaj adopts an accent when she raps as her angry alter ego Roman Zolanski. A rapper's popularity is in part premised on how well he or she defends against haters (including the self). T.I.'s "Motivation" (2004) urges "haters to get on their job" and motivate him to be his best self.

The original hater, *satan* in Hebrew and *diabolos* in Greek, has been variously translated as adversary, obstacle, or slanderer throughout ancient history. According to Wray and Mobley, authors of *The Birth of Satan: Tracing the Devil's Biblical Roots*, "Satan is always a character of opposition; indeed, this is his primary role in the Bible and beyond."[4] Satan's nefarious influence is not lost on rappers who are used to battling with adversaries. Sometimes the adversary is a spiritual demon. More frequently, rappers' devils manifest as other human obstacles—whites, women, rivals, and themselves.

Blue-eyed white devils wreak havoc in rap lyrics and are to be generally avoided. By appropriating Malcolm X and the Nation of Islam's (NOI) 1960s rhetorical practice of publicly referring to white people as devils, rappers acknowledge white supremacy as an oppressive obstacle to progress. White devils are frequently lambasted for exploiting black men. In "The Nigga Trap" (2006) Ice Cube describes impoverished urban neighborhoods as traps where black and brown men are encouraged to "take the cheese." Trapped individuals can acquire their cheese or money in two ways. They can "work all week and give the devil back his loot" as Jeru the Damaja raps in "Ya Playin' Yourself" (1996) or they can enter the underground drug economy. In "Boomerang" (1998) Big Punisher characterizes the cycle of selling drugs and serving time as "the devil's got us by the balls." Ice Cube compares the racist, duplicitous "motherfuckin' devils" that run the

California state penitentiary to slave masters. Prison is a "concrete slave ship" that uses niggas like mules. These rappers explain how white devils' racist acts of tyranny affect black men's everyday lives.

The most explicit visual representation of a white devil in hip hop is also a prison narrative. In the mini-movie music video *Murder Was the Case* (1994), Snoop Dogg cries out for God to save his life when the white devil intercepts his prayers.[5] The devil is a literal obstacle between Snoop and God. The white devil's power guarantees Snoop's gangsta lifestyle until the devil feels disrespected. The devil has been betrayed because Snoop behaves as if his success is a result of his meritorious work ethic. Snoop has forgotten that his success is contingent upon the benevolence of a white devil's access to opportunity. Even as a successful black man, Snoop is controlled by whiteness. Snoop's white devil guides his actions from a position of privilege that is revoked when Snoop forgets his place. Without the assistance of the privileges of whiteness, Snoop fails to successfully navigate urban black life and as punishment Snoop is imprisoned.

In prison, which is a space of death where many black men have languished under white control, Snoop violently retaliates against two white male prison guard escorts who killed his ally. As Snoop shanks one guard, he is shanked by the other. Instead of using the firearm or billy club he is authorized to use, the corrupt guard kills in kind and demonstrates that he and Snoop are not that different with the exception of the privilege granted to the one and denied the other. In this case, power is clearly linked to whiteness within the prison hierarchy.

During the murders, the white devil's eyes flash multiple times to remind audiences that both the devil and the white guard who murders Snoop are connected to the racist power structure. The white devil also reminds audiences that without white benevolence, blacks are vulnerable to death at their whim. Furthermore, the white devil spatially dominates Snoop in death. In the final scene, the devil stands above Snoop's grave near the headstone. In addition to being physically contained by his coffin, Snoop's horizontal position within the confines of the box is contrasted by the devil's vertical position of power above ground where he is free to move wherever he pleases. In rap lingo, urban spaces of death are called traps. Prison is also referred to as a trap or a box. Snoop is still trapped in a box. The confinement is most acute when he opens his eyes wide, turns his head (the only part of his body that can move within the tight box), and stares as us before the feature ends with a loud flatline. Even in his afterlife, Snoop will be subject to white control over his black body. Specifically, white devils represent white supremacy and institutionalized racism as particular obstacles that blacks must overcome.

Tupac Shakur was serving time in prison for a sexual abuse conviction when his third solo album, *Me against the World*, was released in 1995. Tupac maintained his innocence, and his feelings of betrayal were reflected in the song "Fuck the World" (1995), which opens with Tupac rapping, "Who you calling a rapist? . . . You devils . . . wanna see me locked in chains." The mention of chains perpetuates the prison-as-modern-day-slavery motif. Additionally, Tupac comments on the hypocrisy of white devils who accuse him of rape even though white slave masters routinely raped their slaves with impunity. Whites are the initial devil adversaries in "Fuck the World," but the song also focuses on women and peers who also pose a threat. Tupac's paranoia about disingenuous comrades and deceitful women in his lyrics and his real life is legendary. Tupac's "Fuck the World" also portrays a recurring rapper scenario that acknowledges the realities of white supremacy, but also recognizes women and peers as potential devil adversaries.

Women are perceived as devils when they tempt men to sin by having sex with them. Ice Cube adopts NOI white devil ideology in the mean-spirited "Cave Bitch" (1993). He makes no attempt to hide his hatred for the physically unattractive white she-devil adversary sent to tame him via sexual exploitation or false rape accusations. Whereas Ice Cube's white she-devil has stringy hair, no derriere, and silicon breasts, black female devils are physically desirable. Lil Wayne describes an irresistible woman named Helen who is "hot as hell" and "got the devil in her" in "On Fire" (2010). His heat metaphors convey a passionate sexual exchange. Kanye West's "Devil in a New Dress" (2010) earns her moniker because her beauty tempts West to fornication. He is more than willing to acquiesce to the loss of his religion, but, like popular interpretations of the biblical Garden of Eden narrative, Eve listened to the serpent and convinced Adam to sin, and therefore "the fall" is primarily the woman's fault. Lil Wayne and West construct women as sexual temptress adversaries, but their messages seem as if they were intended to be more flattering than derogatory. Tech N9ne and D12, on the other hand, appropriate Eve's biblical role to expresses an extreme hatred toward women in "She Devil" (2002). To Tech N9ne and D12, women are sexually insatiable soul-stealing prostitutes who carry diseases, irresponsibly birth more children than they can care for, and covet cash. Their she-devil has no self-respect, sense of decency, or morals. There are no neutral opinions of she-devils. Men's feelings toward them are either infatuation or hatred. Because she-devils are consistently constructed within the sexual realm, there are few, if any, female rappers who refer to other women as devils. Overall, the devil is primarily masculine in the rapper imagination.

In the cleverly titled track "D'Evils" (1996) Jay-Z discusses the evils that manifest as devils in the narrator's life as a street hustler. He concludes the first verse by identifying money and power as the primary d'evils. The predominant d'evil of verse 2 is Jay-Z's pursuit of a friend turned rival. On one hand, the rival embodies the devil adversary. He is an obstacle to Jay-Z's control of drug distribution territory. On the other hand, Jay-Z is the d'evil kidnapping and pressuring his rival's baby's mother into revealing information. Jay-Z describes himself as possessed by an obsession for money. In the final verse, he articulates his transformation from a pleasant, friendly guy to a liar and murderer beaten down by d'evils. Even as Jay-Z internalizes his d'evils and at times expresses remorse for his actions, he is also subject to d'evils outside of his control.

The track is introduced by two samples from Snoop's *Murder Was the Case* (1994) and Prodigy's verse from the 1995 "I Shot Ya Remix." As audiences hear Snoop say "Dear God I wonder can you save me?" Prodigy responds with "Illuminati want my mind, soul, and body." The paired samples suggest that God may not be able to save Jay-Z from d'evils of the Illuminati. In hip hop circles the Illuminati are a centuries-old influential, international, elite secret society that advocate for a one-world government and control all aspects of American life including its government, global finance, and mainstream media. According to urban lore, the Illuminati maintain their influence because their major adherents are white men with power, privilege, and access to unlimited global resources. The Illuminati recruit individuals willing to dedicate themselves to their plans for global economic domination. This subtle reference to the omnipresent role of white d'evils precedes Jay-Z's articulation of his inherited desire to gain power, privilege, and access to resources by any means necessary. The samples also reiterate the message of white d'evils after each verse. "D'Evils" is the story of a man who becomes a devil in his pursuit of the d'evils presented to him by the rich and powerful white men around him.

Another example of the devil as an external as well as internal adversary is articulated in Jay-Z's "Lucifer" (2003). Because the track is peppered with so many religious references, it is necessary to parse them out before addressing the adversaries within the song. Lucifer, translated from Hebrew as "Day Star" or "Light-Bearer," is now commonly understood as Satan—an arrogant heavenly being who angered God and was cast down to earth from heaven for his irreverence. Lucifer, however, was never linked to Satan in the Hebrew Bible. Instead, "Satan's expulsion from the divine presence for some primordial sin—whether pride, envy, or rebellion—grew out of prophetic oracles that denounced earthly kings in these mythic terms."[6] The primary biblical reference about the fall of Lucifer is Isaiah 14:12: "How you are fallen from heaven, O Lucifer, son of the morning! How you are cut down to the ground, you who weakened the nations!" Isaiah 14 describes the downfall of the King of Babylon, not Satan. The attribution of this verse to Satan is augmented by narratives from the *Life of Adam and Eve*, 2 Enoch, *Paradise Lost*, and Luke 10:18 when Jesus states, "I saw Satan fall like lightning from heaven." Jesus's words have been interpreted to connect Satan and lightening to Lucifer's fall.

The myth of Lucifer's fall permeates popular culture. A female vocalist with a Jamaican lilt opens "Lucifer" singing, "Lucifer, son of the morning! I'm gonna chase you out of earth." Lucifer is immediately connected with light (as son of the morning) and an expulsion. Rap Genius, a website that helps audiences "discover the meaning of rap lyrics," interprets the Lucifer reference as follows: "Satan was originally the light-bearing angel (like the sun) before he pissed off God and was sent to Hades."[7] Although biblically inaccurate, this explanation further reflects the common interpretation of audiences who do not study the Bible but are still familiar with the mythic references that emerge from its narratives.[8] Additionally, the sound and content of Lucifer's expulsion is sampled from Jamaican artist Max Romeo's "Chase the Devil" (1976). The song begins, "Lucifer, son of the morning I'm gonna chase you out of urt (earth)!" Romeo chases the devil to outer space so that he can interfere in the lives of another race.

There are no references to heaven or hell in either the original or the sample. The central message is to chase Lucifer out of earth because Lucifer is clearly vested in earthly activities. Romeo sings: "Satan is an evilous man." Jay-Z's "Lucifer" describes men who are enemies. The human characteristics of the lucifers in this rap include Jay-Z's enemies as well as the homicidal parts of himself. In the first two verses Jay-Z describes himself as a murderous force with dark forces in him and a righteous cause for sinnin'. In the interlude that follows the second verse, Jay-Z expresses a desire to get his soul right and remove the devils from his life. This reference has a double meaning. The devils in his life are within him as well as enemies that pursue him. In the third verse, Jay Z describes the devils responsible for his friend Bob's death. He petitions the Lord to forgive Bob's sins and let him into heaven. He also asks God to blame his lust for

revenge on the son of the mornin'. Throughout the song, Lucifer is a metaphor for life's devils—adversaries that pursue you, the devil you must
become to destroy them, and the devil that fuels vengeful homicidal desires.

Three years after Jay-Z's "Lucifer," Ludacris compares his competition to
Lucifer in "War with God," (2006) a diss track that includes a woman singing the chorus "Lucifer, Oh Lucifer you're the god of evil, you're the god of
hate/Lucifer, Oh Lucifer the darkness is where you find your light." Audiences thought it might have been a direct response to Jay-Z. Others
surmised that Ludacris was taking on southern rapper upstarts like T.I. or
Young Jeezy. The track is less about a battle between good and evil and
more of an appeal to rap audiences' desire for conflict. What better way
to antagonize an enemy than by calling him Lucifer? The idea itself is
unoriginal. The chorus and the beat are directly sampled from Billy Paul's
"War of the Gods" (1973), which is about spiritual warfare.

Nonetheless, Ludacris enjoyed the publicity garnered by the uncertainty
surrounding the object of his disdain. After weeks of suspicion, he finally
told MTV that "War with God" was partially about himself and partially
about his critics. "That record right there is so much more about me being
honest about myself." Luda continued: "I've heard a lot of subliminal things
said from not only rappers but even journalists in magazines [about me].
That record is me taking soft jabs right back at them."[9] While there is no
reason to doubt that Ludacris battles conflicting internal desires, the track
is more of a conversation the rapper is having with his critics in general.
Direct diss lines like "my power's with God" and "I'm hot as the devil/But
I work for the top floor, homie get on my level" are the only direct mentions of God and the devil. In each, "power's with God" and "I work for
the top floor"; the implication is that Ludacris is protected by God (the
man upstairs on the top floor).

While not as sophisticated as Jay-Z's appropriation of Lucifer, "War with
God" is another example of the devil as a human adversary in rap lyrics.
Whether Lucifer represents one's opponents or undesirable aspects of the
self, within these songs the devil is primarily a human being. In addition to
being an external adversary and an internal obstacle to success, rappers characterize the devil as a spiritual being who plays the role of a tempter.

The Tempter

Despite his nefarious reputation, Satan is quoted very infrequently in the
Bible. Samuel Butler proposed "an apology for the Devil—it must be

remembered that we have only heard one side of the case. God has written all the books."[10] The only biblical moments where Satan speaks are when he is acting as a tempter, first regarding God's faithful servant Job and second regarding God's son Jesus. Some would include Satan's role in the Garden of Eden as his first temptation, but this is another instance where common knowledge diverges from the biblical account. "Nowhere in the Hebrew Bible is there any identification made between the serpent and the Devil/Satan; furthermore, the Hebrew Bible does not invest snakes, as a species, with any special qualities of evil."[11] Thus Satan's most significant Old Testament cameo occurs when he tempts Job to curse God, but first Satan asks God's permission in Job 1:6–12, NKJV:

> Now there was a day when the sons of God came to present themselves before the Lord, and Satan also came among them. And the Lord said to Satan, "From where do you come?" So Satan answered the Lord and said, "From going to and fro on the earth, and from walking back and forth on it." Then the Lord said to Satan, "Have you considered my servant Job, that there is none like him on the earth, a blameless and upright man, one who fears God and shuns evil?" So Satan answered the Lord and said, "Does Job fear God for nothing? Have you not made a hedge around him, around his household, and around all that he has on every side? You have blessed the work of his hands, and his possessions have increased in the land. But now, stretch out your hand and touch all that he has, and he will surely curse you to your face!" And the Lord said to Satan, "Behold, all that he has is in your power; only do not lay a hand on his person." So Satan went out from the presence of the Lord.

And when that temptation failed, Satan and God reconvened in Job 2:1–7:

> Again there was a day when the sons of God came to present themselves before the Lord, and Satan came also among them to present himself before the LORD. And the Lord said to Satan, "From where do you come?" Satan answered the Lord and said, "From going to and fro on the earth, and from walking back and forth on it." Then the Lord said to Satan, "Have you considered My servant Job, that there is none like him on the earth, a blameless and upright man, one who fears God and shuns evil? And still he holds fast to his integrity, although you incited me against him, to destroy him without cause." So Satan answered the Lord and said, "Skin for skin! Yes, all that a man has he will give for his life. But stretch out Your hand now, and touch his bone and his flesh, and he will surely curse you to your face!" And the Lord said to Satan, "Behold, he is in your hand, but spare his life." So Satan

went out from the presence of the Lord, and struck Job with painful boils from the sole of his foot to the crown of his head.

After the destruction of his property, the death of his children, and the decline of his health, Job refuses to curse God and die.

The book of Job is a complicated narrative. It is the first instance where Satan intervenes in human affairs, but God is clearly complicit in the exercise. Why would God agree to such machinations? How could a good God allow evil? What is the meaning of suffering? Is God fair? When Job's prosperity and family are restored, Job 42:11 states that his siblings gathered and "consoled him and comforted him for all the adversity that the Lord had brought upon him." Job's suffering is attributed to God and not to Satan. Satan is merely the means through which God measures his servants' faithfulness.

By the time the devil reemerges as a tempter in the New Testament, he is fully mature and acting independently. Mark 1:13 is the most succinct presentation of Jesus's temptation: "And he was there in the wilderness forty days, tempted by Satan, and was with the wild beasts; and the angels ministered to Him." Matthew 4:1–11 and Luke 4:1–13 describe the temptation in more detail. The devil asks for a magic trick. He petitions Jesus to turn stones into bread. Then he requests suicide claiming that if Jesus is the Son of God, angels will rescue him as he jumped from the pinnacle of the temple. Finally, the devil offers Jesus the kingdoms of the world and all of their splendor in exchange for worship. Using the word of God, Jesus rebukes the devil and passes each test.

One significant characteristic of the tempter remains unchanged from his first appearance, and one significant characteristic radically changes. In each instance, Satan is persistent. When the first set of trials do not result in the desired effect with Job, Satan petitions God again. Jesus must rebuke Satan three times before he departs. Satan does not give up easily. Contrastingly, Job's temptation is about faith; Jesus's temptation is about power. Satan had little to gain had Job failed his temptation. Satan was subservient to God and likely suspected that he would lose the end game with Job, but he was happy to wreak as much havoc as possible in the meantime. Satan tempts Jesus without an account of God's prior blessing. Note Satan's claim in Luke 4:6 after he shows Jesus the kingdoms of the earth: "And the devil said to him, 'All this authority I will give you, and their glory; for this has been delivered to me, and I give it to whomever I wish.'" Satan has changed. He is no longer a minion; he has been given power and is eager to wield it. Had Jesus failed, Satan would have triumphed over God.

The shift in Satan's character marks a shift in human character. Less tolerant of a good God who allows evil, the authors of the gospels depict God/Jesus and Satan as disparate antagonistic forces that no longer commune together but war for human souls. As the ultimate antagonistic tempter, the devil's promises of power and glory have proven irresistible throughout history. The appeal of selling one's soul to the devil knows no boundaries. There are various versions of the legend, but the play by Englishman Christopher Marlowe and the dramatic poem by German Johann Wolfgang von Goethe are the most popular.

In Marlowe's version, Faustus is a frustrated doctor who willingly makes a deal with the devil as long as Mephostophilis (the devil's representative) grants his every desire for power. After debating his future with good and evil angels, Faustus seals the deal with a bond in drawn blood. Faustus pranks and pleases a lot of people with his new pal, but at the end of the agreed upon 24 years the devil returns for him, dismembers his body, and takes his soul. In Goethe's version, Faust agrees to deal with the devil in exchange for a full realization of his humanity, but there is no bond drawn in blood. God bets the devil that Faust will return to him. Although Faust never pleads with God to undo his deal, his unselfish actions toward others cause God's angels to redeem him from death and subservience to the devil. The hip hop context does not alter the core Faustian narrative. Humans are tempted by the devil with their ultimate desires. The character of the tempter and the nature of those desires are contingent upon a rapper's personal experiences. Furthermore, rappers oscillate between fates that mimic Marlowe's devastation and fates that embrace Goethe's redemption.

For some rappers, the tempter opposes God. Whereas God allows trials and tribulations to help humans become their best selves, the devil offers an easy way out. Through a series of carefully crafted metaphors about sewing jeans, Lupe Fiasco explains how and why he creates substantive music in "Pressure" (2006). Lupe encourages his listeners not to sell out to drug trafficking or the music industry's superficial expectations. He urges them to follow his mother's advice and "beware of what the devil do/tell 'em that your soul's not for sale like the W's." By referencing the international luxury boutique W hotels, Lupe implies that soul selling can be profitable in the short term. The devil offers an easier financial path to success, but Lupe reminds audiences that the results of honest labor are more rewarding. His lyrical emphasis on jeans represents a rugged unglamorous lifestyle where the rewards lie not in profits but in producing quality work that stands the test of time.

J. Cole and Omen resist the lure of the devil while describing the perils of city living in "Enchanted" (2010). They describe the city as the locus of fatherlessness, poverty, drug addiction, sexual abuse, death, and desperation. They ask God to renegotiate their destiny and hope "God ain't acting unfamiliar" as they play the cards God dealt. The chorus samples Tupac's "Hail Mary" (1996), another rap that expresses profound insecurity about whether God is listening to black men who are trying to survive in the hood. Although little has changed in 14 years, J. Cole cautions that deals with the devil are irrevocable. He warns city dwellers that "the devil out here buying souls, nigga, no refunds" and urges them not to give up on God. Despite his admonition, J. Cole does not minimize the gravity of the temptation. The J. Cole logo from his *Friday Night Lights* mixtape that features "Enchanted" incorporates devil's horns into the "O" and includes an angel's halo resting over the "E." The tempter offers an easier life, but Lupe, J. Cole, and Omen focus on the character building that develops from avoiding the easy route.

In addition to presenting shortcuts to success as God's opposition, the tempter can also be an authority figure who offers notoriety. Snoop expresses no hesitation about selling his soul to the devil in exchange for eternal gangsta status in *Murder Was the Case*. The mini-movie music video and accompanying soundtrack also proved to be an excellent marketing ploy masterminded by Death Row Records CEO Suge Knight. *Murder Was the Case* kept Snoop's name in the media while he faced accessory to murder charges. Initially, Snoop was not a fan of *Murder Was the Case*. Snoop describes working with Knight as a bit like dealing with the devil. "Suge's strong-arm tactics were starting to take a toll. People were afraid to work with the motherfucker and those that did had to do their job in an atmosphere of fear and intimidation."[12] But when *Murder Was the Case* topped the *Billboard* charts, Snoop was pleased. It is no coincidence that rap music's most fully developed deal with the devil appears on a label that depicts a man in an electric chair as its logo. Although Snoop's character faces a Marlowesque demise in the mini-movie music video, Snoop is redeemed by Knight's cunning marketing strategy. Apparently, selling souls sells well.

Despite soul selling's potential profits, sometimes the tempter appears as an intimate partner who appeals to unmet desires for love instead of money. DMX's tempter is his nigga in "The Omen" (1998). DMX and his devil are in a relationship. The devil "scoops up" DMX and "holds him down" when he is in trouble. They kill for each other, gang-rape women, and get high together. The devil is very concerned with DMX's well-being and will kill to make DMX happy. The devil acts like a doting boyfriend who always wants to come over and spend quality time with his girl. And like too many dating scenarios, when the boyfriend decides it's time for the beneficiary of his goodness to reciprocate, DMX feels pressured into delivering the goods. DMX liked the devil's attention. He used the devil to get revenge on the police who killed his family. He felt like his only choice was to let the devil handle the situation for him, but then the devil calls in his favor. DMX claims he never asked for the devil's help. Like an abusive partner, the devil problematizes consent by saying, "You sold your soul when you didn't say no . . . ain't shit for free." The exchange is heterosexual; but the repeated homophobic references to faggots could be covering a same-sex preference, and the homoerotic reference to mixing semen in the lyric—"if one goes soft, we all take the pussy"—implies that the devil could also be tempting DMX to homosexual intimacy. DMX raps as both himself and the devil, but DMX is clearly the subordinate. It suggests the devil has penetrated DMX to the extent that the two of them have become one. Their exchange is a lot like acquaintance rape. It isn't until the very end of their conversation that DMX asks God to forgive him and save him from the devil. Although DMX considers leaving the devil throughout the rap, he prays to God to save him only when he no longer benefits from the exchange. Until that point, the devil's generosity, devotion, and conditional love is worth the selling of his soul.

If the tempter is DMX's nigga, Eminem is the tempter's darling. "My Darling" (2009) communicates similarly abusive relationship themes between the rapper and his tempter's twisted acts of love. Eminem's exchange with the devil follows an obsessive/possessive pattern where intimacy is fraught with violence and love is complete possession. The devil dotes on Eminem in order to draw out Eminem's darker alter ego Slim Shady. He reminds Eminem of the good times the devil and Shady had together and asserts they were meant for each other. He asks Eminem to accept his help and love.

Eminem and the devil feud as the devil tempts Eminem to become Shady again (pun intended). Eminem and Slim Shady war regularly in Eminem's albums. In the introduction to *Slim Shady EP* (1998), a foreboding voice not unlike the one attributed to the devil in "My Darling" taunts Eminem even though Eminem repeatedly states, "I thought I killed you," "what do you want from me," and "leave me alone." The tension between Eminem, Slim Shady, and the devil continues throughout *Relapse* (2009).

Eminem tries to move his life forward but relapses when the devil in him brings him back to his dark places. Eminem violently attempts to destroy the devil in "My Darling." We hear shattering glass, gun cocks, shooting, and a chain saw, but the devil relentlessly returns to remind Eminem that their deal is irrevocable. His fame and fortune are premised on his infamous alter ego. No one loves Eminem. The devil and all the fans love Slim Shady. Ultimately, Eminem cannot resist the allure. The devil's last words to him are "No one's gonna love you like I do." Because there is no other relationship in the song, the devil is the only one caring for Eminem.

During each chorus the devil serenades Eminem with promises to possess his mind, heart, and body. Eminem and the devil recite the chorus together to symbolize Eminem's acquiescence. Finally, they possess each other. Eminem has become the devil's darling. The devil's fame, fortune, and love temptations entice Eminem as he teeters on the precipice of a relapse. Consistent with Marlowe's version of deals with the devil, there is no redemption in the track—only angst and eventual acquiescence. Unlike the traditional horrid death or redemption, however, Eminem expresses the angst felt when the ultimate consequence of being tethered to the devil isn't death, but a life with the devil in the mirror. Eminem's "My Darling" (2009) is less about his temptation to sell his soul and more about living with the devil to whom his soul already belongs.

Even though the temptations are similar, rap's Faustian narratives differ from the traditional tales because rappers are more likely to feel as if they are already in hell while on earth. From the suffering of the city's inhabitants in "Enchanted" to the cautionary tales about drug dealing and artistically selling out in "Pressure" to murder and police oppression in *Murder Was the Case* and "Omen" to drug addiction in "My Darling," the rappers consider dealing with the devil because their lives are already hellish. Death is not the primary deterrent to dealing with the devil. The devil is definitely "down here" and will intervene in human affairs as much as humans allow him to. The trick is to learn to dance with the devil but not on the devil's terms.

Dancing with the devil is a common expression that means engaging in risky behavior. It recurs in lyrics when rappers represent the tension between themselves and the devil's temptations. Dancing is a form of pleasure and a play for power. As a lyric, listeners receive the impression that the devil has his partner in a lockstep, which cannot be disentangled easily. Dancing with the devil seduces a rapper into experiencing the thrill of risky behavior all the while hoping to outmaneuver the devil. Listeners know that the devil is mercurial. At any point, he could reclaim the lead. They await a song's resolution to determine whether the rapper or the devil emerged triumphant.

This is the narrative of Immortal Technique's "Dance with the Devil" (2001). "Dance with the Devil" is a true story of a man named William who violently sexually assaults his own mother to regain the respect of his street crew. Because they cover her face, William does not realize the victim is his mother until he prepares to shoot her after the assault. Once aware of her identity, he commits suicide. His friends kill his mother. No one speaks about the event again until Immortal Technique admits to participating in the assault at the end of the song. This nine minute and thirty-nine second cautionary tale set to the theme from "Love Story" warns that the devil could be anywhere "grow[ing] inside the hearts of the selfish and wicked." The juxtaposition of a beautiful, melodious, incredibly danceable sound with a horrifying narrative represents the seductive complexity of dancing with the devil.

To dance with the devil is to take a great risk. Having spent thousands of years honing his craft, the devil is a tempter who understands human desires. Some of us covet the easy path to success, others want fame and fortune, and some of us need love and respect. William desired all three. Immortal Technique describes young William with an absent father, a drug-addicted mother, "a product of a ghetto bred capitalistic mental" who felt he had everything to gain by proving to his street crew that he was evil. As a tempter, the devil makes death and hell seem far off while the here and now on the dance floor becomes exhilarating. William ended up dancing to a song he had never heard before. Immortal Technique warns, "So when the devil wants to dance with you, you better say never/ because the dance with the devil might last you forever." Dances with the devil are exciting precisely because of their potential to end in death.

The Trickster/Badman

Cautionary tales about the devil depict him as an adversary and a tempter. Trickster/badman tales about the devil depict him as a foil. Tricksters destabilize norms, undermine authority, and upend power structures through the crafty use of language. Contemporary tricksters are outrageously salacious because the more inappropriate an action, the more popular and profitable it is destined to become. Consider Three 6 Mafia. The rap group's name appeals to prurient interests because 666 is popularly recognized as number of the beast/antichrist/devil. They took pride in the fact that mainstream radio refused to play their raw, horror-themed rhymes. Devil discourse is popular in hip hop because it arouses human curiosity, reminds us of our human limitations, and inspires resistance to hegemonic norms.

Generations of black men have compared themselves to the devil as a form of empowerment. Countless rappers have bragged about being as hot as or hotter than the devil. Their content and delivery also have devil attributes. J. Cole merges the influence of angels and demons again when he raps in "Dead Presidents II" (2009) "clever with it, my flow like a devil spit it and heaven sent it." "Suicide" (2008) is Fabolous's single-verse, three-minute, lyrical manifesto. He boasts, "You couldn't hear a hotter flow if the devil said it." Rappers who challenge him "commit suicide." Other rappers similarly brag about sending their enemies and competitors to the devil in hell. J. Cole brags in "Simba" (2008), "Send you to hell, you meet the devil sign a permanent lease." Only weaker individuals sign leases in hell; the baddest rappers wreak havoc there. Half of the six rappers declaring what they would do in Mase's "24 Hours to Live" (1997) describe suicide missions. Styles P. declares he'll "be waitin' to get to hell and bust down Satan." T.I. is robbed and shot in "What Happened?" (2001). The rapper envisions himself in heaven where God tells him that Satan is responsible for his misfortune. T. I. asks God for firearms, ammunition, and strength so he can "ride out on Lucifer's ass" to "bust hell wide open." T.I. wants retribution from the devil who also made Eve eat the apple in the Garden of Eden, enslaved Africans, sanctioned sharecropping scandals, and killed African American martyrs like Malcolm X, Martin Luther King Jr., Tupac, and Biggie. Hell will not be able to hold T.I.'s fury. He enters kicking down doors and spreading rounds. Rappers are such badmen that they willingly go to hell, take others with them, and tell the devil they are too bad to stay.

Few tracks boast better than the late Big L's "Devil's Son" (1993). Big L's first recorded single describes himself as a murdering rapist also known as the devil's son. He raps, "I'm a devil from hell without the tail or the red horns." His stories are outrageous. He gives orders to kill men, women, and babies. He dies and comes back to life. He pistol-whips priests. He gets shot at and spits out the shells. "Devil's Son" is a contemporary badman tale. Big L's lyrics were banned from radio, but revered by his fans in the streets. In his chorus, he sampled Nas's lyrics: "When I was 12, I went to hell for snuffing Jesus" from Main Source's "Live at the Barbeque" (1990) and "I'm waving automatic guns at nuns" from MC Serch's "Back to the Grill" (1992). Sampled devil lyrics further prove that devil comparisons were accepted as well as expected within rap lyrics. Nas and Big L garnered respect by depicting themselves as the "baddest" men in the game. Unfortunately, the two of them never got a chance to battle each other. Big L was shot nine times and violently murdered in 1999 before he could sign with Dame Dash and Jay-Z's Roc-A-Fella Records. Although his murder was never resolved, the 2010 posthumous release of *Return of the Devil's Son* keeps the badman alive and reminds audiences that there is a real difference between devil adversaries in the streets and badman devils in lyrics. Rappers' lives appear to imitate art more often than artists in other musical genres because they experience hell—violence, death, and poverty—on earth.

Imagining oneself as the devil or defeating the devil is one way that a rapper trickster/badman can escape from a hellish reality. Notwithstanding Big L's tragic demise, rapper devil discourse is more rebelliously playful than actually dangerous. Black men who have been demonized in mainstream media flip the script and talk about their devilish ways in their own words, on their own terms. When hip hop critics tell stories about rappers and the devil, however, they describe rappers as actual bad men who have sold their souls. Ironically, the same group of people whose cultural repertoire depicted them confronting the devil at the end of the twentieth century are the devil's victims at the beginning of the twenty-first. When devil narratives are no longer told *by* the artists and are instead told *about* the artists, the narratives shift from empowering to disempowering. Many rappers have unwittingly found themselves enmeshed in the perennial good-versus-evil battle, albeit permanently situated on the evil side.

As the chasm between good and evil grows, the space for discussing the devil as a metaphor for oppression or a trickster/badman shrinks. For many hip hop outsiders, the devil is all evil all the time. The logic follows: if the devil is evil and you are affiliated with the devil in any way, then you must be evil as well. And you must be punished. Under these conditions, one could easily claim that those who are not traditionally Christian are evil and must be marginalized so that order can be restored to faith-based communities with overt Christian agendas. Critics are asserting that: (1) popular culture is a form of mass manipulation; (2) popular artists are agents of the devil, witches, Illuminati, occultists, and/or Masons; (3) hip hop is a demonic subculture; and (4) blood sacrifices are evidence of negative demonic frequencies in hip hop.

The Vigilant Citizen and Marco Ponce are symbologists and conspiracists who maintain eponymous websites that espouse the aforementioned themes. The Vigilant Citizen self-identifies as a mystic Christian and a music producer committed to revealing occult or hidden symbolism in popular culture. He argues that "corporate" occultism appropriates symbols from organized secret societies such as Freemasonry or the Illuminati and deceptively plants them into mass media in order to subliminally desensitize and then manipulate the masses. Vigilant's analyses survey a wide swath of popular culture. Vigilant neither denigrates artists nor directly affiliates them with the devil or the occult. Instead, he encourages his audiences to review the evidence and make their own assessments.

Whereas Vigilant consciously works to conceal his identity, Marco Ponce of marcoponce.com is an exuberant mid-20s extrovert whose site is designed to convince people that (1) there is a true spiritual war, (2) individuals must brace themselves with the full armor of God, and (3) we must stop listening to mainstream music that is demoralizing and leading us astray. Ponce pilfers many of Vigilant's complex arguments and interprets hand gestures, clothing, hairstyles, dances, lyrics, and other symbols as proof that artists are agents of the devil with occult affiliations. The deceived, demoralized slaves to Satan include the rappers Kanye West, Lupe Fiasco, Lil Wayne, Birdman, and Jay-Z. Jay-Z's female protégés, wife Beyoncé and artist Rihanna, are witches. Historically, autonomous women who threatened patriarchal power with their sexual, economic, or intellectual independence were labeled witches. A witch was a woman who had sex with the devil in exchange for power and therefore had to be executed. In an unsurprising affirmation of the lascivious black woman stereotype, the devil most frequently possesses black divas like Beyoncé and Rihanna through sex acts.

Other Christians are dedicating themselves to pointing out hip hop's demonic affiliations. G. Craige Lewis's EX Ministries is vested in spiritual warfare. Lewis is a Christian minister who describes hip hop as a corrupt, anti-American way of life with demonic roots. In his *The Truth behind Hip Hop* series, Lewis uses his revelations from God to highlight the demonic influence of Afrika Bambaataa, Bone Thugs-N-Harmony, DMX, Jay-Z, KRS One, Missy Elliott, Snoop, and Wu Tang among others. The Forerunner Chronicles proclaim the truth in the name of Jesus. They are most infamous for a documentary titled *The Jay-Z Deception*. These are some of the more sophisticated sites. Other media outlets including urban radio shows, online and print magazines, and homemade YouTube videos have acknowledged these conspiracy claims.

Kanye West and Jay-Z publicly deny any Iluminati, Masonic, occult, or devil worship affiliations. Kanye West has publicly refuted claims that he sold his soul to the devil. During an October 24, 2010, MTV interview about the release of his mini-movie, *Runaway*, Sway asked West if he felt society's expectations for him were limiting. West responded:

> There's this line where I say, "I sold my soul to the devil that's a crappy deal." And all these people said what you mean, you sold your soul to the devil? And when I say it, I'm saying when I allow other people's ideals to interfere with what I know is true to myself, that's the devil. So it's like people talking mess on the blogs is the devil or telling me or you know, trying to call me names. That's what the devil is. And me thinking twice about what it is that's really in my heart because of what people's reaction will be, is me selling my soul to the devil.[13]

Literal interpretations miss West's message. For him, doubt is demonic.

In interviews, Jay-Z has also refuted claims that he is Illuminati, a devil worshipper, and/or Mason. Jay-Z makes a lyrical appearance on Rick Ross's "Free Mason" (2010) to further refute the claims. "Free Mason" is about black men moving up from the ghetto to worldwide fame. It's the typical hip hop success story. Ross's verse brags about being the best, and through references to symbols and math, he alludes to Illuminati, Masonry, and the Five Percent Nation. Jay-Z's verse, on the other hand, directly denies these claims. Because Ross is trying to get on Jay-Z's level, he attempts to create buzz about himself by appropriating the claims that Jay-Z is in a position to deny. Jay-Z is already so successful that he can refute what people say about him. Ross needs people to talk about him, period. Being in a position to refute rumors about oneself instead of creating them about oneself truly signifies worldwide status.

Jay-Z claims haters created outlandish fairy tales that link him to the devil because they fear and resent his success. He says that he is amazing, not a Mason, and that God engineered his accomplishments. The verse is a denial, but it is not repentant. True to the badman's braggadocio, near the end of his verse Jay-Z raps, "Bitch I'm red hot, I'm on my third six but the devil I'm not/my Jesus piece flooded but thou shall not covet." Even as he refutes the claims, Jay-Z tantalizes the audience with the possibility that he is on this third six proudly marked with the number of the beast and wearing expensive jewelry paid for with the price of his soul. True fans interpret these words differently. "I'm on my third six" is Jay-Z rapping on the 18th bar of his verse ($3 \times 6 = 18$), and "thou shall not covet" is a biblical reference to the Ten Commandments. In fact, the verse alludes to prayer, baptism, the necessity of sin and forgiveness, thankfulness to God, and an admission from John 8:7 that he without sin should cast the first stone. In both his lyrical text and context, Jay-Z refutes claims that he is a Mason or an agent of the devil.

It is no accident that talented, powerful, popular, and rich African Americans are being targeted by these claims. Black male moguls and entrepreneurs from the entertainment industry are especially threatening to white male dominance. Calling them agents of the devil is designed to undermine their success, discredit them, and restore order. There is no better way to temper black men's influence on tween and teen audiences than by claiming they are evil. Notably, there was no mainstream outrage when Snoop made *Murder Was the Case*, an explicit video depicting him selling his soul to a white devil in 1994. Similar silence surrounded Three 6 Mafia's horrorcore debut in 1995. The protests were limited because hip hop was not nearly as economically viable then as it became 10 years later. Since rappers have been rapping regularly about the devil since the 1990s, the emergent backlash from the first decade of the twenty-first century is best explained by social conditions, namely the economic crisis known as the Great Recession, which I am calling the Greater Depression until the accuracy and the levity of the crisis catches on.

The U.S. banking system experienced a "liquidity crisis" that came to a head in late 2007. Subprime mortgage delinquencies and foreclosures led to the collapse of the securities backing those mortgages. Subsequent government bailouts and stimulus packages salvaged big business but not the average American. The economy lost over eight million jobs. Every state reported an increase in unemployment. There were over 800,000 foreclosures in the first quarter of 2009. As of January 2010, U.S. customers were carrying $2.46 trillion in consumer debt. Unemployment rates in 2010 were higher than they were during the Great Depression. One in seven Americans was living in poverty.[14]

When people are poor, they want to know how the other half (or upper 1% as the case may be) stays so rich. Hip hop artists known for their bling are a popular target. If poorer people begin to believe that the rich are rich only because they made a deal with the devil, they won't feel so badly about being poor. At least they still have their morals. Furthermore, Jay-Z and

Beyoncé are a top-earning couple who average approximately $100 million a year. If Beyoncé and Jay Z keep doing what they're doing, their great-grandchildren will have old money one day—wealth that has been passed down through generations. Jay-Z's enterprise is named Roc Nation as a nod to the Rothschilds and the Rockefellers. It could certainly be said that many of these upwardly mobile rap stars pose a direct threat to the *color* of wealth in our society. Claiming their money was an ill-gotten gain is another form of restoring order.

During times of recession, people are more inclined to conspiracy. Conspiracy theories ebb and flow in waves associated with how confident people feel about their social environments. When times are hard and unemployment rates are high, individuals get creative about where they look for explanations. It is no coincidence that Lewis released his six-disc *The Truth behind Hip Hop* exposé in 2007. Vigilant Citizen's first post appeared in November 2008. Marco Ponce's followed in August 2009. These were the core years of economic decline. Professor Joshua Gunn, author of *Modern Occult Rhetoric*, explains, "Whenever there's a sense of social anomie and crisis these things do tend to flare up." He also noted that "white guys who feel disempowered in some way" are most likely to be conspiracy theorists.[15] Moreover, classic conspiracy rhetoric relishes mystery. Conspiracy theories are deliberately ambiguous so that their validity evades empirical proof. Race and class status often contribute to whether individuals believe the claims. The selective nature of these vitriolic assertions reflects social anxieties. The perceived precarious position of white Christian patriarchal supremacy requires its adherents to protect their identity by being intolerant of others. Ostracizing undesirables (i.e., rich black men and the women with whom they affiliate) is consistent with the Tea Party's conspiracy claims, resistance to diversity, and desire to take back our country. The important unspoken questions are: Who are we? And, take back our country from whom?

Similar accusations of popular culture artists with occult affiliations were raised during the social upheaval of the '60s and the '80s. During those times, rock music and heavy metal were the respective targets. Those artists were primarily white men. Vigilant Citizen and Ponce also identify white businessmen and religious leaders who they believe maintain IIlluminati and occult affiliations. Because white men are represented so positively in other cultural arenas, no one dares surmise that most white men are under satanic influence. Because black men still endure negative cultural representations in and outside of hip hop, it is much more likely that claims about their occult affiliations could affirm negative stereotypes about the race. The latent racism is further perpetuated by a lack of contemporary exposés about Eminem. Neither Vigilant Citizen nor Marco Ponce have written substantive treatises about Eminem. Hip hop's model of white boy angst is simply frustrated whereas African Americans are demonic. Because Eminem has few notable white rapper competitors, no matter how many devil allusions he might make, he is essentially a good old boy when he lyrically decimates black rappers. His tortured conversations with the devil are mere art whereas black men are real devils.

Conspiracy claims about rapper occult affiliations are not limited to whites and Christians. Increasingly, well-known rap legends are accusing contemporary rappers of devil worship. Professor Griff, formerly of Public Enemy, is known for speaking his mind. He was the PE member repri- manded by Chuck D for making anti-Semitic remarks in 1989. In 2009, videos began circulating on the Internet where Griff claimed that hip hop industry insiders made blood sacrifices in attempts to secure fame and for- tune. Suge Knight sacrificed Tupac Shakur; Sean "Diddy" Combs sacrificed the Notorious B.I.G.; Dame Dash sacrificed AAliyah; Jay-Z sacrificed his nephew; Kanye West sacrificed his mother. Griff declares that these artists are part of a diabolical plan to control hip hop. In January 2001, hip hop founding father Afrika Bambaataa told the *Chicago Sun-Times*, "Hip-hop has been hijacked by a Luciferian conspiracy."[16]

MC Hammer, an ordained minister who is still rapping, released the video "Better Run Run" (2010). In verses couched between a chorus of "that's the fire" (alluding to hell fires and the supposed hotness of the track) Hammer disses Jay-Z by accusing him of selling his soul to the devil for the world and a girl. The video depicts a Jay-Z look-alike being pursued by a red-faced, black-cloaked, horned devil. At the end of the video, Hammer rebukes the devil, ministers to the Jay-Z look-alike, and baptizes him.

Jay-Z never responded in kind and stated that Hammer would be embarrassed when he read the great things said about him in his book, *Decoded*. Less than two weeks after the video's premier, Hammer announced that he was ending his beef with Jay-Z. Most of the blogosphere was appalled by Hammer's wayward attempt to create beef to boost his dated career. Hammer was primarily seeking publicity, but his moralistic bent sent a familiar message to Christians. The devil is an adversarial embodiment of evil who will tempt the weak to sell their souls in exchange for wealth and power. Ironically, this is the same message that rappers who portray the devil as an adversary and a tempter have been communicating for years. The baptism in Hammer's final scene is redemptive and not malicious. Hammer's message was not a condemnation. This Hammer versus Jay-Z hiccup in hip hop history is important because it raises questions about power and rap music. Lesser known rappers and white rappers are not being accused of devil associations. Rappers whose rap lyrics are words that matter are the ones being undermined. Hip hop occult rumors are gifts to racist critics seeking to further demonize black men, but how do black hip hop artists benefit from said demonization? Other rapper-on-rapper devil accusations come from angry rappers who feel ignored by their record labels, cheated out of money, or generally frustrated that, despite all of their hard work, their lyrics are still not perceived as words that matter. Jealousy is the deadly sin behind any arbitrary accusation.

In addition to promoting Christian morals and jealousy, there is another reason well-respected rappers like Griff and Bambaataa may contribute to hip hop conspiracy theories. Travis Gosa, a professor at Cornell University, told me:

> There may be a positive function to hip hop conspiracy theory... artists accusing Jay-Z of occult activities do so in an attempt to problematize the issue of control over black cultural production. Who controls hip hop? The white man/devil? Do you have to sell your soul to the whiteman/devil to make it in hip hop? Who controls the "evil" messages in the music?[17]

Any discussion of rappers claiming to be agents of the devil should acknowledge that there are devil worshippers. But before accusations are attached to rappers, one must also acknowledge the African American historical precedent for alluding to the devil as a symbol of oppression especially in the face of attempts to control black cultural production.

When Griff posits that the most successful rappers must have sold their souls to a (white) devil because they are closest to having "white" wealth, "white" access to resources, and more power than your average black fan, he problematizes whiteness as the standard by which success is measured. He also provides whites who feel threatened by black upward mobility an opportunity to demonize black men as a group. Simultaneously, he offers black rappers a road map to fame as long as they play into the popular trickster/badman/devil braggadocio. In a scenario like this, who really has power? Griff for telling the truth about white control over black cultural production? Whites for demonizing black men? Rappers for capitalizing

Chapter 5

Godly Power

There is no image of God except what we create for ourselves. Throughout God's existence, God's identity has been mutable. As a benevolent and malevolent, omniscient and fallible, impartial and preferential, compassionate and vengeful, white, black, raceless, faceless father and mother, ideas about God evolved as humans evolved. Religions create God to make sense of the senseless. Rap creates God to justify contradictions. In the Abrahamic religious imagination, God is omnipotent. God does what God does. Humans learn to accept the things they cannot change. In the hip hop imagination, God's power is not limited to a supernatural realm. It can be appropriated for personal gain to change the things individuals cannot accept. The black man as God "down here" represents the omnipotence of God "out there" wrestled to earth and resurrected in human form. When God "out there" refuses to account for the misuse of power in His name, God "down here" takes over where He left off. The righteous intent of black men who call themselves Gods is evident in their bolstered self-esteem, but absolute power whether in the hands of a God created by humans, or men who call themselves Gods will corrupt absolutely without accountability.

Power is like energy. It is never depleted; it simply changes its locus. Power in itself is neither good nor bad; its evaluation depends on its use. God's power can liberate individuals from oppression or grant some individuals oppressive power over others. Consistent with the contradictory nature of rap, God's power whether "out there" or "down here" has been appropriated to liberate and oppress at the same time. Rhetorically, there is no better way to gain power than to claim that God is on your side, your God is better than everyone else's, and only God can judge you.

The providence of God "out there" grants power over one's oppressors and the power to love God, oneself, and others. As God "down here," black men gain power over white supremacy through self-deification. But when God's empowerment chooses sides and grants heterosexual men power

over women and gay men, the liberatory nature of power is utterly compromised. This chapter explores the complexities of the God-sanctioned power
over domination and the God-sanctioned power to dominate as God's
gangstas resist oppression, establish hierarchies, and regulate intimate
relationships.

Resisting Oppression

In order for God to truly liberate the gangsta, the gangsta has to first liberate him or herself from oppressive ideas about God. Monotheistic traditions like Judaism, Christianity, or Islam maintain power over others by
insisting that individuals worship one God. Theologian Kelly Brown Douglas argues that "a closed monotheism is *absolutely* and inherently intolerant
of other claims to divine truth. It is concerned not simply with the loyalty
of its adherents to a single God, but also with the beliefs of others."[1] Individuals who fail to convert to the faith associated with political power have
routinely been persecuted throughout the religious history of Judaism,
Christianity, and Islam. Power combined with monotheism, especially
closed monotheism, is always oppressive.

Oppression, as defined by bell hooks, is the complete eradication of one's
choices. Exploitation and discrimination may limit one's choices, but they
do not completely obliterate them.[2] Paulo Friere argues that oppression
"constitutes violence . . . because it interferes with the individual's . . . voca-
tion to be more fully human."[3] Per these definitions, Christianity can be
considered oppressive when it removes an individual's choice to believe
in other deities or the divine potential within human beings. Christian
adherents who believe that their God is the only God and that nonbelievers
will be persecuted on earth and/or via the eternal fires of hell are oppressing
those who would choose to believe otherwise. The violent persecution of
Jews and the enslavement of stolen Africans are global historical examples
of Christian oppression. Because the Jews failed to convert and because
the Africans were deemed incapable of conversion, political authorities justified their dehumanization and the murder of hundreds of thousands of
innocent people in the name of God. Douglas is right. "Power and a closed
monotheism present a potentially deadly combination."[4] Furthermore,
when political power aligns itself with the power of God, other manifestations of authority like white supremacy and patriarchy are easily justifiable.

Christians may not be inherently oppressive or violent, but the closed
monotheism of Christianity has certainly been oppressive for individuals
of other faiths, people of color, women, homosexuals, and a large segment

of the hip hop generation who inherited a Christian God "out there" but cannot reconcile His oppressive actions or the oppressive actions of His religious representatives down here. Within three verses and no chorus on "When I Get to Heaven" (1993), Ice Cube lambasts Christianity for its hypocrisy, moneygrubbing, and racism. The melodious sound and simplicity of the song belies the complexity of Ice Cube's claims. The church is a fashion show, the priest is a beast in sheep's clothing, and the preacher is concerned only with tithes and wealth. Ice Cube's pithy phrases astutely link white supremacy to Christianity when he raps, "400 years gettin' our ass kicked/By so called Christians and Catholics." He boldly asserts that because God is just a man, "a killer from the start," He shouldn't mind if Ice Cube threatens to murder whites who mete out justice by imprisoning black men, bombing black churches, and killing innocent black children.[5]

Sampling the sound and the frustration of Marvin Gaye's "Inner City Blues"(1971), Ice Cube conveys that in 22 years Christianity has done nothing to ameliorate the oppression of inner-city residents. Inflation, the draft, rising bills and taxes, and police brutality makes Gaye "wanna holler." Immediately after the Gaye sample, Ice Cube samples NOI leader Louis Farrakhan urging blacks not to lay down and back away from their struggles. By incorporating other NOI references in the song like the prohibition against eating swine, knowledge of self, and Elijah's plan, Ice Cube suggests it is time for a black alternative to Christianity that stands up to white supremacy. He drives the point home with the refrain, "they won't call me a nigga when I get to heaven."

For many rappers, resisting oppression requires resisting religion. It demands that they abandon oppressive ideas about God and replace them with new ones. Ice Cube abandons the Christian God "out there," but only hints at His replacement. Rappers from the Five Percent Nation fully manifest the black man as God's replacement. The primary belief of the Five Percent Nation, also known as the Nation of Gods and Earths, is that the black man is God and the black woman is an Earth. Founded by former NOI member Clarence 13X aka Father Allah in 1964, the organization inherited many NOI precepts including the belief that 85 percent of the population is misguided, 10 percent of the population is actively misguiding the 85 percent, but 5 percent are the poor righteous teachers who understand the truth and can save the 85 percent by sharing the knowledge that the black man is God. The Five Percent teachings include an alphabet and mathematics that are compiled into lessons that members memorize and share "the knowledge" with each other.

Five Percent doctrine appeals to the disenfranchised who desperately need to believe in themselves. Juan Floyd-Thomas writes, "The underlying message of the Five Percenters is that the disorder they had experienced up until then had been caused by outside forces beyond their control, evil influences they were now able to overcome through self-mastery." He explains that even women in the Five Percent Nation who were regulated to the position of the God's fertile Earths could appreciate the protection, security, and stability engendered by "a strong nuclear family and traditional gender roles."[6] The self-empowerment taught by the Five Percent Nation served to break the mental chains of inferiority for a black community suffering from poverty, disenfranchisement, racism, and other forms of oppression. Because each man is God, however, the nation is characterized by decentralized leadership and permissiveness. Individual Gods set their own codes of conduct, which frequently leaves members unaccountable for their own acts of oppression and open to critiques of hypocrisy because of behavioral inconsistency. It also leaves Earths vulnerable to mistreatment and abuse.

Adherents argue that the Five Percent Nation should not be held to the same standards as Islam because it is not a religion. Members do not consider themselves NOI or Muslim; neither Five Percent nor NOI are considered orthodox Islam, but both are often grouped with Sunni Islam as representing the Muslim presence in hip hop because all three are stereotyped by outsiders as "threats to American civilization" and considered by insiders to be personally transformative forces. Rejecting the submission demanded of orthodox Islam, Five Percenters interpret Islam as I Self Lord Am Master or Independent Source of Life and Matter and Allah as Arm, Leg, Leg, Arm, Head representing a man's core body structure.

Five Percent was a way of life adopted by many hip hop heads predominantly on the East Coast during the late '80s and early '90s. Five Percent influence is not limited to self-empowerment. Its language about sharing information permeates hip hop via commonplace phrases like "entering the cipher," "dropping knowledge," praising something as "the bomb," or demanding that someone "show and prove." Because of its influence, some argue that Five Percent was the original spiritual presence in hip hop until rap became more mainstream, more diverse, less about dropping knowledge, and more about the blinged out prosperity gospel of Christianity. Of course, anti-Islamic sentiment and the War on Terror made many Americans wary of anything slightly Islamic.

As terrified as most cursory interpreters of Islam are of *jihad* (holy war), linguist and hip hop scholar H. Samy Alim helps contextualize it as sometimes an armed struggle but also a struggle for "self-determination in the face of persecution, oppression, and occupation."[7] If there were a *jihad* for the Five Percent Nation, it would be a struggle to wrest power away from a white mystery God "out there" and return it to black men "down here" on earth. Many black men refused to petition a white mystery God "out there" for earthly assistance because the reverence would invest white men with a supremacy that they believed was reprehensible and directly responsible for their impoverished living conditions.

Five Percent rap group Brand Nubian released "Ain't No Mystery" in 1993. In the song, Sadat X characterizes the mystery God as a big white man on a throne with a magic wand who arbitrarily decides who goes to heaven and who goes to hell. God is characterized as either invisible or inept throughout the verses. Brand Nubian lists the mystery God's complicity in poverty, slavery, police brutality, and the hypocrisy of church culture. Brand Nubian concludes that it ain't no mystery; the supreme black man is God. In 1997, Five Percent rap godfather Rakim returned to the game with *The 18th Letter*. The track "Mystery (Who Is God?)" (1997) describes the creation of the earth, cites the Bible and the Qur'an, and concludes that as a black man, he and the Creator are one.

Both tracks resist the oppressive nature of a white mystery God but in divergent ways. Like Ice Cube's "When I Get to Heaven," Brand Nubian denounces the white mystery God responsible for their oppression and concludes with relative certainty that the black man is God. Rakim acknowledges a God "out there" absent the white supremacist characteristics of his peers' mystery God. When he asks "who is God," he forces audiences to rethink what they know about God. When he raps "we are Gods," he forces audiences to rethink what they know about themselves. Rakim celebrates the beauty, power, and creativity of God and then associates it with blackness. Brand Nubian resists white supremacy by demonstrating their power over the white mystery God. Rakim resists white supremacy by offering blacks the power to think of themselves in empowering ways.

Five Percenter God talk resists oppression by disassociating God from the oppressive tactics of white supremacy. Common and Cee Lo Green, on the other hand, resist oppression by disassociating God from His power. They encourage audiences to seek the understanding and wisdom that will help them gain their own definitions for God in "G.O.D. (Gaining One's Definition)" (1997). Common rejects closed monotheism, celebrates "different branches of belief," and urges individuals to acknowledge any supreme being that helps people be their best selves. Cee Lo's verse seeks the truth about the role of race in religion. He learns that Jesus was not white, but cannot accept that black men are Gods when the title contradicts their actions. He concludes that the devil is not white but a color-blind mind-set that "evil white folk and evil niggas" share. Without naming Five Percenters, Cee Lo demands their accountability when he concludes his verse with "If you God, then save your own, don't mentally enslave your own." For Common and Cee Lo redistributing God's power means gaining one's own definition by fully interrogating established belief systems.

In addition to race, the other traditional aspect of God that rappers have interrogated is His identity as a patriarch. Tiye Phoenix disentangles God from the power of patriarchy on "Half Woman, Half Amazin'." On one hand, the single's title (which is also the title of her 2009 debut album) is a simple boast. On another, the declaration of half woman, half amazin' resists patriarchal oppression by embodying God "down here" in the body of a woman. Lyrically sampling Nas's half-man, half-amazin' boast from "It Ain't Hard to Tell" (1994), Tiye acknowledges the men who have come before her as she demands that they recognize her power as a woman. Imani Perry describes Nas's half-man, half-amazing claim as "a statement of the divinity in the flesh-and-blood person, a radical concept when embodied by a black man, the member of a group often demonized, stereotyped, and abused by society."[8] Tiye's claim is even more radical as a member of a group further demonized, stereotyped, and abused by men within hip hop.

Like many of Nas's religiously ambiguous lyrics, "Half Woman, Half Amazin' " is a mystical track that never directly addresses God, but Tiye divinely positions herself through her spiritual and religious allusions. As a phoenix rising from her ashes, Tiye's moniker references the universal myth of a bird that ignites itself to be reborn. The life-after-death theme is further substantiated by her Jesus allusions. In a twenty-first-century throwback to the year Jesus was born, Tiye raps, "Follow my tweets like the wise men did baby Jesus." When she identifies herself as the truth, she recalls Jesus's words from John 14:6a: "I am the way, the truth, and the life." Describing herself as something the world has never seen and attributing her topics to the voices of higher prophets, Tiye, like Jesus, is fulfilling prophecy. She boasts of miracles like walking on the sea, turning water into wine, and making a blind man see with her mind.

Tiye demands that men who are oblivious to her skills recognize that she is the long-awaited, amazing female rapper who cannot be eliminated because of her divine power to keep coming back. Furthermore, her references to slum gods and goddesses as well as her self-deification are Five Percent characteristics. She represents the handful of female members who were courageous enough to reject their position as Earths and declare themselves Gods, a position equal to that of their men. Additionally, her "math" or recited statistics about the numbers of cells in the brain and other facts about the human body are reminiscent of the numerical evidence often recited by Five Percent rappers.

Tiye disaffiliates God from patriarchy by highlighting her divinity and by eschewing oppression. Without threatening violence, disrespecting anyone, or reducing her skills to sexual prowess, Tiye appropriates God's power to elevate herself above the stereotypes about women rappers by celebrating the miraculous nature of the human body. She celebrates the divinity in all of humanity. In contrast to most empowering tracks by men, Tiye does not put others down to raise her status. Instead, she begins at the top by appropriating God and demands that her haters meet her on her higher level. Because the power of God "out there" resides in Tiye "down here" she is half woman, half amazing.

Establishing Hierarchies

The most effective strategy for a rapper to amass power over white supremacy and patriarchy, especially as they are manifested through Christianity, is to declare that he or she is God or half God. When oppressive authorities wield power over the oppressed, the resistance strategies intended to invert an established hierarchy must be bold. When power is horizontal, however, and distributed relatively equally among peers, the power necessary to establish a hierarchy is less audacious. Instead of being God, rappers access a relationship with God "out there" to establish power over peers. These relationships include being a child of the God, receiving blessings from God, and enacting violence with God's approval.

The hip hop generation has been indelibly shaped by deindustrialization and draconian federal policies that have defunded essential social services and criminalized large swaths of the African American population. An additional defining characteristic of the hip hop generation is a familial one, marked by the absence of fathers. Approximately 70 percent of African American children are born to single mothers. Fatherlack describes youth who desired yet were denied affirming relationships with their biological fathers. Because mothers are the stabilizing parental force for the hip hop generation and because power is still predominantly male identified, rappers are more likely to describe themselves as children of daddy God rather than a mother God. Women rappers like Lil' Kim, Foxy Brown, Trina, Lady of Rage, and Lauryn Hill have all alluded to God as a father. In "Sunlight" (2007) RZA declares Allah's omnipotence as the father of all. While many God the father rap references are generic, there is a consistent sentiment that God is watching over, protecting, and providing for His children. His presence empowers them to love themselves and to think of themselves as maintaining power over those who do not acknowledge God as their father.

Nas is perhaps the most readily recognizable God's son since the words are tattooed across his stomach and denote the title of his 2002 album. Nas frequently raps about God as his protector/provider father figure. As a father, God gives gangstas the power to love themselves and the depressed environments from which they come. In "God Love Us" (1999) Nas describes a neighborhood where death is in the air. Its inhabitants are armed, dodge stray bullets, and encounter death daily as they attend each other's funerals. Nas catalogues the good and bad of his hood where people work, eat, and play and where people use drugs, sell drugs, are in and out of prison, birth babies too early, betray each other, and contract AIDS. But at the end of it all, Nas concludes, "Our lives are the worst, on top of that, we broke/That's the main reason why God love us the most." Nas's God does not condemn hood residents for their predicament; he loves them because of it. In the first two verses Nas recounts near-death moments, when he knew God was watching over him. In the chorus, Nas describes a God who feels, listens to, forgives, and ultimately loves "hood niggas." Just as Jesus forgave the "crook nigga" who died on the adjacent cross in Luke 23:43, Nas knows God will forgive him and his comrades. Nas describes God's love as an "inner love" that provides him with the power to elevate himself above the stereotypes, return God's love, love himself, and love his hood.

Tupac Shakur aka Makaveli also acknowledges the importance of a father during the hellish times of crisis narrated in "Blasphemy" (1996). The introduction along with verses 1 and 2 conclude with variations of the line, "Remember what my papa told me, blasphemy." The fatherly advice of "money over bitches" and "watch for phonies" is offered to protect the son from poverty, iniquitous women, friends turned enemies, disingenuous preachers, and anyone else pretending to be someone who they are not. Although there is no reason to question the lyric's authenticity, Tupac frequently lamented his biological father's absence in his interviews. It is more likely that the fatherly advice came from a father figure. After careful consideration of a line in verse 3 where Tupac raps, "Tell me I ain't God's son, nigga mama a virgin," it is also possible that the father figure is God-like. Tupac was not literally born of a virgin, but his bold claims about being God's son demand that audiences reconsider what constitutes blasphemy. The track is aptly titled because it exposes Christian hypocrisy by blurring the boundaries of blasphemy. Tupac asks, is it blasphemy to use God to justify the suffering of others? Or, is it blasphemy to identify oneself as God's son?

His claim to be God's son serves an empowering function for a man who struggled through fatherlack, poverty, addiction, eviction, and persecution. He survived like only a son of God could. Tupac's audacious claims to be the son of a God who understands the plight of the oppressed are augmented by Prince Ital's strong Jamaican accent, which gives the chorus a reggae vibe. Historically, reggae has been progressive in its popular denunciations of the white man's Christianity, and many Rastafarians believe in the black man as God. According to William David Spencer,

> For God to be revealed as a black male is to place an exorbitant value upon one who has been stolen, subjected, despised and—now dramatically—reasserted. The concept may seem blasphemous, but it comes from the depths of a psyche whose identity was supposedly irretrievably taken and had substituted in its place a "Quashie" mentality of self-loathing servility. Rather than irretrievable, the true identity of diasporan black males is seen to have been safe in God's keeping.[9]

"Blasphemy's" soundtrack communicates this Rastafarian belief that further empowers Tupac to resist oppressive stereotypes about black men. It gives him power over his oppressors whether they be bitches, phonies, or other enemies. "Blasphemy" pursues power over others by reestablishing hierarchies. Unfortunately, those hierarchies ultimately leave enemies and women at the bottom.

Unlike Nas's God "out there" who uniformly distributes His love to the hood, Tupac's God does not offer equal protection to His children. Daddy God is powerful, but He is not perfect. As effortlessly as God makes men feel more secure, the God created in man's image can undermine his daughters' self-esteem. God's blessings further perpetuate gendered distinctions. Men establish hierarchies with the material possessions they receive from God. Women establish hierarchies through their God-given talent.

An account of God's blessings is a surefire strategy for maintaining power over one's peers. Busta Rhymes's "Make It Clap" (2002) and "Arab Money Remix Part 1" (2009) are paradigmatic examples of how money is seen as a gift from God in Christian and Islamic contexts. In "Make It Clap" Busta and his sidekick Spliff Star become rich by scamming people at Clap Studios—their physical fitness facility. They decide to go to church to get a blessing (and to get acquainted with the attractive women there). In order to appropriately repent for his sins, Pastor Offering tells Busta that the blessing will cost about $100,000.

Audiences note that even ill-gotten money (whether from an urban scam or a pastor's manipulations) can be blessed by God. Money blessed by God is sanctioned power over others. Pastor Offering wields power over Busta. Busta cannot be forgiven for his sins without paying a hefty price. Busta earns his money by wielding power over the women at Clap Studios. Until they learn how to make it clap (dance suggestively with an emphasis on "clapping" the buttocks together), the women will not be desirable to men. Women who can make it clap wield power over men who desire their bodies and will be willing to pay for the pleasure. Appropriately Busta plays both himself and the pastor in the video. In verse 3, while still in the church sanctuary, he and Spliff explicitly describe their expectations for women's sexual performance. A hierarchy of exploitation is firmly established with God's blessings as the ultimate authority and men in the primary position of power over women. Additionally, the chorus goes out to "soldiers that be flippin' them birds" and "shorties shakin' they curves." The money earned by men who deal drugs and women who strip is a blessing from God no matter how questionable the ethics because it establishes the earners at the top of the hierarchy above those who are willing to part with their money to obtain their vices.

The Christian God is not the only one to bless via material wealth. Allah does the same in Busta's "Arab Money Remix Part 1." Busta and a host of other rappers boast about their wealth in between Ron Browz's infectious Arabic hook "Bismillahi r-rahmani r-rahim. Al-hamdu lillahi rabbil 'ala-min." It translates as "In the name of Allah, most Gracious most Merciful. All Praise is due to Allah, Lord of the worlds." Critics accused Busta of racism for irreverently quoting the Qur'an out of context and mispronouncing Arab as Ay-rab. Busta corrected the pronunciation and explained that he never intended to be irreverent. "I have a lot of Arab friends and love and respect the Arab culture. I'm Islamic and I respect their close relationship with God and the value and significance of their financial and economic stability."[10] Arab money, for Busta, is not disrespectful; it is a preferred means for accumulating generational wealth. Notably, garnering this wealth is still considered a blessing from Allah who deserves praise for his beneficence and mercy.

Busta is one of many rappers including Jay-Z, Nas, Lil Wayne, and others who rap about money as a gift from above. Lavish Jesus pieces with canary yellow diamonds and other fanciful accessories are further evidence of the belief that God approves of public displays of prosperity. Familiar refrains of "only God can judge me" suggest that God can bless any endeavor—even participation in an illicit underground economy. While God's blessings are indeed personally gratifying, their purpose is the solidi-fication of one's place within a social hierarchy. The one with the most blessings has the greatest favor from God.

Whereas men focus on material possessions as their primary blessing from God, women's claims center on their lyricism as God's primary bless-ing. Women rappers who must prove themselves superior to their male peers boast about God-given talent. The Lady of Rage appropriates Genesis 1:1 when she raps in "Some Shit" (1997): "for in the book of Genesis it reads/in the beginning God created Heaven and then he created me." Queen Latifah appropriates John 3:16 in her "Wrath of My Madness" (1989) lyric, "For God so loved the world, he gave ya me." Inserting themselves within biblical narratives situates the women as God's divine daughters who consider themselves blessings from God who have also been blessed with mad lyrical skills.

Throughout hip hop history, rap divas have made claims about their divinely inspired lyrical talent. In "Get with Da Wikedness (Flow Like That Remix)" (1997) Rage raps, "Slaughter by the daughter of God that makes me a goddess/The one who rocks the hardest." In "I Can't Understand" (1993) Queen Latifah spits, "Forgive me Father for I have sinned/I just destroyed a phony ass rapper again." Tiye Phoenix satirically asks God's forgiveness for "Killing Everybody" in her 2009 boast about being the best. She describes her lyrics as "a blessing and a threat to humanity." Monie Love rapped in "Mo Monie" (1993), "Blessed when the Lord snipped my microphone cord/And said rock it any way you can, you got the whole world in ya hand." Eve notes in "Be Me" (2001), "She spits mean, God def-initely blessed her right."

The devaluation of women within hip hop motivates these artists to dis-prove the stereotype that "girls can't rap" and hype their talents as equal to that of their male peers. Notably, it is God's masculine power that allows them to express rage, slaughter, destroy, kill, rock the hardest, and be mean. The aggressiveness with which they convey how God's power elevates their status is typical of hip hop's hegemonic masculinity. God gives them access to the masculine power that they need to be successful in a man's world.

Because power is masculine in hip hop, women rarely rap about a female God. Furthermore, women rappers have always been extremely ambivalent about self-identifying as feminists. Rah Digga's "Tight" (1999) lyric is certainly an exception. She brags, "Baby, I'm hard, represent the feminist God." All of Rah Digga's companions in the video are men. She raps about "taking mad niggas' titles" and decomposing XY chromosomes. Men are under attack. The feminist God elevates Rah Digga over her male competitors, but the feminist God remains masculine in Her ability to make Rah Digga hard in the ways that men are hard-bodied, experience hard erections, and rap as hard-core rappers whose singular goal is to obliterate the competition. God gives women rappers the masculine power they need to compete with the men who are their major competitors and to erase the doubts of anyone who may question their skills. Women appropriate God's power to destabilize hip hop's typical gender hierarchies and venerate women's God-given talents.

Both women and men benefit from God's masculinity albeit in different ways. Women appropriate God's masculine power to oppose men's stereotypes about women in the game. Men appropriate God's masculine power to sanction aggressive violence against other male enemies. Few artists have perfected the performance of hypermasculinity like 50 Cent. His 2003 album *Get Rich or Die Tryin'* resurrected hip hop's gangsta ethos embodied by his muscular physique and hood narratives of dealing crack, being imprisoned, and surviving multiple gunshot wounds. A theatrical version of 50's come-up story is reenacted in his video "Many Men." He survives a shooting and plots revenge. The video opens with the line "I need you to pray for me." The chorus is a prayer. In it, 50 notes that he no longer cries or looks to the sky, but still desires God's mercy when he does what he has to do to survive. Verse 3 opens with 50 rapping, "Every night I talk to God, but he don't say nothing back/I know he protecting me, but I still stay with my gat." The verse ends with 50 confirming God's purpose for his life because he is alive and his enemies are dead.

Placing equal faith in God and one's gun is a common theme in men's rap music. Both represent power over life and death. Many rappers rap about being caught up in an environment not of their own making and engaging in disreputable and oftentimes violent actions with the sole comfort that God understands and will have mercy on them. Living a life where the threat of death is imminent requires as Nas rapped in "Halftime" (1994) "wait[ing] for God wit the fo' fo' [.44 magnum firearm]." This sentiment conveys a gangsta's belief that God understands the precariousness of a gangsta's existence and expects a man to defend himself by violent means if necessary. Through the gun, God gives gangstas power over their enemies by granting them the power to protect their lives and end the lives of others. One's God-given life is worth living and dying for. As a general rule, rappers do not evoke God to enact violence for fun. Instead, they describe themselves as embattled by enemies. When Ice Cube rapped in "When I Get to Heaven" "God is a killer from the start/Why you think Noah had to build his ark," he points out God's destructive and murderous tendencies. Noel Leo Erskine confirms, "God takes sides and identifies with rappers in their attempt to confront violence with counterviolence. Their God is the God of the Old Testament who uses violence as a midwife to give birth to new possibilities and realities."[11]

In "Creation and Destruction" (2001) Immortal Technique relocates God's power to create and destroy within himself. Throughout the aggressive battle rap, Immortal Technique depicts himself as a supreme figure, a spiritual witch who created life with his spit, made the sun shine, regulated time, and cooled lava by merely walking on it. His cleverest boasts are when he bests God. Immortal Technique raps, "When God said 'Let there be light,' I turned it the fuck off." He concludes verse 1 with the line "I allowed God to let you motherfuckers exist." During the second and final verse he brags that his power to destroy is iller than a mutated virus or a plague that God gave Moses.

Immortal Technique's name alone makes claims to his supremacy. As a battle rapper, his lyrics are dense, and his disses are hard. Being more destructive than God is a lyrical strategy that gives him power over his enemies and power over ideas about God. When he claims to be stronger than "the fake image of God" he cautions listeners to be wary of a mystery (white) God that may not have their best interests at heart. The nature of the rap, however, prevents Immortal Technique from considering anyone's interests but his own. His power over competitors includes a discernible hatred of bitches and "feminine men." Empowering oneself by appropriating God's violence establishes a hierarchy that assures the obliteration of one's enemies.

God's power resists, establishes, and maintains hierarchies. When a rapper is battling (lyrically or physically) to be the best, his or her God is more powerful than the God of his or her enemies. In these situations, the saying "my God is your God's God" has never been more relevant. Although the imposition of hierarchies keeps competitors and enemies in their place, hierarchies also permeate rap's more intimate relationships.

Regulating Intimate Relationships

Unfortunately, appropriations of God's power in regulating intimate relationships are usually explicitly exploitative. For instance, when Gudda Gudda raps in Young Money's "Every Girl in the World" (2009) "these hoes is God's gift like Christmas," he implies that women are possessions that God gives to men like parents give children toys during the holiday. Whereas Young Money wants to fuck every girl in the world, Nas just wants to create a perfect one in "The Makings of a Perfect Bitch" (2004). In true Frankenstein fashion, Nas pieces together his perfect bitch and describes his power over her: "I'm her daddy, I'm her messiah, I'm God/ Cause I injected obedience and loyalty in her heart." Like God, Nas exercises his power to create but unfortunately he creates a creature he can have complete power over.

Ghostface Killah regains power over a woman he believes has committed infidelity and betrayed him by verbally assaulting her in "Wildflower" (1996). As a Five Percenter who refers to himself as God in the track, Ghostface further self-deifies when he raps, "I came to you as a blessin' " and "sexually you worshipped my di-dick like a cross." Ghostface is more than the man in the relationship; he is God and vengeance is his. Acting as a moral force that prevents further harm, Ghostface's friends, other Gods, encourage him to rap about his anger instead of physically attacking his woman. His lyrical descriptions of sex are so violent, however, that one cannot help but wonder if Ghostface describes rape. As a God, Ghostface is not invincible. He is deeply hurt by his woman's actions, but being God does not give him the power to forgive her as much as it gives him the desire to exert (sexual) control over her.

Perhaps the most layered appropriation of God's power over a sexual partner is Lil B's "Look Like Jesus" (2010). Rapping from a church sanctuary, Lil B repeats the first line of the hook "hoes on my dick 'cause I look like Jesus." The hook previews a single verse where Lil B describes himself as a pretty bitch princess who fucks women all night and/or convinces them to suck his dick. During the two-minute song, the word *bitch* is used approximately every eight seconds. The video consists of alternating shots of Lil B and stained glass windows and sculptures that depict the life of a white, forlorn, effeminate-looking Jesus. Lil B also claims to dress like Jesus.

Because Lil B looks and dresses like Jesus, women cannot resist his sexual power over them; they are expendable conquests that boost his ego. It matters not that Lil B does not look or dress anything like the Jesus images in his video. In that sense, "Look Like Jesus" is an attention-grabbing marketing ploy of a savvy young rapper who directs all of his own videos and maintains hundreds of MySpace pages to distribute his stream of consciousness "based" music. Lil B told MTV, "Based music is being yourself, staying positive and you can be negative too, but you have to show both sides."[12] One positive attribute of "Look Like Jesus" is that his lyrics describe consensual sex. Unfortunately, there is no mutual pleasure. The hoes are on *his* dick. Lil B appropriates Jesus's power over women, but the greatest potential for positivity resides in a Jesus who provides Lil B with the power to redefine masculinity.

Lil B describes himself as a pretty bitch and a princess who wears tiny shirts and tiny jeans that sag below his behind. These are nonnormative descriptors of hip hop's traditional hypermasculinity. It is no accident that the Jesus Lil B appropriates is similarly "pretty," a man with a slim build, long flowing hair, and robes to match. This is not the powerful resurrected Jesus, the blinged out Jesus, or the Trap Jesus of Lil B's peers. This is a Jesus made in Lil B's image to serve competing interests—overemphasizing heterosexuality (i.e., sexual conquests) while queering masculinity.

In other tracks, Lil B has self-identified as a fag, a lesbian, and a lesbian man. Lil B titled his debut album *I'm Gay* (2011). He frequently acknowledges rumors that he is gay but refutes them by counting the number of hoes on his dick. At one point, he bragged he would have 100 hoes on his dick when he died. His series of freestyle raps where he claims to be other people including but not limited to James Worthy, Bill Clinton, J. K. Rowling, and Paris Hilton denote the playfulness of a young man desperate for attention with a knack for renegotiating language. When Lil B declares in "I'm God" (2009) that he always wanted to be God, he's claiming that he wants to be better than the best. When Lil B calls himself the Based God, he declares that he is the best at making based music, which is technically true because he is the only one making it. Lil B uses God's power over women to garner enough power to be based—confident, independent, and operating outside of the normative descriptors of masculinity.

To be clear, Lil B does not embrace homosexuality. From subtle interjections of "no homo" (which in hip hop slang means "do not mistake me as homosexual") to use of the word *fag*, and explicit claims about his sexual exploits suggest that heterosexuality is still the norm. But as a Jesus and a Based God, Lil B is empowered to do whatever he wants. As he does so, he redefines hip hop's expectations for masculinity and creates space for conversations about homosexuality that other rappers shut down in God's name. For example, when Byron Hurt asked Busta Rhymes about homophobia in hip hop during his documentary *Beyond Beats and Rhymes*, Busta replied, "I can't partake in that conversation, homes. That homoshit? That's what you talking about? I can't talk to you about that. . . . cause with all due respect, I mean, I'm not trying to offend nobody. What I represent culturally doesn't condone it whatsoever."[13] The cultural belief Busta referred to was the Five Percent condemnation of gays and lesbians. As Five Percent Gods, procreation is the norm and homosexuality is unnatural at best and devilish at worst. When asked if a gay rapper would ever be accepted in hip hop culture, Busta ignored the question and exited the room. Lil B's power over women and his homophobia are disgusting, but his power to invite conversations about homosexuality and nonnormative masculinity is inspiring.

Whether rappers consider themselves a family, nation, clan, pack, crew, fellow convicts, or death row associates, the homosocial bond among male rappers is their primary intimate relationship. Oftentimes, these male friendships degrade the feminine as part of their bonding ritual. Whether it's the heterosexual exploitation of "it ain't no fun if the homies can't have none" or the homophobia of "faggot-ass niggas," intimate relationships among men in hip hop are too often precipitated on a virulent distancing from the feminine embodied by both women and gay men. The power of God is appropriated to justify these exploitative heterosexual relationships and condemn homosexual relationships, but interestingly enough the power of a female God helps rappers learn to truly love God, themselves, and others.

Hip hop is notorious for perpetuating relational hierarchies wherein one partner wields power over another. However, the most redemptive moments have emerged through those rare occasions when rappers create intimacy with female Gods. Charles Hamilton has "Conversations with God" (2008). He respectfully calls her Miss and asks if she is offended by his disrespectful lyrics about women. God admits that his delivery is brash, but She encourages him. As Hamilton laments about life's difficulties, God tells him that She is watching, listening, and supporting him even as She pressures him to be his best. Hamilton learns that God's love is unconditional. She empowers Hamilton to express himself. Unfortunately, Hamilton's expression includes power over "bitches' sexual exploits and niggas who don't understand." Despite these references, the track as a whole is not about the degradation of others. God demands that Hamilton face his "inner beast." Overall, it is extremely unusual and incredibly progressive for men to rap about female Gods without relying on the stereotypical tropes of femininity. Charles Hamilton's God grants audiences permission to reimagine God's identity outside of the constraints of masculinity.

Perhaps his inspiration came from Common who encourages fidelity in "Faithful" (2005) by envisioning his female partner as God. Initially, he is uncertain about his ability to remain faithful, but ultimately concludes that he could give God's love back to her. Because she would die for him, he would ride for her, be grateful for her, reflect her, and wear her cross/heart around his neck. Thinking and then speaking of his woman as God gives Common the power to be faithful. His reverence for God gives him the power to respect his woman. That power is further reflected in the second verse where a man is tempted by his mistress but has a moment of clarity, returns home, confesses his indiscretions to his wife, and declares his love for her. At the song's end, the voices of John Legend and Bilal harmonize to declare their commitment to being faithful. Common foreshadowed these paradigm shifts at the beginning of the song when he said, "God moves." God has indeed moved the men from a desire to be faithful toward a commitment to being faithful. Being faithful to God requires being faithful to oneself as well as loved ones.

Unfortunately, this power to love emerging from intimacy with a female God is an exception to the rule. The distribution of the masculine God's power whether "out there" or "down here" is almost always uneven. A majority of the raps discussed in this chapter resulted in an uneasy combination of the power to love oneself and wielding power over others. Achieving the power to believe in oneself almost always results in an unfair exercise of power over someone else. Because our God-given senses fail us when it comes to knowing God, the profound uncertainty about God's power is negotiated in various ways. Some gangstas self-deify. Others encourage audiences to acquire their own definitions. Others identify as God's children, recipients of God's blessings, or executors of God's violence. Irrespective of the approach to God's power, God is consistently seen by rappers as an irrevocable reservoir of power that can be appropriated to resist oppression, establish hierarchies, and regulate intimate relationships.

Chapter 6

The Rap on Rap and Religion

Religious beliefs often choose us before we can choose them. Religion, the ritualized practice of (re)establishing a relationship between human beings and the transcendent (something or someone greater than the human situation), is communicated through family, culture, media, and other social institutions. Religious habitus is a phrase that describes a learned and shared religious consciousness that shapes how humans perceive the world.[1] Although individuals are not genetically predisposed to a particular religious belief, a child's earliest interactions predetermine his or her religious attitudes. The familial religious habitus of children is most seriously interrogated when they mature into adolescence. According to the authors of *How God Changes Your Brain*, "religious interests rapidly decline during adolescence and . . . many teens will reject their parents' values as they attempt to redefine their spiritual beliefs. Indeed, for many people religiosity continues to decline through the rest of life, a trend that has continued since 1970."[2] One of the many factors that contribute to this reevaluation of belief is exposure to religious themes within popular culture. Although understudied and perhaps underestimated, youth interactions with religion in popular culture have the potential to influence their religious beliefs.

This chapter considers rap's ability to inform, affirm, or oppose the religious attitudes of its audiences by asking the genre's youthful fans about their experiences with rap and religion. These survey data complement and invigorate the book's textual analyses of God talk in rap music by mimicking a hip hop cipha. A cipha (linguistically derived from cipher, also spelled cypher in some communities) is a group performance where each participant takes turns displaying his or her talent, which is usually rapping or dancing. Because each contributor's rhyme or dance is inspired by the previous participant, the goal of these spontaneous freestyle performances is to create a completely original unbroken circle of creative energy. This book presents a hip hop scholarship cipha by combining the perspectives of artists and audiences in an original format. The questions posed to the youth in this survey chapter were inspired by the texts examined throughout this book. In turn, the survey responses provide nuanced interpretations of the rappers mentioned in other parts of the book. The lyrical and visual analyses combined with an audience reception study provide a glimpse into a cipha filled with unique and yet interdependent performances of religious habitus. The distinct perspectives expressed within this hip hop scholarship cipha provide a fuller picture of how religious habitus influences rap, how rap impacts religious habitus, and how audiences interpret the relationship between the two. This groundbreaking approach to studying rap and religion is exploratory but essential for discerning how audiences perceive and interpret the function of religion in rap.

The Survey

Participants were recruited from fall 2011 popular culture and hip hop courses at my university—California State University, Long Beach (CSULB). The courses included a 200-level "Introduction to Hip Hop" taught in Africana Studies, two sections of the 300-level course "Popular Culture: Women, Gender, and Sexuality" taught in the department of Women, Gender, and Sexuality Studies, and two of my own 400-level communication courses, "Hip Hop Criticism" as well as "Communication and Popular Culture." I actively recruited students who were predisposed to think about and be interested in popular culture and hip hop. Data were collected midsemester so the hip hop students would have already gained a fundamental understanding of hip hop history. Although all of the students were informed that I was writing a book on rap and religion, I did not preview specific content within the book or lecture on the subject.[3]

Students were informed that the purpose of the Rap and Religion Survey (RARS) was to gather data about how individuals interested in popular culture and familiar with rap music think about and interpret rappers' use of the devil, Jesus, and God. They were given a survey that required them to select from multiple-choice options and write short-answer responses to questions about themselves, their beliefs about the devil, Jesus, and God, as well as their opinions on the relationship between rap and religion. Students took anywhere from 10 to 30 minutes to complete the survey. Since students were not required to participate and could submit incomplete surveys if they preferred, there were varying levels of completion. There were a total of 175 submitted surveys.

Despite the fact that 175 is a reasonable sample size, the study had several limitations. The current convenience sample would have been greatly enhanced by recruiting various populations. Surveying noncollege students would have provided an opportunity to compare and contrast the responses of those formally trained to think critically about the culture they enjoy and those who have not been formally trained to do so. Although slightly more difficult to recruit because of Institutional Review Board limitations, the perspectives of teenagers ages 13 to 17 would have added an additional layer of complexity. Finally, interviews or focus groups would have offered an opportunity for follow-up conversations and expanded discussions of the brief comments made in the surveys. Nonetheless, these RARS results are an essential first step toward determining what hip hop fans believe about God and religion and, furthermore, how they interpret rappers' beliefs about God and religion. Please note that the study's descriptive statistics may not always add up to 100 because of rounding, and student quotes were only edited for clarity.

Demographics

Survey respondents represent a diverse subject pool, which is attributable to the diverse nature of CSULB and Long Beach, California. Nearly half of the participants lived in Long Beach. Students who lived outside of Long Beach commuted an average of 19 miles. Of the 175 students surveyed, 49 identified as white, 44 identified as Hispanic or Latino/a, 26 identified as Asian or Pacific Islander, 26 identified as black or African American, 24 identified as bi/multiracial, 2 identified as American Indian, 1 identified as other, and 3 chose not to respond. No single race or ethnicity represented over half of the sample. However, 70 percent of participants were nonwhite. In general, both hip hop classes included a majority of nonwhite students. They were likely drawn by the subject matter and/or the fact that the courses were taught by African American professors—one of whom was an Africana studies professor. The inclusion of this overwhelming minority population is important because the face of rap music remains largely African American and convenience samples of college students rarely reflect this diversity.

Although racial diversity was ensured, gender diversity was not. Recruiting from gender studies courses where women students outnumbered men helped ensure that 63 percent of survey respondents were women and only 36 percent were men. The higher number of women participants, however, did not skew student interest in hip hop. Forty-one percent expressed a high interest in hip hop, 43 percent expressed a medium interest in hip hop, and the minority of 15 percent expressed a low interest in hip hop. Additionally, approximately 30 percent were currently enrolled in a hip hop course. The oldest respondent was 43, and the youngest respondent was 17. The average age of the respondents was 22. Overall, this participant diversity reflects the diversity of hip hop audiences.

The respondents also reflected an impressive religious diversity. Approximately 38 percent of the students self-identified as religious, 33 percent self-identified as not religious, and 30 percent self-identified as spiritual but not religious. Sixty-six percent of the religious students identified as Christian, while 23 percent identified as Catholic. Other represented religious affiliations included Buddhist, Egyptian Pagan, Hindu, Jewish, Muslim, Satanist, and Wiccan. In addition to noting their religious affiliation, students were asked whether religion was an important part of their family or their culture. Of the nonreligious students, only 12 percent noted no familial or cultural religious affiliations. Catholicism and Christianity were overrepresented as religions that impacted nonreligious students, but Buddhism and Judaism were also included. Sixty-four percent of the spiritual but not religious students did not note a familial or cultural religion, but mentions included Buddhism, Catholicism, Christianity, Islam, and Judaism.

Religious and nonreligious students alike appear to be impacted by the religious habitus of their communities. One could justifiably surmise that both embracing a religion and rejecting one are likely impacted by the religious beliefs encountered during childhood. Whereas the spiritual students were less likely to note a familial or cultural religious affiliation, declaring oneself spiritual and not religious still engages religious habitus. For example, distinguishing between spiritual and religious is a common phenomenon. In the book *America's Four Gods*, Paul Froese and Christopher Bader observe that when people say "I'm spiritual but not religious" they usually mean "they do not affiliate with a specific church but still believe in God and the supernatural."[4] Mark Lewis Taylor suggests the distinction becomes necessary when individuals perceive that established religions are "ineffective communicators—silent about social trauma or actively complicit in systematic dehumanization."[5] Disassociation from organized religion and the embrace of alternative and affirming "spiritual" practices and communities continue to reflect the social nature of religion.

Because individuals do not have to be religious or spiritual to believe in God, students were specifically asked about their beliefs in God. Response options were inspired by the 2006 Baylor Religion Survey (BRS), an extensive national study of Americans' religious affiliations and beliefs. Thirty-seven percent of participants surveyed had no doubts that God exists, and 29 percent believed in a higher power or cosmic force. Twenty-one percent of surveyed individuals believed in God but with some doubts, 7 percent sometimes believed in God, 3 percent did not believe in God, 2 percent had no opinion, and 1 percent believed humans were gods. Overall, 94 percent of the surveyed population maintained some belief in God or a higher power.

These descriptive statistics are not generalizable to the entire hip hop fan population, but the participants represent a diverse subject pool that mirrors rap's audiences. Moreover, their responses to questions about religious beliefs resonate with national findings. In alignment with the 94 percent of students who believe in God or a higher power, the BRS reports that "85–90% of Americans routinely respond 'yes' when asked 'Do you, personally, believe in God?'" Even individuals unaffiliated with a religious tradition are still inclined to believe in God or a higher power.[6] The 2002–3 "National Survey of Youth and Religion" (NSYR) reports that "more than 80% [of American teenagers ages 13–17] do believe in God, slightly more than 10 percent are unsure about their belief in God, and . . . only 3 percent definitely do not believe in God."[7] The 28 percent of the RARS participants who acknowledged doubts about God's existence is certainly higher than the NSYR, but the majority still believed in God or a higher power, and the percentage of teenagers and college students who do not believe in God was the same. Froese and Bader explain the higher rates of doubt among the older youth: "Once an image of God is introduced to our minds (usually by a parent), it takes on a life of its own. And as we age, our image of God develops more fully and continues to be influenced by new experiences, which are reconciled with—or completely undermine—our earliest image of God."[8] The negotiations with religious habitus that occur when thinking more critically and independently about inherited religious beliefs might also explain why more NSYR respondents self-identified as religious than RARS respondents. While BRS confirms that youth between the ages of 18 and 30 are less likely to have a religious affiliation, in both instances the predominant religions were Protestant and Catholic.[9]

Rap and Religion

When students were asked to list "what religions are represented in rap music," their responses mirrored their personal, familial, and cultural religious affiliations. Eighteen students left the question blank or wrote that they were unsure. This perplexity was articulated by a Christian student who observed, "I hear a lot about God and Jesus, but not a lot about what kind of religion that is—not a clear, 'I'm Catholic' or 'I'm a non-denominational Christian.'" The student astutely observed that references to God and Jesus do not ensure adherence to a particular religion. However, 91 percent of the respondents listed Christianity as the dominant religion represented in rap. Perhaps these students were more willing to make the assumption that mentioning God and Jesus denoted a Christian religious affiliation or, as another Christian student explained, "Christianity is the religion I see most in music, or maybe I want to see that most so it stands out to me." Religious habitus could partially explain why most students readily identify Christianity in rap music, even if rappers rarely explicitly identify as Christian.

The majority of students listed several religions, but the second most frequently recorded religion was Islam, noted by 26 percent of the students, with Catholicism listed by 21 percent of the respondents. Within the Islamic category, one student specifically named the Five Percent Nation, and two students identified the Nation of Islam. Of the 33 students who listed Catholicism, 6 of them wrote "Christianity/Catholicism" as if the two were similar/synonymous while another 6 used *or* to distinguish between Christianity and Catholicism. The others simply listed them horizontally with commas or vertically, suggesting that the religions deserve separate indicators. Despite the fact that Protestant and Catholic are commonly used designators to differentiate between two branches of Christianity, no student ever used Protestant as a distinguishing term. Judaism followed Islam and Catholicism with 10 percent recognition. The top five religions rounded out with an "all religions are represented" category noted by 8 percent of the respondents.

A spiritual but not religious student described the breakdown: "Mostly in America, it would be Judeo-Christian belief systems, but sometimes American rap may reflect Islamic values as well. However, religious beliefs and lyrics in rap music may vary depending upon who the artist is, their background, and who their targeted audience is." A Catholic student further confirmed the potential for multiple religious representations in rap but was less confident about audience response: "Almost all religions can be found in rap music dependent on the origin of the music. In the American mainstream, Christianity is most prominently displayed. I couldn't see the public at large being receptive to Jewish, Muslim, or any other religious rappers. It was difficult enough for the radio to play 'Jesus Walks' by Kanye." This student explained that rappers can adhere to any religion, but audiences may reject their religious articulations. His example of the "Jesus Walks" megahit, however, is ironic proof that audiences can be quickly persuaded to embrace religion within rap.

A 21-year-old Catholic with a high interest in hip hop implied in a lengthy additional missive on the back of his survey that rap was like a religion. In this excerpt he explained,

> This music, it provides us with many uplifting feelings; motivation to work harder, how to deal with a relationship, how to make money, as tough as things may get, you can make it through, someone who's ready to commit suicide, but some Eminem song comes on and they're like, "Shit, why am I doing this?" Many critics despise rap and hip hop as a negative influence, but this is the reason why we have different genres. Rap and hip hop is for everybody; it comes down to being true to yourself.

In his defense of rap music, he describes its benefits in the same way that many religious people describe the benefits of their religion. For this respondent, rap, like religion, provides motivation, practical advice, and hope. Similarly, his reference to various rap genres can be interpreted as paralleling the various religious denominations that advocate the notion that there truly is a religious practice for everybody.

In addition to being asked what religions are represented in rap, students were asked, "Do you think rappers can be religious?" and "How do you know when rappers are being religious?" Two individuals did not answer the question. Three individuals marked "no" because rap contradicts religion. A 21-year-old who did not consider himself religious and reported listening to rap several times every day justified why rappers cannot be religious. He wrote, "I don't think rappers are religious because most religions don't stand for what rappers represent." A 29-year-old who claimed to listen to rap a few times a week differentiated religious from spiritual in her answer: "I don't think they can be religious; spiritual maybe, but not religious. It's a contradiction to (most) religions to act the way rappers do or speak the way they do. As a spiritual (not religious) person, I think it's ok to reference a higher being and acknowledge a greater existence than your own." Her explanation suggests as previously noted that spirituality has more permeable boundaries than organized religion.

Thirteen individuals were perplexed by the contradictions and marked that they were unsure whether rappers could be religious. A woman who claimed not to be religious and who listened to rap once every two or three months wrote, "I usually cannot tell if they are being religious. It's hard to see that they take a stand when all they seem to rap about is sex, money, and cars." It's possible that her low interest in hip hop contributed to her uncertainty, but a 21-year-old Christian with a high interest in hip hop observed, "There is no way to know if a rapper is religious. Just because he talks about God or references any beliefs doesn't make him religious." Perhaps because he self-identified as Christian, his expectations for fellow believers demanded more than a mere mention of God. His observation is important because in addition to claims about contradiction, he echoed a popular sentiment among the students that merely listening to rap does not make an audience privy to a rap artist's private thoughts.

An overwhelming majority of respondents (90%), however, reported that yes, rap can be religious. Students ascertained that rappers were religious by paying attention to what the rappers said and did. Words and actions emerged as two distinct categories although some responses referenced both. Support for the action category included appearance, imagery, and lifestyle. Students claimed to know rappers were religious based upon their appearance, which included religious clothing, jewelry such as crosses and Jesus pieces, and tattoos (often of crosses). They identified religious imagery in videos and cover art, but besides a cross, no one specified or elaborated upon what else this religious imagery might include. They also noted that a rapper's lifestyle was important. To truly know, one would have to follow the rapper, observe what kind of volunteering he or she did, and pay attention to his or her associates.

Words overwhelmed actions within the responses. Despite the 21-year-old Christian student's claim that mentioning God does not make a rapper religious, 114 students overwhelmingly said they knew rappers were religious when they referenced a higher power including God, Jesus, or Allah. (Ironically, neither of the two Allah references were made by Muslim students.) A spiritual but not religious "recovering Catholic" noted rappers were being religious "when they made specific references to a higher authority that sustains them regardless of the judgmental criticisms and other injustices they encounter in society." Not only is the aforementioned higher authority reference evidence of religion but evidence of rapper resistance to injustice. A 26-year-old Catholic summed up the students' two approaches to measuring religiosity through God talk when he described rappers as being religious when "speaking <u>TO</u> God as well as about Him." Students regularly mentioned prayer as a form of speaking to God. A 20-year-old Catholic distinguished between the ways rappers could talk about God: "I believe rappers are being religious both when they praise and deny the existence of God or anything intangible/unexplained." This Catholic student's short response expanded the stereotypical boundaries of what counts as religious. First, he noted that anything inexplicable could be considered religious. It appears that praise for "anything intangible" counts as a religious act. Second, denying the existence of God is also considered a religious act. In contrast to the student who said a simple mention of God does not make one religious, this student includes traditionally nonreligious mentions of God within his definition of religious acts. In addition to God talk, a majority of students observed that rappers are being religious when they make lyrical references to religion. Mentions of confessions, faith, and morals as well as discussions of hard times, death, and the afterlife were offered as recurring evidence of rappers being religious.

Although 157 students agreed rappers could be religious, only 115 of them could actually name religious rappers. Of that 115, only 17 could name 10 religious rappers, and only 2 of the 17 were students enrolled in hip hop courses. Despite their confidence in religious behavior, even students studying hip hop faltered when asked to actually name religious rappers. The top five religious rappers were Kanye West with 69 references, Tupac Shakur with 63 references, Jay-Z with 38 references, Lil Wayne with 32 references, and Nas with 26 references. For a complete list of rappers with more than two votes, see Appendix B. Although students were not asked to list songs, many of them noted "Jesus Walks," which must contribute to West's ranking as their number one religious rapper.

The second most religious rapper was Tupac Shakur. The average age of respondents was 22, which means they were born in 1989, were two years old when Tupac released his first album and seven years old when he was murdered. These young adults do not have memories of being in the club when a new Tupac joint was released, did not wait for his videos to appear on *Yo! MTV Raps*, nor did they see live interviews of Tupac on television. All of their knowledge about him and his music comes to them second-hand, primarily through YouTube videos, posthumous releases, and commentary. Yet 15 years after his death, he is considered their second most religious rapper. Tupac regularly incorporated religious themes in his music, and while conspiracy theories surrounding his death fuel the perception of his potential resurrection, it appears that Tupac's legacy as a religious rapper is best described as the result of a hip hop habitus. These youth have inherited religious interpretations of Tupac that they were too young to experience for themselves when his music was first released. As an "old school" rapper, Nas (like Tupac) also likely inherited a hip hop religiosity habitus because his more recent work lacks the religious themes that permeated his earliest records.

West's, Jay-Z's, and Lil Wayne's presence among the top five religious rappers should come as no surprise, primarily because the sheer glut of product from these three men increases the potential for audiences to recognize religious themes in their music. During the week of September 8th in 2011 alone, Lil Wayne placed 12 simultaneous singles on the Billboard Hot 100.[10] Without such chart domination, audiences would have more difficulty recognizing the religious themes of artists who only occasionally have a hot single. A lack of exposure partially explains the absence of women rappers from this list. Because there are so few mainstream women rappers, there are fewer opportunities for audiences to recognize their religious themes. Lauryn Hill and Nicki Minaj were the only women to make the religious rappers list, but neither of them fell within the top 25. Perhaps the fact that most prominent religious leaders are men provides a social expectation for men's overrepresentation as religious rappers. Nonetheless, the fact that three of the top religious rappers are also the most popular rappers suggests that according to this population, there is certainly a place for religiosity in mainstream rap music.

Even though students were not asked why rappers felt the need to be religious, several of them volunteered that rap music and religion have always had a symbiotic relationship that could result in either a contrived or a genuine expression of religiosity. A 19-year-old who claimed to not be religious despite being reared Catholic opined, "I feel rappers are only using God to make their words have a more powerful impact." A 21-year-old Christian expressed a similar sentiment: "Sometimes they're just saying stuff to sound cool." A spiritual but not religious 29-year-old expounded,

> Well many like to appear to be as part of the cliché uniform image that people are used to seeing. If they do not accept an award and thank God, then they are viewed differently. It's like it is part of the formula to balance any violent imagery they use in their raps—it's "okay" because they still believe

in God. But truly religious rappers would probably have more progressive lyrics without the violence and degradation of women common in many raps.

For these three students, rappers' contrived relationships with religion allow them to sound more impactful and appear more respectable without necessarily expressing any specific religious allegiance.

Other students suggested that because rap and religion naturally coalesce, they have the potential to inform rappers' more authentic expressions of religiosity. For example, a 22-year-old who came from a Christian family observed, "I believe rappers write music to express themselves. By expressing themselves, they often highlight their vulnerabilities, which showcases a level of openness between artist and listener. To be religious, one has to be open with their vulnerabilities." A 21-year-old Christian suggested religion plays a particularly impactful role in the neighborhoods where rappers were reared. She explained, "Rap started on the street, and religion is everywhere too, even on the streets. So they grew together in some sense." Although the evidence for religiosity may vary and although the rationales for incorporating religious themes may diverge, the students agreed that rap and religion could certainly coexist. Students were asked to offer more in-depth characterizations of the relationship between rap and religion by identifying the presence of the devil, Jesus, and God in rap.

Dealing with the Devil

Because of the late 2000s surge of Internet conspiracy theories about rappers' affiliations with the devil, students were asked about their personal beliefs in the devil, whether they thought rappers worshipped the devil, what evidence they had of rappers who worshipped the devil, and which rappers worshipped the devil. Twenty-seven percent of students had no doubts that the devil exists, 12 percent believed in the devil with some doubts, 8 percent sometimes believed in the devil, 18 percent believed the devil is a fictional character, 18 percent believed evil humans are the real devils, and 18 percent had no opinion about the devil. Nearly half (47%) harbored some belief about the devil as a nonhuman entity. Because there is so little written about the devil in the Judeo-Christian and Islamic sacred texts, most individuals' knowledge about the devil emerges from popular culture.

According to the surveyed participants, rap's relationship to the devil is largely illusory. It appears that the devil's influence in popular culture films like *The Omen* is much easier to identify than the devil's role in rap music. Whereas 90 percent of students believed rappers could be religious, 41 percent were unsure whether rappers worship the devil, 39 percent did not think rappers worship the devil, and 19 percent believed rappers worship the devil.

A 21-year-old man who believed humans are the real devils characterized the common uncertain responses when he wrote, "You honestly can't know. Unless you follow them around 24/7 and know exactly what they do behind closed doors, there's no way of knowing." By contrast, a 25-year-old man who believed in the devil with some doubts was sure that rappers do not worship the devil: "I believe that rappers grew up believing in God, so therefore they recognize that the devil is somebody to not worship. They acknowledge that they have devilish tendencies, but that is not the equivalent of worshiping the devil." Contrasting his opinion is a 21-year-old woman who had no doubt that the devil exists. She supported the "yes" responses by referencing a familiar (yet biblically unsubstantiated) Christian myth: "The devil was the head of music in heaven; there's no doubt that he's controlling ours down here."

Regardless of their beliefs about rappers and devil worship, 54 percent of the students agreed that the best burden of proof would be if rappers said they worshipped the devil, 20 percent said audiences would not know with any certainty, 12 percent said rappers would not publicly worship the devil because it would be unpopular, and 11 percent suggested audiences could discern potential devil worshipping through a rapper's use of symbols, including tattoos, gestures, and clothing. Additionally, a handful of students made astute claims about the devilish nature of rappers' lived experiences.

Similar to the proof of being religious, the proof of devil worship is in the articulation of it. A 21-year-old male hip hop student who believed in the devil with some doubts was sure rappers worship the devil. He wrote, "If you really listen to rap, they be sending subliminals, and basically tellin' us that there is a Illuminati out there." Also similar to the uncomfortable contradictions noted in the difficulty of determining whether rappers are religious, a 20-year-old woman who believed the devil is a fictional character mused, "I wouldn't <u>know</u>. . . . If I said truthfully though I would think most mainstream rappers do worship the devil. Common scenarios of killing, raping, drugs, crime—all ungodly activities—are continuously found among mainstream rap today."

For many students, the uncertainty is augmented by the fact that rappers will never publically affiliate with the devil because it would be unpopular.

A 23-year-old who sometimes believed in the devil posited, "I probably won't know if any mainstream rappers worshipped the devil because, in my opinion, it is not something that would be openly talked about, and even if a rapper did rap about worshiping the devil, I'm sure it would not reach a mainstream audience considering it is such a taboo topic." A substitute for not saying anything directly would be the use of symbols. A 21-year-old woman who had no doubts that the devil exists asserted, "We would never know for sure, but rappers like Jay-Z and Kanye West make [their affiliations with the devil] pretty obvious through their clothing labels, hand gestures in photos, and even lyrics in their songs."

For other students, this evidence is immaterial because hell is experienced on earth. A 21-year-old who had no opinion about the devil broke down its definition outside of a religious context: " 'Devil' is associated with malicious acts that society has frowned upon. For example, being part of a gang can be associated with the 'devil,' but it is not to necessarily say that the rapper worships these activities. <u>Sometimes</u> it is the only way that they can escape harsh realities like poverty or abuse." Another 19-year-old who believed in the devil with some doubts likened the devil to "the bad in life growing up in the ghettos."

Nonetheless, 37 students named rappers who they believe worshipped the devil. Overall, the top five rapper devil worshippers were Jay-Z with 24 references, Kanye West with 14 references, Odd Future Wolf Gang Kill Them All (OFWGKTA) and front man Tyler the Creator with 8 references, Three 6 Mafia with 7 references, and Eminem with 5 references. Student claims that Jay-Z and West are religious rappers and devil worshippers most likely mean that rapping about the devil is seen as a religious act by some audiences and seen as proof of devil worship for other audiences. Jay-Z's and West's cultural caché, which was only augmented by *Watch the Throne* (2011) sales figures, made them targets for Internet devil accusations (see chapter 4) that students repeated in their lists like a meme. One woman student seemed to have inherited her vague evidence of demonic practices when she claimed, "Kanye, Jay-Z, (I don't know much about the names). Maybe not worship the devil but for sure engages in demonic practices that goes hand in hand with walking with the devil." This 21-year-old woman had no doubts that the devil exists, and she was sure rappers engage in demonic practices, but she could not name the rappers with any certainty nor could she identify these demonic practices. Her certainty is shrouded by the uncertainty most likely aided by hearsay, which also informs the aforementioned comments about "subliminals" and the Illuminati that happen to be entirely unrelated to devil worship. Without definitions, these claims are simply reiterations of popular yet unfounded discourse. Several students conceded that when OFWGKTA and Tyler the Creator refer to demonic themes they seem to be doing so for shock value; the same could easily be said of Three 6 Mafia horrorcore rappers who named the group after the number of the beast/antichrist/devil. Eminem's nod on the devil worshipper list is likely attributable to his generally provocative material or, more specifically, his tracks where he has conversations with the devil like on "My Darling" (2009). A 21-year-old woman who had no opinion about the devil wrote, "The only rapper who could possibly be evil would be Eminem; he has issues. (Raps about stuffing [ex-wife] Kim in a trunk for Christ sake)."

The scant data about rappers who worship the devil are interesting but certainly inconclusive outside of the claim that the students as a whole are more sure about the devil's presence in general than they are about rappers' relationship with the devil. In a statement left in the additional comments section of the survey, a 21-year-old who believed in the devil with no doubts expressed skepticism about the role of the devil: "I believe the Illuminati and devil worshipers are putting on acts to cause controversy and be more relevant, but at the same time, I do believe behind the scenes there is more going on than the public knows." The student astutely identifies the constructed nature of both rap and religion—neither audiences nor believers have full access to all that is going on "behind the scenes." Audience uncertainty about rappers' religious beliefs likely reflects difficulties in defining and describing their own religious beliefs. Incertitude seems to characterize the experiences of fandom and faith.

The Jesus Piece

Jesus's hip hop presence as a "blinged out" Jesus piece of jewelry suggests an influence worthy of interrogation. Students were asked about their personal beliefs in Jesus, whether they thought rappers believed in Jesus, what evidence they had of rapper belief in Jesus, and which rappers rapped about or compared themselves to Jesus. Fifty-four percent of students believed Jesus is the Son of God, 13 percent believed Jesus was one of many messengers of God, 6 percent believed Jesus was an extraordinary person but not a messenger of God, 6 percent believed Jesus probably existed but was not special, 8 percent believed Jesus was a fictional character from the Bible, and 12 percent had no opinion.

Unlike the devil data, which lacked a single majority vote, over half of the students checked the "Jesus is the Son of God" box despite five other viable options. Based on the selection of the other options, 73 percent of the surveyed participants seemed certain that Jesus existed. These data are certainly curious considering the fact that only 34 percent identified as Christian or Catholic, and 37 percent had no doubts that God exists. In essence, at least 17 percent of students were not sure God exists but were certain that Jesus is the Son of God. Beliefs about Jesus not only transcend beliefs about the devil and religious affiliation but also transcend beliefs about God. In reports relatively consistent with their personal beliefs, 79 percent of those questioned thought that rappers believe in Jesus, 16 percent were unsure, 1 percent did not think rappers believe in Jesus, and 4 percent chose not to answer.

Overwhelmingly, students wrote that they knew rappers believe in Jesus if the rappers said so. Fewer students provided evidence for rapper belief in Jesus perhaps because it was one of the last questions on the survey, and they may have been experiencing fatigue, or perhaps because they felt they had already answered the question in other responses. Of the 124 descriptions of evidence for rapper belief in Jesus (which were indeed similar to evidence for religious rappers and devil-worshipping rappers), there were 88 references to verbally expressing belief in Jesus; 20 references to symbols like crosses, the Jesus piece, and Jesus tattoos; 7 references to award shows; 7 references to audiences not knowing about rapper belief in Jesus with any certainty; and 2 references to a rapper's lifestyle as evidence of belief in Jesus. A 25-year-old who had no opinion about Jesus suggested, "Many of these rappers grew up in a religious household or had family members who are religious or grew up around people who are religious. So they are exposed to that. As a result they could not help but become connected and believe in Jesus. Just because these guys have a Jesus piece does not mean they believe in Jesus however." His response accurately sums the study's recurring themes. He acknowledged Jesus's presence in hip hop as a form of habitus, noted Jesus's symbolic appeal via the Jesus piece, but emphasized that audiences cannot know with any certainty about a rapper's personal beliefs.

The list of rappers that rap about or compare themselves to Jesus was also familiar. Out of 98 responses, Kanye West had 84 references, Jay-Z had 30, Lil Wayne had 15, Tupac Shakur had 9, and Nas had 8. Most likely, West's "Jesus Walks" (2004), his 2006 *Rolling Stone* cover as Jesus, and his famous Jesus piece continue to ensure his Jesus affinity for audiences. In fact, many younger fans mistakenly locate the origins of the Jesus piece with West instead of the Notorious B.I.G. Several students' tongue-in-cheek commentaries affirm the Kanye West-Jesus connection:

"I am pretty sure Kanye thinks he's Jesus."
"Kanye thinks he's a God (insert eye roll)"
"Praise Kanyesus Christ!"

Other students further elaborated on why rappers might compare themselves to Jesus. A 27-year-old who believed Jesus was one of many messengers or prophets of God wrote, "Can't think of any names, but anyone arrogant enough to compare themselves (as I have heard before) or anyone trying to make a statement by doing so." A 21-year-old Catholic who believed Jesus is the Son of God stated, "Kanye, Lil Wayne, Jay-Z, most top rappers because their ego is boosted because they are on top of the industry." A 23-year-old who believed Jesus probably existed but was not special posited, "Seems to me that many rappers consider themselves to be very special and should be worshipped by women and men because they are rich. In that way they compare themselves to Jesus."

Taken together, these comments suggest that the relationship between rappers and Jesus is about power. Comparing oneself to Jesus makes a powerful statement. Moreover, comparisons occur when rappers reach industry heights that make them feel powerful. Comparisons imply that an individual's material success means that he has been chosen (by God). This uniqueness justifies wielding power over those that are less (financially) privileged. Despite Jesus's biblical humble beginnings and affinity for the downtrodden, these students, who each held different beliefs about Jesus, seemed to suggest that the popular culture Jesus is primarily powerful. The same power that attracts rappers to Jesus may also explain why so many students who are not religious and unsure of God's existence are also attracted to Jesus. Irrespective of the clear affinity for Jesus contrasted by doubts about God, the college students still believed in rappers' belief in God.

The Gangsta's God

Students were more certain that rappers believe in God than they were sure rappers believe in Jesus or worship the devil. Eighty-six percent of participants felt that rappers believe in God, 13 percent were unsure, 1 student did not think rappers believe in God, and 2 students left the question blank. Despite students' personal affinity for Jesus, there was a slight distinction between thoughts about rapper belief in God and rapper belief in Jesus; 150 students supported rapper belief in God; only 138 students supported rapper belief in Jesus. Twenty-eight students were unsure about rapper belief in Jesus whereas only 22 students were unsure about rapper belief in God.

The evidence that rappers believe in God resonates with the evidence for religious rappers, devil worship, and belief in Jesus. Proof included God talk (thanking especially when receiving an award, praying, rapping about the afterlife, and discussing one's upbringing), symbols, and the audience cannot know with any certainty. Ninety students listed rappers who believe in God—that is 53 more than those who listed rappers who are devil worshippers, 25 fewer than those who noted religious rappers, and 8 fewer than those who could name rappers who rap about or compare themselves to Jesus. Only 15 students could name 10 rappers who rap about God, and only 1 of the 15 was currently enrolled in a hip hop course. The slightly lower response for this item could be another example of fatigue, but perhaps it was more difficult for students to identify tangible references to a very intangible God. Their doubts about God's existence may also be attributable to an indeterminate presence, which is very different from images of Jesus, the devil, and other easily identifiable religious symbols.

Nonetheless, the final list was exactly the same as the list for religious rappers although the number of references varied slightly. The top five religious rappers were Kanye West with 59 references, Tupac Shakur with 54 references, Jay-Z with 37 references, Lil Wayne with 26 references, and Nas with 20 references. Beyond the top five, the lists of religious rappers remained comparable (see Appendix B).

Students were then asked to comment on the relationship between God talk in rap music and real-life rapper behavior through the following item: "Do you think it's possible for rappers to acknowledge God (in their lives and/or music) while rapping about sex, selling drugs, violence, and other morally questionable activities? Please explain your answer." Three percent of students left the item blank, 7 percent did not think it was possible, 11 percent were unsure, and 78 percent said yes, it was possible.

For some students, acknowledging God and rapping about morally questionable activities was not possible because it posed a contradiction. Several additional students who were unsure or who voted yes, it is possible, offered responses that explained their discomfort with the contradictions. Only 9 of the 31 contradiction statements came from self-proclaimed religious students (7 Christians and 2 Catholics). Being religious seemed not to be the prime indicator of who would be disturbed by the rap hypocrisy. Answers to this question seem to have emerged from a moral but nonreligious compass. A 25-year-old woman with a low interest in hip hop who was spiritual but not religious opined, "I think it sounds ignorant when you're rapping about selling drugs and then say forgive me God and thank you God, bless me, etc. For one, you know it's wrong; that's why you're asking for forgiveness and habitual sin is supposedly not forgiven." A 27-year-old woman with a medium interest in hip hop who was not religious but whose family was Christian expounded, "I think it's 'possible' but not ethical. Even if God isn't mentioned in the song, don't rap about killing bitches and then thank God for your award." A 20-year-old woman with a low interest in hip hop who was not religious but came from a Catholic family argued, "They are opposite ends of the religious spectrum. The sex usually in rap music is adulterous, unconsented, or before marriage: each of which fall out from under the religion of God. As well as drugs and stealing. These are all said in the Ten Commandments. Thou shalt not steal. Thou shall not harm thy neighbor. Even envying. These are uncomplimentary." A 21-year-old woman with a medium interest in hip hop who was spiritual but not religious commented, "These acts are unmoral. With sex it is an acceptable act because God wants us to do it (with certain criteria) but with other morally questionable activities you cannot rap about participating in these acts and still talk about God because these are not godly activities."

These representative quotes reflect the most stringent criticisms. Interestingly, they all came from women respondents without a high interest in hip hop, although two of the four were currently enrolled in hip hop courses, which meant they were not part of the women's studies cohort. A lower interest in rap may explain a higher intolerance for apparent contradictions. More women than men expressed discomfort with rap hypocrisy, but because women were oversampled in the study, it is impossible to conclude that women were more sensitive to rap music misogyny and sexual exploitation although the argument is plausible.

The following quote from a 26-year-old cultural Catholic with a high interest in hip hop represented a more thoughtful rationale for the contradictions. His musings were more reflective of the majority perspectives.

I feel that them mentioning Jesus or God can be hypocrisy. I mean, I love rap and all, but you can't talk about womanizing, killing, and other vile acts. Then when they go up to accept an award for an album in which you mention all of those things and thank God for everything. But then again if they only rapped about God, they wouldn't have won that very same award. That's an internal struggle that they may have or that the record labels just don't allow.

Whether an intentional mixed message, an internal struggle, or a negotiation of industry expectations, the inconsistency can contribute to the uncertainty of some audiences. Nonetheless, not only did a majority of students believe rappers could acknowledge God and still rap about morally questionable activities, but they also justified the rappers' behavior. There were five categories of justifications offered within the yes, it's possible responses: I've seen the evidence, rapping is a job, it's normal, everyone deserves forgiveness, and dear God can you hear me?

Instead of fully explaining their answers, students within the "I've seen the evidence" category offered examples of rappers who rapped about God and morally questionable activities. Nas, Tupac, and Kanye West references recurred although DMX and Scarface were each mentioned once. For example, a 25-year-old with a medium interest in rap noted, "Tupac was a rapper that rapped about all of the above including God. He talked about his life, which included sex, drugs, and violence. At the same time he also knew that these things were not right and wondered if heaven has a ghetto. Just because someone experiences these morally questionable activities does not mean that they do not believe in God." A 20-year-old with a low interest in hip hop wrote, "In 'Hell of a Life' Kanye says pussy and religion is all he needs!" A 27-year-old with a low interest in hip hop did not drop names, but explained the combination thusly: "Because they rap about whatever is important to them, relevant to them and their lives and their audiences." Even students without a high interest in rap could provide evidence for mixing God talk with morally questionable activities. Several students further affirmed that rapping about relevant issues is part of a rapper's job description.

In the "rapping is a job" category, students noted that the mainstream music industry encourages rappers to embody personas that engage in illicit sex, sell drugs, and commit violent acts in order to sell their product even though those actions may not accurately reflect rappers' personal lives. They also noted that rapping is an artistic expression that should not be mistaken for reality. A spiritual but not religious 22-year-old who listened to rap several times a day described industry influence: "One aspect of this conflicting behavior has to deal with the performance and monetary side of the 'rap game.' Music labels push artists' image to present what will sell the most records—regardless of the artists' personal beliefs. It's the nature of the beast." A 21-year-old whose family was Buddhist and who also listened to rap several times a day justified rappers' artistic license: "Because it is an artistic form of expression, they can be living through those experiences solely through their music. They may see such things going on in their communities. Just because they rap about such things doesn't mean that they act that way in reality." A 25-year-old cultural Jew who never listened to rap explained, "I think that the lifestyle rappers have has a public face—they talk about sex and drugs, etc. and in their private life they are closer to God—I think sometimes the line gets faded and God makes it into the lyrics."

Whereas the other avid rap listeners alluded to industry pressure and the nature of artistic performances, a student who never listened to rap offered the most nuanced rationale by suggesting God accidentally appears in lyrics while rappers are busy working as rappers. God's unintentional presence is reminiscent of a Christian "witness," wherein if an individual truly believes in God, God's goodness will emanate from that person without explicit acknowledgment. Ironically, this proselytizing perspective emerges from a cultural Jew. Again, the study seems to suggest that an individual's personal religious affiliation has little bearing on his or her interpretation of the mash up between rappers' God talk and their morally questionable activities.

While a rapper may have a unique job, the students considered contradictions to be a normal part of everyone's daily struggles. In the "it's normal" category, they explained that all of us have been guilty of saying one thing and doing another. A 21-year-old Catholic wrote, "Rappers or really anyone can engage in controversial/questionable activities like selling drugs, violence, having sex, etc. and still have a strong faith and concept of God. Everyday people often do this. They may act one way but their faith never falters, only their actions do." Another 21-year-old Catholic concurred: "They all have flaws but it doesn't mean they lack faith." A 19-year-old who grew up Catholic but no longer considered herself religious cautioned, "We need to keep in mind that rappers are like any other human in the fact that they are multidimensional. Rappers have the right to talk about bitches and drugs one minute and then about God the next minute." A 23-year-old Christian man contributed to the thread about human complexity when he argued, "I feel that the lives we live are layered with so many thoughts and feelings and contradictions that I feel more comfortable with an artist who feels they can touch on multiple subjects, including religion, because these are thoughts that run through my mind daily." A 20-year-old Christian confessed, "Sex, selling drugs, violence, and other morally questionable activities are something that tempt and affect people every day. You would be lying if you said you have never done something morally questionable, so I think it's good that they acknowledge what the world is but still believe in God. Helps you realize you aren't the only one."

Each quote was chosen because it best represented the rationales for contradictions as a form of normalcy. It so happened that a student who grew up or currently was Christian or Catholic proffered each justification. It may be that religious individuals who are immersed in sin, repentance, and redemption narratives display the most sympathy toward imperfect multifaceted individuals who "have flaws but do not lack faith." Not only does the tension resonate with the students, but the last two felt comforted by rappers who acknowledge a familiar struggle.

Forgiveness is the key aspect of religion whether adherents are instructed to forgive themselves, others, or seek forgiveness from God. In the "everyone deserves forgiveness" category, students emphasized that rappers are entitled to seek forgiveness no matter how heinous the infraction. A spiritual but not religious 20-year-old whose family was Christian claimed, "God, if you believe, is all about forgiveness. So it can be used as a way to live with the bad things you've done." A nonreligious 21-year-old who was culturally Catholic and whose family was also Catholic explained, "I believe rappers acknowledge God because they know that some of the things they take part in are sins. They want God's forgiveness, however, they are not going to stop doing these things either." A spiritual but not religious 21-year-old man who came from a Christian family quipped, "The minority (Black) version of [Christianity] allows for hope, healing, praise, and forgiveness. Allowing people to do what they do, repent and praise, and then ask for forgiveness. A cleaning of the slate like Catholic communion and confession but easier." A nonreligious 21-year-old whose family members were Protestant and Catholic questioned, "Why should a rapper who believes in God be exempt from morally questionable activities? Would their God not forgive them?"

Unlike the "it's normal" responses, the illustrative quotes from the forgiveness category come from students who were not religious but were connected to religious families or cultures. On the whole, the quotes' tones were also much more cynical than the previous "yes, it's possible" responses. Students noted that rappers use God to assuage guilty consciences, that forgiveness does not have to lead to repentance, that the appeal of forgiveness is its ease, and that it makes sense to believe in a God that will forgive. The final quote references "their God" as if to emphasize that each individual can choose to believe in a God that best suits her or his interests. The students' emphases on forgiveness may have developed from personal experiences of feeling constrained by a childhood religious habitus even though their lives were shifting in a different direction. It is conceivable that individuals who chose to be spiritual or nonreligious also chose to pursue a more permissible belief system that would underscore the importance of forgiveness and deemphasize judgment, punishment, and suffering.

Whereas student perceptions of forgiveness may have been tongue-in-cheek, responses within the "dear God, can you hear me?" category were serious expressions of how God helped rappers through hard times. In this category, the youth did not perceive contradictions as readily as they offered explanations linked to lived human experiences, especially the struggles faced by many rappers. A 22-year-old who came from a Catholic family but was not religious yet believed in a higher power discerned, "Most people do believe in God because it comforts them, so why would rappers be any different? They talk about their dead homies being up there with God and God helping them through other hard times." She continued this theme in the additional comments portion of her survey: "Because many rappers come from a lower socioeconomic status, they were raised with at least a semi-close affiliation with God because that is how people deal with their situations. They need to feel like there is a purpose to hardship as most humans do." A 43-year-old self-described "recovering Catholic" who believed in a higher power commented, "Some of them mention God as being the only judge. Many rappers speak of how society labels them, stereotypes them, judges them wrongly, oppresses them. They often make references to their belief that all these hypocrites will find out in the end on judgment day that they were wrong and these rappers have faith that God accepts them as freely as anyone else." A 21-year-old Catholic who believed in God with some doubts observed, "Being humans aren't perfect, we all commit sins. Sometimes we look at this higher power during hard times as many of these rappers did when they had fear they might die or they or their parents are hooked on drugs and have no other solution but to pray." A 20-year-old nonreligious cultural Catholic who believed in God with no doubts acknowledged, "It's known that rappers do stand on the fence about religion and questionable activities. But I think it has to do with how they grew up. Yes, there could be violence and whatnot surrounding their lives but they also grew up with a foundation and focus on God. They did not choose the violence, but they choose to follow a God." A nonreligious 23-year-old whose family was Catholic but who did not believe in God deduced, "I think rappers will rap about God and violence and the other topics all in one song. I don't think they think what they do is immoral. They think it's the hand they were dealt and that God watches over them." A 19-year-old cultural Catholic who believed in God with some doubts concluded, "Yes, I believe it is possible for rappers to acknowledge God while speaking about sex, selling drugs, violence because some rappers will rap about how the violence is destroying society but there is hope, faith, and the belief that God will give us another day."

Despite the fact that only one of them believed in God with no doubts, the students identified a "habitus in the hood." All of them were able to appreciate a rapper's relationship to God abstracted from religion and focused on providing hope and comfort during hard times. They believed that God understood rappers were "dealt a hand" and, therefore, not responsible for their environments. Students noted that rapper experiences with death, drugs, violence, stereotypes, and oppression were outside of a rapper's purview but within the realm of possible change for God. Instead of asking the rappers to elevate themselves to God's status "out there," students situated God "down here" within the environments from which the rappers emerged.

Recognizing how oppressive environments demanded more permissible understandings of God led three students to claim that rappers may need to access their own God who departs from traditional religious concepts. A 21-year-old who was not religious but came from a Catholic family and believed in a higher power or cosmic force deliberated, "This is tough because it's two conflicting ideas for a lot of people; believing strongly in God means you stay away from things as sex, selling drugs, and especially violence. But it really depends on what sort of God the artist believes in." A nonreligious 23-year-old who believed in a higher power or cosmic force and believed humans can be gods, yet came from a Catholic family acknowledged, "They do it because I believe they have a concept of God that in their mind makes it okay." A 21-year-old Christian who had no doubt that God exists suggested, "Rappers incorporate religion in their music both by direct praise/mention or by the personification of God as an individual (often themselves)." The last quote above does not belong to one of the two students who believed humans are gods. Ironically, it comes from a Christian student who has no doubt that God exists, and yet it is the only reference from the entire subject pool that acknowledged rappers who self-deify. Although students seem to understand that permissible and flexible ideas of God are necessary for rappers who emerge from depressed environments, there is a general reluctance to perceive humans as gods "down here." Quite possibly, the inability to escape or ameliorate these environments affirms the limited power of humanity and the necessity of a higher power "out there" to orchestrate change.

Discussion

This cohort of survey participants was not particularly religious. However, they largely believed in God or a higher power and were widely convinced that rappers can be religious and can still acknowledge God while rapping about morally questionable activities. Despite the overall confidence that rappers can be religious and that they can demonstrate belief in Jesus and God via words and actions, students were quick to caution that an outsider can never really know what someone else believes. This may explain why so many of them were comparatively unsure whether rappers worshipped the devil. Whereas expressing religious belief is acceptable in our society, advocating devil worship is not. Rappers cannot publicly thank the devil and be perceived as respectable in the same ways that they can thank God and be celebrated by their communities. Additionally, the students' penchant for believing rappers' literal/lyrical expressions over any other claims could also support their doubts about devil worship. Rappers rarely (if ever) explicitly say they worship the devil. Instead, devil affiliations are said *about* the rappers—not by them. When students repeated those assertions, they came across as fragmented claims characteristic of hearsay.

Nevertheless, Kanye West, Jay-Z, and Lil Wayne consistently topped the list of rappers who are religious, who worship the devil, who rap about or compare themselves to Jesus, and who rap about God. Their popularity ensures that their music is heard by a wide swath of the population that interprets their religious themes in various ways. Their lyrics and imagery prove that rap and religion can and do coalesce in mainstream popular culture. The fact that the same three rappers, however, are considered Christian by some and devil worshippers by others proves that rap and religion's coexistence is not without contradiction.

Consistent with this pattern of accommodating contradiction, survey results rendered an unanticipated discrepancy among the students' personal beliefs. Despite doubt about God's existence, students were more certain that Jesus is the Son of God. A 21-year-old student who believed in a higher power or cosmic force and believed Jesus was one of many messengers or prophets of God pondered, "I think that if rappers believe in God then they have to believe in Jesus." And yet, 17 percent of the students believed in Jesus while maintaining serious doubts about God. This 21-year-old slightly contradicted her own statement. It would seem that if she believed Jesus was one of God's prophets, then she would also state that she believed in God, but instead she was willing to commit only to a belief in a higher power.

Jesus maintains a popular culture caché that God lacks. Theologian and university chaplain Bernard Chris Dorsey proffered the following rationale in a personal conversation:

> It sounds like some kind of new age monophysitism with the twist being the agnostic leaning of many college students. People really like Jesus and want him to be of divine origin, but they are often uncomfortable with the seemingly capricious God they grew up being indoctrinated with. So it sounds like the solution is to ascribe to Christ a divine nature of some sort, but the results seem not to be fully human and fully divine but fully human and contingently divine.[11]

Jesus is accessible because there are images of him and stories about his life that resonate with human beings unlike the authoritarian God who, at least in biblical narratives, has wielded His power rather erratically over humanity. The fact that Jesus seems more accessible than God to the students may in part explain some rappers' affinity for the Jesus of the disinherited over a capricious God.

Student differentiation between God and Jesus may also be interpreted within the God "out there" and God "down here" paradigm established throughout this book. Overall, students appear to be most comfortable with the idea of God "down here." For instance, they expressed more personal doubts about the distant God "out there" than the God who was sent "down here" as Jesus. When students justified the connection between rap and religion, they described a tolerant God who understands life "down here." Furthermore, they associated rapper comparisons to Jesus as manifestations of earthly power. Although only one respondent explicitly mentioned that humans could be gods, students' personal and interpretive ideas about God pulled God closer to the human experience, not further away.

Within this rap and religion cipha, student doubts about God "out there" and their affinity for imagining a God closer "down here" reflect the characterizations of God noted throughout the lyrics and videos analyzed within this book. For artists and audiences, acknowledging the gangsta's God means embracing ambiguity. The mystery of the gangsta's God is reflected within the discrepancies among the students' personal beliefs about Jesus and God and their cautionary claims that audiences cannot be certain about a rapper's personal beliefs. Appreciating an enigmatic God requires interpreting the incertitude of everyday life as a normal and healthy aspect of one's lived experiences. Students reflected this perspective when they claimed the conjoining of God and morally questionable activities was in a rapper's a job description, declared the potential hypocrisy as normal, suggested everyone deserves forgiveness, and noted the social conditions that urged rappers to petition God for assistance. The responsibility of the gangsta's God is to normalize rather than ameliorate uncertainty.

The most significant insight from this study is that what might appear to be irresolvable contradictions to rap's critics are actually held comfortably in tension not only by the artists but also by their audiences. Rap music has been widely critiqued for its hypocrisy, but the 84 percent of these students with high or medium interest in rap music were not disturbed by rap's potentially contradictory messages about religion. Students perceived the relationship between rap and religion as no more incongruous or complex than other aspects of their lives. This racially diverse group of hip hop fans characterized the ambiguity and uncertainty that accompanies rappers' paradoxical use of religion as essential features of human life.

Since religion is a social process, rap music does indeed have the potential to socialize religious behaviors. When accessed through rap music, the gangsta's God gives the genre's fans permission to discover God and religion outside of institutionalized religious habitus like churches, mosques, and temples. Instead fans find religion everywhere—from the streets to the Billboard Hot 100. Fans' religious backgrounds help them interpret artists' religious themes and, through the flow of the cipha, new ways of thinking about religion may be formed. Though this descriptive research is neither generalizable nor representative, it remains valuable because it provides an appreciable first peek at the thoughts of this population. What has been proven with absolute certainty is the fact that rap and religion are not antithetical; rather, the rap on rap and religion has only just begun.

Conclusion

Meaning, Power, and Money

Come experience life as a hustler knows it. Some of you should already know it. Our hustler isn't born; he is made out of a little boy's coming-of-age realization that rapping would not earn him the dead presidents that he desires. He starts to hustle everything from crack to opium. When people question his choices he responds, "Can I live? You can't knock the hustle." The street life is politics as usual. He learns to distinguish friend from foe. He challenges his enemies to bring it on. He knows beyond a reasonable doubt that he is doing what he has to do. D'evils be damned. He becomes one of Brooklyn's finest hustlers rolling on 22s, making his cashmere thoughts come true. Ain't no nigga around can do it better. He lives his life to the limit and loves it. He has only a few regrets. Our hustler is feelin' it. So much so that he christens himself Jay-Hova.

Jay-Hova is prescient. He expands his hustle to realize his childhood dream. Instead of drugs, he peddles knowledge about street life. He releases several volumes of the Book of Hov. He builds a dynasty with his *familia*. Despite the ambivalence about his gift being a curse, he carefully lays out a blueprint for his career. The $450 million man's albums have sold over 50 million copies worldwide. He has more number one albums than anyone but The Beatles. As of 2011, Jay-Z has earned 13 Grammys, 10 MTV Video Awards, 9 BET Hip Hop awards, and 3 American Music Awards. Jay-Z sold his Roc-A-Fella and Rocawear companies for millions. He has stakes in the New Jersey Nets, the cosmetic company Carol's Daughter, the chicken wing restaurant Buffalo Boss, the gastropub The Spotted Pig, and the upscale 40/40 sports bars. The former president of Def Jam Records, spokesman for multiple products, and investor signed a $150 million deal with Live Nation to continue to advance his entrepreneurial ventures. Those ventures also include television and film production.

Jay-Z is hip hop's mogul. Following the footsteps of Russell Simmons but doing it bigger and deffer, Jay-Z is the consummate businessman. In fact, he's a business, man. And his humble beginnings are like so many others in the hip hop world. They grew up in depressed environments. Too many of them watched their working-poor parents struggle, their friends die, and their dreams disappear until some found upward mobility via the underground economy. Hip hop may have started as a hobby, but it became, for so many youth, a way of life and an economic means to sustain one's life. Jay-Z credits his success to his hustler mentality, but as Jay-Hova his success can also be credited to his Jehovah/God mentality.

Jay-Z's lyrics are appropriate exemplars of the gangsta's God because his career longevity offers a sustained body of work that reflects many of the recurring God perspectives within rap music in general. His songs are dedicated to contextualizing the gangsta persona through personal reflections on his life. Growing up in Marcy Projects in Bed-Stuy, Brooklyn, New York, Jay-Z describes himself as the consummate drug dealer and American gangster. Additionally, his environment exposed him to various ideas about God that inform lyrics about his perpetual quest for meaning and power.

In his interview at the New York Public Library with Cornel West and Paul Holdengräber, Jay-Z overemphasized the importance of context when he said "any music without context is a lie." Critics of rap music too often separate the music from its ecology. Seismic shifts in the urban American landscape inspired the lyrics of rappers who personally survived those conditions or were representing those who had. Of course, rappers should be held accountable for perpetuating oppression, but understanding its origin provides perspective on how and why certain hierarchies developed and were sustained. Jay-Z's body of work accesses the complexity of human emotions as he balances the adrenaline rush and capitalist successes of the hustler's life with his internal struggles and regrets. Many of Jay-Z's suffering, sin, and salvation narratives are appealing because his lyrical characters do wrong for all the right reasons. Understanding their emotions requires attention to their unique environments.

Jay-Z would not be considered a religious rapper per anyone's definition (including his own). Yet he came of age with religion in the air. His paternal grandparents were heavily involved in the Church of God in Christ. In his book *Decoded*, Jay-Z explains, "Church wasn't a major part of my life growing up, as it had been for my father. . . . But when you grow up in a place like Bed-Stuy, church is everywhere. So is mosque. So are a thousand other ways of believing."[1] Jay-Z is merely one of many rappers who embrace these religio-cultural influences and incorporate them into their music.

In addition to his emphasis on context and the role of religion in the neighborhood, Jay-Z's popularity suggests that his appeal traverses boundaries of time, geography, and social class. The universal acceptance of his content makes his work an appropriate frame for summarizing variations of the gangsta's God. I am not claiming that other rappers merely imitate Jay-Z's style. I am claiming that over the past 15 plus years of his sustained career, Jay-Z has consistently incorporated God "out there" and God "down here" figures.

God "Out There"

Jay-Z's lyrics construct a traditional masculine God who desires to remain "out there" and chooses to be inactive in human affairs. Jay-Z is often lambasted for his "D'Evils" (1996) line "never prayed to God, I prayed to Gotti." Christians interpret it as blasphemy. Jay-Z interprets it as depicting a character so driven by capitalism that he worships the mafia instead of God. Throughout the track, Jay-Z describes a man who is increasingly possessed by a desire to amass more money. From betrayal to kidnapping to bribery to murder, the character becomes so cocky that the song concludes with, "And even if Jehovah witness, bet he'll never testify." Jehovah would never snitch. Not because he observes a code of the streets, but because Jehovah is a silent God. The song's conclusion communicates the limited utility of God as well as the limited efficacy of a religious faith (Jehovah Witnesses) to prevent moral evil. Moreover in each chorus, Jay-Z samples Snoop's "Murder Was the Case" when he raps "Dear God I wonda can you save me?" The traditional God in "D'Evils" is not depicted as less omnipotent. He simply withholds his power and influence.

Jay-Z further ponders God's choices in "Lucifer" (2003). In another song that critics offer as proof of Jay-Z's blasphemy, Jay-Z describes his loss of faith after the death of his friend the Notorious B.I.G. His desire for revenge culminates in a violent encounter. Jay-Z breaks down his lyrics. "I'm coming like a force of nature, or even something supernatural, something you can't oppose or prevent, because my cause is righteous and my intent is pure. All you can do is make sure your casket's picked out and you've gotten right with God because death is inevitable."[2] Jay-Z's God "down here" is unstoppable, but his victim should still pray to the God "out there" who remains powerful enough to grant entrance into heaven but chooses not to exercise his power and stop Jay-Z. "Lucifer" is bracketed by prayers for forgiveness. The introduction asks God to forgive a murder. The conclusion petitions God to forgive a victim and admit him to heaven. Even though Jay-Z temporarily appropriates God's power to exact revenge, the song still locates power within the concept of a God "out there" who does not interfere with free will but can still be approached for forgiveness regardless of the circumstances. The profound uncertainty surrounding God "out there's" desire to be an active force in human affairs persists, but apparently, it never hurts to ask.

In other Jay-Z lyrics, God "out there" embodies characteristics of a father figure. Jay-Z's father left his family when he was 11. Jay-Z claimed "that sense of loss and abandonment . . . affected who I was as a person for years even today."[3] Three months before his father died, Jay-Z had the opportunity to ask him why he left, and why he never returned. Jay-Z said his father never offered satisfying answers, but he felt better after asking for them. Jay-Z has similar lyrical moments with daddy God in his lyrics. In his quest for meaning, he interrogates God in "D'Evils" (1996), "Where I'm From" (2007), "Lucifer" (2003), "Beach Chair"(2006), and "Young Gifted and Black" (2009). He asks God questions to which there are no answers, but through reflecting and asking, Jay-Z learns to mature as a man. In this sense, daddy God is like his biological father—imperfect and silent. The songs' contradictions and silences mirror the chaos of lived experiences. When God "out there" fails to explain, humans are left asking questions, knowing that there are no forthcoming answers.

God "Down Here"

In Jay-Z's lyrics, God "down here" takes the form of Jesus or himself. When Jay-Z rapped in "Empire State of Mind" (2009) "Hail Mary to the city, you're a virgin/Jesus can't save you, life starts when the church ends," he wrestles Jesus away from Christianity and returns him to the streets. The problem, for Jay-Z, is that the church limits Jesus's accessibility. For example, despite criticisms that wearing a platinum Jesus piece is disingenuous, Jay-Z habitually wears a Jesus piece while recording an album. Symbolically wearing Jesus close to his heart is not a show of Christian devotion as much as it is a prophetic statement of future profits as well as an opportunity to be inspired by the memory of a God "down here" who spoke truth when it was not popular. For Jay-Z, Jesus must be removed from the church and moved into the streets where people live their lives.

Jay-Z's final "Empire State of Mind" verse is dedicated to a woman turned out by the appeal of the city's fast life. Stereotypically, black church men have appropriated the power of Jesus to overcome various obstacles. Stereotypically, black church women have appropriated Jesus as a surrogate boyfriend to save them from their sinful natures. Jay-Z discourages the "mami" in his verse from seeking redemption in the arms of an unrealistic Jesus boyfriend who will not physically save her from her already complicated set of circumstances. Jay-Z reigns over the empire of New York City, created and sustained by human ingenuity where "there's nothin' you can't do." Humans give Jesus meaning not vice versa. Jesus can't save you because the power of Jesus resides in the interpretations of human beings. Although critics have interpreted Jay-Z as dismissing Jesus, the lines can also be read as increasing the possibilities for imagining the meaning and power of Jesus outside of Christianity.

God "down here" also presents an opportunity for Jay-Z to allude to himself as God. In "Breathe Easy (Lyrical Exercise)" (2001) Jay-Z composes lyrics about exercise and extends the metaphor into practically every line of the track. Through his lyrical braggadocio, he runs circles around his rapper athlete competitors. He raps, "Run suicide drills over and over with the weight of the world on my shoulder that's why they call me Hova/I'm far from being God, but I work goddamn hard." When Jay-Z decodes the song he notes, "Hova, is of course, short for Jay-Hova, which is a play on Jehovah—a piece of wordplay that irritates the fuck out of some religious people. They should relax and listen to the next line."[4]

His lyrical exercise is also an exercise in recalling religious history. In ancient Greek mythology, Atlas was condemned to support the heavens on his shoulders as punishment for defying Zeus. Later depictions of Atlas show him as a symbol of strength and endurance by carrying the earth on his shoulders. In Christianity, Jesus metaphorically carried the world on his shoulders when he hoisted the cross and bore the burden of humankind's sin. Combining secular and sacred legends to depict himself as the simultaneously rebellious Atlas and the obediently selfless Jesus, Jay-Z lyrically elevates himself over his enemies by referring to himself as Jehovah. Despite the denial of his divinity, Jay-Z empowers himself by creating new understandings for what it means to be God.

Although he retracted his God claim in "Breathe Easy," at other times, Jay-Z fully embodies God "down here" as Jay-Hova, Hov the God, King Hov, Hov, or Hovito. Each moniker further reiterates Jay-Z's self-identification with God. Moreover, his album titles imply divinity. His three volumes (1997–99) are often referred to as Books of Hov, which allude to Books of the Bible. His four *Blueprint* albums reference his power of creation—the divine ability to manifest something out of nothing as God did when he spoke the world into existence. He describes himself as hip hop's savior on his return from retirement album *Kingdom Come* (2006), which samples a phrase from the Lord's Prayer: "Your kingdom come, Your will be done on earth as it is in heaven." Jay-Z frequently refers to himself and other black men as Gods. He pays homage to Rakim when he borrows the moniker Rakim made famous—the God MC. Jay-Z's God "down here" appropriation comes no clearer than in his Usher Raymond collaboration "Hot Tottie" (2010) when Jay-Z raps "but I'm Godbody, ya'll better ask somebody." Jay-Z has repeatedly very publicly said, "I believe in God." His presentation as a premier rapper has been established through his God "down here" appropriations of God "out there."

The aforementioned Jay-Z tracks are exemplars of the conditions that gave rise to one gangsta's God. His quests for meaning and power can be extrapolated from his God "out there" and "down here" lyrical references. God, however, is not Jay-Z's only source for meaning and power. His other model is money. Jay-Z is world renowned for his music and his wife (Beyoncé Knowles), but his business savvy makes him a mogul. After the murders of Tupac Shakur (September 1996) and Notorious B.I.G. (March 1997), the hip hop world experienced a void. In part, it was filled by the gruff barks and prayers of DMX. In part, it was filled by southern hip hop led by pioneering Outkast's *ATLiens*. And in part, it was filled by Jay-Z's propagandizing of bling as a central form of worship.

God Meets Money

Jay-Z's body of work lives religion by connecting it with capitalism. As Jay-Hova, Jay-Z's power to profit is endless. As he boasts on "U Don't Know" (2001), "Put me anywhere on God's green Earth/I'll triple my worth." Jay-Z believes in God, and he believes he can be God when it suits him. His presentation as a peerless entrepreneur is secured through these appropriations of an Absolute authority. Jay-Z's lyrical characters often ask God to support their attempts to make money by any means necessary. In "Pray" (2007), the gangster asks the Lord to forgive and guide him as he enters the unscrupulous world of drug distribution and corrupt police. The final verse alludes to shame and regret but contextualizes the drug profession as a response to oppression. In "Public Service Announcement"

(2003), a song that also traffics in the drug distribution theme, Jay-Z makes it clear that "only God can judge me, so I'm gone/Either love me, or leave me alone." God understands, and can be petitioned with any request—even for help in an illicit underground economy. Part of Jay-Z's legacy is the marriage between the gangsta's God and money as a lifetime partnership for the pursuit of meaning and power.

The value of hip hop's commercial viability is highly contested. Jay-Z has been critiqued for his role in hip hop's mass commercialization. Hip hop purists believe that as long as market forces dictate rappers' persistent dribble about cash, cars, and hoes, rap music will never be prophetic. Others argue that hip hop has an inherent entrepreneurial spirit that will continue to inspire lyrical ingenuity about the path to (monetary) success. Both sides must concede that the crossroads where rap meets religion has been marked by market forces for many years. The sheer popularity of Lil Wayne's record label Young Money Entertainment, featuring Drake and Nicki Minaj as its headliners, suggests that money is the foremost priority of the next generation. Young money represents the divine promise of prosperity to hip hop's heirs.

Predicting the role of the gangsta's God in the future requires attention to socioeconomic conditions. The pirating of digital music has decimated music industry sales. Declining profits means record label executives expect artists to create their own followings before they are signed. Artists who control their products are freer to generate greater diversity in their music and incorporate religious content that includes but is not limited to Islamic and Christian God talk. Greater economic disparity between the haves and the have-nots often leads to a racial entrenchment. Whites who paid little attention to the amount of money made by black and brown hip hop entrepreneurs before being affected by the foreclosure and unemployment crisis, now readily accuse them of devil worship. In response, hip hop may see more God "out there" references to defend against these claims of occultism or hip hop may see more playfully blasphemous God "down here" references that, as Jay-Z says, "fucks with you for the fun of it."[5] As protests emerge around the world due to economic injustices like unemployment, the lack of a living wage, unequal access to water, and rising food prices, we should anticipate more global demands for diverse Gods "out there" to help individuals achieve economic advancement and/or more Gods "down here" that justify economic gain by any means necessary.

In *Decoded* Jay-Z writes, "I think for hip hop to grow to its potential and stay relevant for another generation we have to keep pushing deeper and deeper into the biggest subjects."[6] These subjects should include variations on the God figures discussed in this book. Unfortunately, hip hop is in trouble. Hip hop is not dead, but it is getting dumber. The underfunding of public education in the United States has done a grand disservice to popular culture. Children who are no longer taught music in school, and who graduate barely literate cannot make sophisticated contributions to hip hop culture. Emerging rap artists are becoming popular at younger and younger ages. We cannot expect impassioned musings about meaning and power akin to those bestowed upon us by Jay-Z from someone who is 16 years old. Of course, not all hip hop is young, and not all of it is dumb, but the current critiques of hip hop must place their concerns in the appropriate places. The commodification of hip hop does not curtail conversations about God. Economic shifts should create more God talk, not less in the coming decades. In order for American youth to substantively contribute to this discourse, they must acquire the necessary historical, cultural, literary, and religious vocabularies.

Consistent with the descriptions of the gangsta's God in this book, God will not directly intervene in humans' messy state of affairs. There will be no benevolent disbursement of cash from the heavens to employ the unemployed and educate the uneducated. Whereas the gangsta's God's silence can be understood as evidence of God's absence or disinterest, most gangstas interpret God's silence as an opportunity to celebrate human ingenuity. Communing with God "out there" creates community with like-minded individuals "down here." God's children become each other's allies. As a father, daddy God encourages independence, responsibility, and accountability. He empowers His children to emerge victorious over their various trials and tribulations. He does not fight battles for them.

The characteristics of the gangsta's God vary depending on the gangsta, but ultimately, the gangsta's God understands when humans do what they feel they have to do. Gangstas' Gods have blessed good sex, sanctioned violence, and supported capitalism. Whether "out there" or "down here" the gangsta's God is never unaware of humans' earthly endeavors. Jesus was, after all, gangsta. Sent from "out there" to "down here," he got beat down, but he got back up. Gangstas appropriate Jesus to piece together their own salvation. They recognize devil adversaries and temptations as part of the persistent battle between good and evil. By embodying God's power, they see themselves as exercising power over their oppressors and manifesting the power to love God, themselves, and one another. Gangstas' articulations of their experiences remind us that the gangsta's God can be a force that's bigger that you, but the gangsta's God can also be you.

Appendix A

God Talks

This appendix includes a series of "God Talks"—interviews I conducted with a music producer, a hip hop pastor, a choreographer and artistic director, as well as other hip hop scholars who think regularly about rap and religion.

Brian Taylor
(Music Producer)

What kind of music do you produce?
    Various genres mainly in the Christian industry. A little hip hop and pop.

Can you describe your creative process when working on a new track?
    Usually taking your life and the way you feel at the time and just putting it out into the music. Basically start with a thought and the melody will come from what you feel or what you happen to stumble upon while just playing around. It's really an organic process when it comes to creation.

Do you usually create with yourself or others?
    Usually I'll work with a team—me, a songwriter, and another producer. We'll go in and try to catch a vibe, or sometimes we'll have a specific artist we are working for and we'll actually try to cater the song to that artist.

Do some emotions inspire you more than others?
    Definitely. It depends on how you're feeling. If you're feeling good, it will be very hard to make that song that is supposed to be sad or very melancholy or thought provoking. Sometimes a bad mood brings that pain out that you need to create the sad songs. It's hard to make a break up song or a song about being unappreciated when you're feeling very good or loved. And it's hard to make a song about being on top of the world when you are going through a detrimental trial.

In your opinion what is music supposed to do?
It's supposed to relay a message.

Would you say there is a spiritual or religious component to producing music, and if so how would you describe it?
I will say there is some type of spiritual component or a religious component depending on the person. From spirit mainly like I said, it could be from the feelings or the emotions that you have, and then the religious component can be, depending on the person, how far you go talking about certain subjects. So this religious component could limit you as far as language or morality, and content of your music.

How is producing for hip hop different from producing for Christian music?
There is no difference at all. If it's a contemporary R&B artist, a Christian artist, whatever, it's the same type of sound that you're looking for and same type of music you're creating just for a different person. The only thing that changes is the content really.

Is there a such thing as "God sound" in music?
You mean like a sound that people readily identify with God, or a certain religion?

Yes, a sound that people readily identify with God.
I wouldn't say that there is, but I do think certain cultures identify sounds with the religions of their culture. Like African Americans relate organs to the church. Certain drums are related to tribes, and certain key sounds are related to Indian worship. It just depends on the culture, but if you were somebody who was from maybe Asia and listening to the organs, you wouldn't say that sounds like church. Cultures identify with certain sounds. I wouldn't say there is a God sound universally, though.

Do you think that music can invoke the presence of God?
I do.

Can you describe what happens when music does invoke the presence of God?
Music is supposed to relay a message, but everybody receives the message differently so it's like reading a book or looking at a painting. Everybody can receive the message in their own context. If a song does invoke the presence of God for a person, then they will have a certain feeling, or

they'll be attached to that song some kind of way. Something will speak to them which creates a feeling of maybe comfort or maybe joy. For me, if a song evokes the presence of God, then I'll probably feel at peace but at the same time very joyful. I have heard people say they feel very quiet, very reserved when they feel that presence because they're trying listen to hear what it's saying. Music can invoke the presence of God, but again it will be received differently.

Rap music is notoriously loud and raucous, so can you still find the peace of God in its sound?

Yeah, I definitely think you can. Like I said, part of it depends on the message and what they were trying to do with the song. A lot of people feel that you can find God in different ways. Some people are pressed by certain words and the right words with the right sounds can appeal to people in a God aspect.

Does it work the opposite way? Are there sounds that can invoke the presence of evil?

It depends on what the person thinks is evil. An alcoholic may receive a song saying get tipsy different from someone who has a father who is an alcoholic, but then a social drinker may enjoy that song. Music is very personal to people. Although it is one song, one product that was created, a lot of people receive things differently. Some people will think it's empowering; some people will think it's derogatory.

Would you consider yourself a fan of rap music?

Yeah, definitely. I'm not a fanatic though. Being from the South, I'm mainly a fan of country and soft rock, stuff like that.

So when it comes to music is it more the content, the sound, or the perfect combination of both that appeals to you?

It's the combination of both.

What do you think is the most popular misconception about rap music?

That it's reality. People have taken that particular form of entertainment and classified it as reality, when it's really entertainment like any other genre of music or any other form of entertainment whether it's movies or books, but for some reason people have grabbed hold of rap music as reality, and I don't think that's true.

Where do you think that misconception comes from?

The way the marketing is handled? I can't really explain it. People have gravitated towards that genre of music, and they made it valid in their heads. Perception has become reality and for some reason that one area of music has really taken a stronghold.

How do you think rap will change in the future?

I think it will circle back around into what they call hip hop as opposed to just rap. Certain things will phase out like it does with any other music, and it does with fashion as well. It's gonna go back to more of a conscious type of music.

You just distinguished between hip hop and rap; what's the difference to you?

I feel like hip hop and rap they are one in the same, but hip hop is the roots. Where the tree branched off is what you call rap music now. Hip hop was the beginning; it has become more commercialized, and as a result rap music was created. What you see—all the branches and the leaves—are rap music, but the roots of the tree are hip hop, and it will go back to the roots.

Do you believe that hip hop at its roots, the conscious-level hip hop, do you think that's inherently spiritual?

I do truthfully. Hip hop is a form of relaying a message—what was going on in life at the time, what was surrounding the artist, what wasn't being said, what people needed to discuss—it was a sounding board for issues, whether it was politics or problems in the neighborhood, or even just we worked hard, let's have fun. It was just a sounding board in the form of music. Now certain artists may have had a spiritual aspect to them, but I wouldn't know who that would be unless I knew their background. Artists can bring a spiritual aspect to their music, but I don't think that hip hop as a whole is designed to put people's spiritual views out in the public.

Do you identify with a religious faith? If so, which one?

Yes, I am Christian.

Is there anything else you would like to add?

Nope.

Dr. Andre Johnson
(Dr. James L. Netters Assistant Professor of Rhetoric and Religion and African American Studies at Memphis Theological Seminary, pastor of Gifts of Life Ministries in Memphis, Tennessee, and editor of *Urban God Talk: Rap Religion and a Spirituality of Hip Hop*)

Dr. Johnson, thanks for joining me. You've got quite a few titles. How do you identify yourself?

I am a pastor first. Everything I do starts with the fact that I am a pastor and everything flows from that standpoint. I am a pastor who is hip hop.

From your pastor perspective, who or what is God?

God for me is the Creator of the Universe who incarnated into the man known as Jesus of Nazareth. This is not a small thing for me. To say God dwells on earth as Jesus is to say that God was/is Jesus, and to say that means that if one attempts to understand (as humanly possible) the mind and action of God, one will have to look to Jesus's words and actions. In addition, the fact that this Jesus hung out with the despised, marginalized, ostracized, and poor folks of society also says that God was intentional about God's actions. To be a follower of this God, I must be intentional about who I surround myself with as well.

Per your definition, what is God's relationship to religion?

Good question. I believe that God is not related to any religion. Authentic, healthy, nontoxic forms of religion can serve as a vehicle in discerning and discovering the Divine, but are not God in any way.

What is God's relationship to hip hop?

God's relationship with hip hop is the same as God's relationship with anything or anyone else. God is the Creator of everything, and as one practicing the Christian faith, what God creates is good.

What is the relationship between rap and religion?

This has taken on more significance as of late. However, looking back, maybe it should not have. "Rap" is the spoken word, a way to articulate thoughts, ideas, concerns, etc. to the public. Religion is the vehicle through which we experience the Divine. However, that experience is typically mediated through speech. Therefore it should not be surprising (or it should not have surprised people) that rap and religion would naturally be a fit.

Please describe the work that you do with hip hop.

First, as a pastor, I am intimately influenced, shaped, and surrounded by hip hop. My congregation is hip hop! I also write and study hip hop as an academic. I had the opportunity to teach (as far as I know from my own research) the very first hip hop theology/religion class [at Memphis Theological Seminary] in a seminary or divinity school back in 2005 as a graduate student at the University of Memphis. Since there were no books, articles, etc., out at that time other than Anthony Pinn's volume, *Noise and Spirit*, I had to draw from my own experiences and listen carefully to the music. By the way, when I teach the hip hop theology class, I teach more from the "secular" side of hip hop because that's what most of my students (pastors and church leaders) will encounter in their churches.

As a pastor, why do you do pursue your hip hop interests?

It is part of the culture. It is an important vehicle for many people young and old, and finally, from a religious standpoint, it speaks volumes to many people on a spiritual level.

How do you respond to critics that claim hip hop should have no relationship with the church?

I don't! Really, I gave that up a long time ago. If a pastor or church leader cannot see that the study and examination of hip hop will help her or his overall ministry and help her or him be more effective at reaching out and identifying with both young and older members of the congregation, then so be it. Besides, as I tell my students, hip hop is already in your church no matter where you are—rural Mississippi or urban Memphis. Whether you recognize it or not is immaterial.

Times are changing; the economy is crashing; wars are continuing; unemployment is rising; citizens are occupying. What should we expect from rap and religion in the future?

Good question again. Just like times past, people who are struggling to make sense out of life are going to turn to the spiritual. It is already happening. However, also like the past, people will use what is at their disposal to discern God in their lives. What will help many appreciate the relevance of hip hop is to understand that all theology is contextual. Many still perceive theology as something God handed down from on high. However, that is so far from the truth. Theology is "God Talk," or how humans talk about God. Thus as I write elsewhere, theology is profoundly rhetorical and is shaped, constructed, and lived out in community. Therefore people with an association and appreciation of hip hop will speak, discern, and think on theological precepts that emanate from their own contexts. Because I see myself as a public theologian, my job is to discern and discover that theology and engage it on its own terms, and finally, become part of the conversation.

What hip hop are you listening to these days?

Mostly old-school stuff!! I am currently listening to hip hop old-school mixes when turntables were used! Being a former DJ and rapper, I still appreciate the skill that turntablists still use. Also been listening to LeCrae. I think he is beginning to redefine the holy hip hop scene. By the way, there is really no such thing as holy hip hop; it's all hip hop.

Thanks again for joining me. Is there anything else you'd like to add?

No, other than may God bless you in your work and may you find the peace that passes all understanding. And let the church say AMEN!

Dr. Daniel White Hodge
(Assistant Professor of Youth Culture and Director of the Center for Youth Ministry Studies at North Park University as well as author of *The Hostile Gospel: Finding Religion in the Post Soul Theology of Hip Hop*)

Dr. Hodge, in your opinion, who or what is God?

Well, that's a really good question. I think God can be a lot of different things. For me, God is an unknown entity. I don't want to say genderless, but I also don't want to necessarily put a gender on God. So, I see God as this Being who has been able to create the universe. The function of God is another question that I am still working through and pondering. Once upon a time in my fundamental Christian years, I looked at God as always involved with human life. But as I've mulled around I'm not sure what the function of God is. I'm not necessarily agnostic in that sense or atheist for that matter, but I'm also not completely like "Oh God is in every bush." But I do see God as good, seeking peace and seeking justice, someone who has put together a marvelous universe and stuff that we will probably never understand in this lifetime. God or gods plural will probably show us more when we pass on from this life.

In that context, how do you define religion?

Well, I'll try to stay away from the textbook definition of religion. I see religion as practicing spiritual belief and figuring out what is sacred, profane, evil. I know in some churches, particularly Christian churches, they say this is not about religion, this is about a spiritual walk. But I do believe religion is an important function in life, because it does help organize some of those belief systems or those structures particularly as it pertains to morals, ethics. For me, religion helps organize some of those beliefs around God or gods for that matter and helps to make sense of life.

In your response, you contrasted spirituality and religion. How exactly is spirituality different from religion?

Spirituality in a nutshell is a lot more personal than I think religion is. I could take it even a step further. It's often the difference between rap and hip hop. Rap is something that is being done; hip hop is something that we live. I think religion can be done very good and very easy, but spirituality requires connecting to my family, to friends, to community, and to engage in those things of life and death and right and wrong and morals and immorality.

You just hinted at this, but can you say more about the relationship between rap and religion and rap and spirituality?

Absolutely. I think it's an interesting dynamic. Some rappers' religion is very fundamental, very rigid in their religious beliefs, very Old Testament in their approach to God. Like God is their avenger and He's going to avenge my this and my that. They see God in that sense, yet they are very critical of the religious manifestations of white theology and white patriarchal religion, which is dominating our cultural landscape. I think about David Banner's album, *Baptized in Dirty Water*. Yes, of course he talks about the booty and hoes—those old relics of patriarchy and misogyny—and at the same time still comes across in this kind of sacred neo-secular profane arena. Tupac issues a really strong criticism of the African American church in the U.S. He basically says why does God need a bigger church? Why does God need a pastor with all of the bling? Hip hop continually questions authority. They come out and criticize religion just as quick as they would any other social institution, be it economic, education, etc. It's that juxtaposition. You're going to call me a heathen and savage but yet you want to bring me into your church. So, it's interesting to hear some of those criticisms come out because it's a rejection of religion.

At the same time, I do find hip hop very spiritual in the sense that they're looking for a God—something that's pure, that hasn't been desecrated with race. Something that hasn't been tore up with gender saying that only men can do this and women can't. Or something that hasn't been tainted by money like tithing a certain amount of money will help you make it into heaven. Hip hop really begins to say wait a minute now, what are you bringing to me? Who are you bringing to me? I mean, I had one kid tell me, "I can't even go back to Christianity." There's too much stuff messed up. One young lady even told me, she said, "It's like everything has been f-ed up in the Bible. Everything's been rewritten a thousand times. I want to go to a more pure religion. I want to check out Zulu. I'm going to check out Five Percenters because that's a little bit more pure. It hasn't been f-ed up as much." I'm like it's an interesting position when you start thinking about it because there's a lot of stuff to contend with. I do think that spirituality is forming, but anytime you have an oppressive religion coming in and saying basically worship our God or we'll kill you, people will say all right I'll worship your God on the surface but behind closed doors I'm going to be doing my own thing. Hip hop is trying to seek God in all of this mess.

What is it about rap music that helps it become so critical of religion?

Its roots in marginalized communities that say we're going to stand up. We've been left out. We've been left behind. We're going to actually take back some of our identity. Hip hop poses a very fundamental and profound sociological question of, am I going to continue to get slapped and kicked around by the system or am I actually going to stand up and do something about it? If all I can do is just stand on this corner and say don't follow this person, then that's what I'll do. Rock and hip hop really look at organized religion very suspiciously.

Times are changing; the economy's crashing. We've got perpetual wars, we've got unemployment rising, cities being occupied. What does all this mean for rap and religion and the future?

Man, that is a really good question. You can't ignore the list that you just listed. I think a lot more people now are starting to understand what a lot of hip hoppers have been saying for a long time. But most of them looked at us as if we were crazy. Hip hop has been asking, "What's going on here?" But they're doing it in such a way that is scary to some folks. It's loud. It's aggressive. It is hostile. It is. But essentially combining the hostility with gospel, which literally translated means good news. Hip hop speaks to this current economic and social and cultural crisis that we're experiencing. I'm hoping that society is able to listen, but I don't know. Unfortunately, right now I still think it's on the underground. I don't know where the Tupacs are in the mainstream. I'm always leery when I see people like Common doing commercials for Target. You know, commercialization is an SOB, man. It'll overwhelm you.

You're clearly a hip hop fan. Who are you listening to?

I'll start with the old school: A Tribe Called Quest. I was fortunate enough to work on Bone Thugs-N-Harmony's album *E 1999 Eternal*, so I still listen to those cats. I think their ecclesiastical approach to death, the devil, and God are very interesting. I think it cannot be overlooked because it's essentially where Western theology has not been willing to go. We tend to use things that are dark and 666 as very evil and bad. While there may be areas of that, I still think it's a dialogue that most rappers wouldn't normally have taken up. You can't overlook Common. De La Soul, I think what they did was beyond their time. Digable Planets. *The Miseducation of Lauryn Hill* was one of the best rap albums out ever. I still listen to that and marvel. Mobb Deep, I'm always a fan of their first album, *The Infamous*. I can't vouch for their current stuff but that first album, man. There's so many references to life, death, God, and street living, which really reminds me a lot of The Geto Boys and Scarface. Of course, I can't overlook the females. I've always been a fan of MC Lyte. Any of Sista Souljah's old stuff. Tupac, for sure. Currently, I listen a little more on the religious side: LeCrae, Odd Thomas, Propaganda. Of course, Jasiri X, I listen to a lot of his music. He's current and contemporary. Nas, Jay-Z, and Kanye. Those are the artists that really catch my attention. I listen to the commercial stuff only because I've got to keep up with some of the kids that I work with out in the communities.

Is there anything else you'd like to add?

Oh, no. I appreciate what you're doing. I think that this scholarship is starting to really blow up. I'm really encouraged by that. I know when I first, at least in the circles that I ran in, started the conversation of hip hop, religion, and spirituality it was very much frowned upon and there just weren't that many resources. So, the fact that within the next three years there are going to be a significant amount, and when I say significant, I mean like 10, 15 good resources out there for students and scholars alike to really engage and have conversations with is really encouraging. I'm looking forward to reading the manuscript and seeing it bound and shelved with the books in the library.

Christopher Eclipse
(Artistic Director and Choreographer)

What kind of creative work do you do?

I'm an artistic director. I conceptualize shows. I bring together the production team to execute concepts. I also choreograph, which entails basically putting dance moves to music. Creating the steps or the story through music and dance for music artists. I direct or choreograph for theater stages, concert stages, film, and television.

Who have you worked with?

Some of the bigger names have been Jay-Z, Kanye West, Adam Sandler, Tom Cruise, Madonna. I've worked with a lot of people. I went to Columbia College; I did a lot of theater. But since I've been out here in L.A. I've been working more in the industry. So, those are industry people I've worked with. I also work with dance companies such as Deeply Rooted, which is a black modern dance company based in Chicago. Kevin Iega Jeff and Gary Abbott of Deeply Rooted who are both world-renowned artistic directors/choreographers and two of my mentors. Elana Anderson. She's also a dance teacher and world-renowned dancer. I've worked with High Hat, who is one of the largest hip hop choreographers in the world. I've worked with Fatima, who is also one of the biggest hip hop choreographers in the world. Who else? Jeffrey Page, who is an up-and-coming hip hop choreographer. He won a VMA for choreographing Beyoncé's "Who Run the World" video. That's enough, right?

Definitely. Can you describe your creative process when you work on new choreography?

Well honestly, it changes from job to job. I will have the production send the music and then I have to meditate. Honestly, I have to listen to the music, meditate on it. By that I mean sit down with my eyes closed and visualize what I see for the music. That's the first part of my choreographing creative process. After I do that I kind of see the steps inside of my head, what it is that I want to do. I see the vision for the steps. The next part is the hardest part for me, bringing it out of my head to the physical world. That's when I go into the studio or sometimes in my living room or my bedroom, which is my favorite place to work when I'm creating. I start to play with the movement on my own body first. From there, it kind of comes out. It's cool because when I'm doing that I experience the movement first and I experience it from the audience's perspective while it's coming out. Somebody once told me when you're creating in this creative process you're your first audience. I keep putting the work out, using myself, my body until I feel the right feeling inside, until it feels right. At that point, I put the count to a move. I take that piece to the artist or the production and then I teach them what I created.

The artistic direction is similar except the producers usually come to me with a blank canvas, and I have more creative freedom. So at that point, I just come up with the total concept. Pretty much the same creative process. Not only do I get to conceptualize and create the steps, but I create the show. I like to be able to create the whole vision and then as a choreographer I like to come inside that vision and put the steps to it. It works hand in hand.

Would you say that there's a spiritual or a religious component to your creative work?

Yeah. When I use words like *vision* and *meditate*, I'm not using them lightly. That's really what happens in the process. I literally have visions, and I literally have to meditate. Some people call it prayer. The creativity comes from somewhere. The visions come from somewhere. The ideas come from somewhere. I'm one that thinks that they come from a higher source. As cliché as it sounds, I know that these ideas coming through me are bigger than me. Sometimes I don't even feel like choreographing or art directing, even though I love to do it. Sometimes I'm in the middle of my sleep, just knocked out, and I'll have to wake up to write down something I just saw in a dream that I know is supposed to come to fruition. So, it's definitely spiritual. For some people it may be religious. For me, I don't consider myself a religious person anymore, but in some ways dance and choreography and artistic direction are my religion because it's what I live by. It maps out who I am. I'm sure whenever the day comes where it's time for me to transition and go into the next realm and leave this world I'm sure that's one of the things that people are going to identify me with and people are going to say I was. That's going to be part of my legacy.

Do you think that you're unique or do you think a lot of people that do the creative work that you do have the same sort of spiritual feelings about it?

If there is any way that I am unique it's probably in the fact that I carry through on my concepts. For the most part, the visions that come to me that are important, I really take the time and the discipline to bring them to the Earth. I don't know if I would call myself unique because I think everybody has visions. I think everybody has dreams and has an artistic side. I just don't think everyone follows through with bringing their visions to Earth. And yes, I think everyone in my field experiences similar spiritual things, but I don't know if they recognize them as spiritual feelings like I do.

Your higher power seems to be benevolent, helps you do good in the world. Do you think there are evil powers that are using folks within hip hop to do evil in the world?

I don't know if my higher power is making me do good or making me do bad. It kind of all works together. Hip hop artists who are doing what people consider bad are following through with their vision and following through with what they know and what they've been exposed to. I don't look at what they're doing as bad or negative. I just think it's from their perspective and that's what art is about. Whatever higher power that's running me to do bad or good in my mind is the same kind of power that's running them. I don't think there's a different higher power. But for instance, I don't know if there's a devil that's running Jay-Z or Kanye West. These men are working in their reality, the way they know how to work in it. They're doing what they do the best they know how. But then you have to think about the people who are listening to it. They don't live in the same reality as Jay-Z and Kanye West, so they're going to only work out of their perspectives. To answer your question: no, I don't think there is an evil power running them. I think there's a higher power running them. I think that the stuff that people consider evil that comes out of them is based upon their own perspectives. It's pretty much judgment. I think that's evil. I think judgment's evil. If there is something that's evil.

So far you haven't called your higher power God. Why is that?

Sometimes when I use the word *God* people get afraid. To me, it's just politically correct sometimes to say higher power. I feel like I'm talking about the same entity. God and the higher power is the same thing for me. But I battle with that a lot in my work. A lot of my work is based around sexuality and religion, because that's the stuff I battle with the most. Like for instance, this piece I do with my hip hop dance company [Untitled Dance Company] is called "The Conductor." In this piece, it's a symphony of dancers, and I play the conductor. The conductor represents my life and how humans try to conduct each other to be a certain way. So, what happens in this piece is he's conducting and the orchestra is moving together. The music is all harmonized, and it's all working together. But then at some point, the conductor loses control and a higher force takes over and it creates chaos with the symphony. He realizes he has to release control in order for the symphony to come back together. When it comes back together they're back in harmony but he's dancing with the symphony. He's not conducting them. The higher being or God is always in control even over the conductor. That's kind of how I think about the word *God* and higher being. I don't really have enough information to even really give God a name. But for the sake of conversation I will go with higher being because I feel like I'm talking to a huge audience of people and I don't want them to be offended by the word *God.*

Do you think that God has a place in hip hop?

I think that God is hip hop. Hip hop is just another channel for God to work through. To say that God is not a part of hip hop is crazy. I mean hip hop is all about creativity, and it's all about coming from one's true self and one's true personality. To me that's God. Whether people recognize it or not, to create, to bring things forward, to bring things to life, to bring things to the Earth that people might not have otherwise known or experienced is a form of Godliness. When I say God is hip hop I don't mean that I'm going to get on my knees and to pray to hip hop. But at the same time, like I said before, in my process I do have to meditate to get things out. What am I doing when I'm meditating? Some kind of praying. I'm trying to figure out what the vision is. Meditation and prayer work hand in hand.

Do you think there's a "God sound" when it comes to the music or "God movement" when it comes to dance?

Any artist that will read this interview knows exactly what I'm talking about when I'm talking about the chill factor. It just happens, and you know it's right. In that moment you realize that God is in it. Not only is God in it, but the rest of the people who are supposed to connect to this are going to feel the exact same way. It's like you connect with millions of people in one instant second, and it causes you to have chills. You get these chills and it's like damn what was that? It's better than an orgasm. When you have that moment that's that God sound. That's that God feeling. That's that Godliness. You're connecting with a million souls all around the world. That's something hip hop has done. So yeah, there is a God sound.

There's definitely a God dance. Anything happening in choreography or when I come up with a good concept, I literally experience. I mean I literally experience it in my body, in my soul. I feel it. I know if it's going to make people cry because I cry first. If it's going to make people laugh, I'll laugh first. Like, I don't want to say I'm giving myself my own show, but it's like God is projecting a show in my mind and I'm watching it. I'm feeling it the same way you would feel it as an audience. When you have those moments you can say that's a God sound, that's a God dance. I don't think most people would call it that, but that's what it is. I mean there's no way around it.

Do you consider yourself a hip hop fan?
I consider myself a hip hop baby. I feel like I was born into hip hop.

Can you say more about that?
I was born into an era when hip hop was getting big, and I'm just a child of it. I'm a baby of it. I've come here with my own ideas, but I haven't lost the original concept. It was instilled in me. I took it into my heart, into my soul. I have a real connection with it, to the point where the stuff that I do now maybe doesn't look like my father's stuff but I am a child of it. I feel like I have the right to move this way and move that way with it. I'm not going to disrespect it; I'm not going to take it out of context. I'm a hip hop artist in my heart. What I do with hip hop, especially dance, is just like hip hop originally did. I took from my culture and all the experiences that I've come in contact with, and I put it into those dances. That's my voice. It's a very true hip hop voice, even though some people who think they know hip hop, think they really have an understanding of it, would totally disagree with me. But those people who do that, I'm already aware that they don't really know what hip hop really is and where it resonates from.

Who are some of your favorite hip hop artists, performers, dancers? Who's the best of the best overall?
I don't know if I have favorites. So many people have inspired me. I've danced many nights to Slick Rick, Black Thought of The Roots, Digable

Planets, Grandmaster Flash, Nas, Biggie, of course Tupac, J Dilla, Outkast, Digital Underground, Redman, Jay-Z, Kanye, Slum Village, The Last Poets, Talib Kweli, and Lauryn Hill. They were all fresh. These are all people that I work to. Man, who else? There's so many. I've been inspired by so many hip hop artists.

Earlier you said you don't see yourself as a religious person anymore.
    Yeah.

So that means you have no current religious affiliation?
    No. Not at this point. I don't go to church. I don't go to any spiritual institution right now at all. Because I am a gay man, I haven't been able to really find my place inside of religion. Even though I'm not a religious person, I've had music and dance to express myself. At the same time, hip hop is similar because it hasn't fully looked at the gay hip hop artist and accepted them into their realm. We've been ostracized. I do want hip hop to open up to artists like myself who love men. I'm a man who loves another man. My voice is just as valid.

I'd like to unpack that idea a little bit more about being gay in hip hop and how that ties into religion. You said that hip hop ostracized you. Is it true that religion is ostracizing you too?
    Yeah. It is. It is. I feel like I'm like a rebel almost. I feel like a fighter when it comes to being heard inside of religious circles or some hip hop circles. Not physically fight, but it's like a hip hop mentality. I'm coming in with "This is who I am. This is what I do. Love it or leave it." When I'm in the church or I'm sitting around a group of guys who are all supposedly straight or whatever . . . for them to hear me I have to put on a little extra. I feel like I have to be on my A-game just a little bit more because they're already looking at me as something less or a sinner who has committed the ultimate sin. They're already waiting to ostracize me because I'm the gay black man. They're already looking at me.

It's ironic because hip hop and religion can be ostracizing to you as a gay man. But at the same time, if you combine the aggressive aspects of hip hop with the inspiration of your higher power you can use hip hop and religion to critique hip hop and religion.
    That's exactly what I mean. I can come into it with the ideas that I've gained from hip hop and religion/spirituality and be heard. It is that

structure that gives me my voice inside of hip hop, even though they don't sometimes realize it. That's what it is. I feel very confident and proud to say that, yeah, I'm a gay man. I'm a gay man who loves hip hop. I've been loving hip hop. I am hip hop. It's like one of the proudest things I can ever say. The only reason I have to use the term *gay* is because there's really no other term to explain who I am and what I am. I'm really more than that. It's important that the people hear that. It's important that people know because otherwise we could just be erased. "Oh, these people don't exist." Quietly, there's so many of us inside that industry dealing with and battling with religion and who God is and all of these real oppressive thoughts. They're afraid to come out, but you know what? There's people like me here. Until that time comes, I'm going to be the one that stands there.

Do you have any advice for the ones that feel like they really can't say what they want to say or be who they want to be? What would you tell those folks who are struggling?

Be strong. You're going to have to be regardless of what you are—straight, gay, or whatever. You have to be that. You're going to have some moments where you have to be strong. Don't be scared. Who cares what people have to say about you? At the end of the day, you have a voice. You have something valid to say that your audience needs to hear. Say it. If you want to think of your voice or gift as a religion, save those people. Save your audience. They need you. They're waiting on you. That's truth. To me, that's the real meaning of getting saved because you truly are saving lives.

Dr. Monica Miller
(Scholar of religion at Lewis & Clark College, Department of Religion and author of *Religion and Hip Hop*)

Dr. Miller, who is God?

Well, I would answer the questions in two ways. First, I would answer the question as a scholar of religion. God is a human projection and construction, a social construction, and so in this sense God is an empty signifier by which humans then project meaning on to. That is not to deny any type of confessional claims to belief that people might have in God around their own religiosity, but I feel scholars of religion are limited to the types of claims they can make theologically about the concept of God. Personally, I would leave metaphysical understandings and explications of God as something that is higher than the self to pastors and theologians.

How do you define rap?

I define rap music as the more the lyrical wing of hip hop culture. Yeah, the lyrical expressions of hip hop culture.

Can rap help us understand God, and if so how?

Absolutely. I do think that concepts of God, as your work has shown, are pervasive in rap music, and these concepts can certainly help theologians working in the area of constructive theology. I think they help show the ways in which humans are playing around with concepts of God. And how concepts of God change over time, space, and place. We can see the types of weights that are given to constructs of God in cultural products, in pop culture, and in rap music in particular.

What kind of work are you doing in relation to hip hop, rap music, and religion?

In the third project that I have now, the forthcoming book, I tried to move the discipline of religion away from solely excavating rap lyrics. So that is to say, existing literature that looks at religion and hip hop, religion and rap music, more specifically, focuses on lyrics—their claims rely on textual analysis. I think that has been great; it has produced a lot of conversations. Now, the area of religion and hip hop needs to go beyond solely apprehending rap lyrics to look at other domains of hip hop culture. The question has been what is religious about hip hop culture? That question assumes something self-evident about religion. It assumes that religion is something that is real in the world, in a phenomenological sense, and so I apply poststructural analysis, postmodern thought to that question and flipped it on its head. I am asking what do the uses of religion in hip hop culture accomplish for competing social and cultural interests? The latter question gets us to a more robust analysis of class, race, gender, region, sexuality. It allows us to do much more than assume religion as self-evident in rap music or hip hop culture.

I'm really playing with the theory behind the study of hip hop and religion. What are the different approaches? What have been the prevailing questions? How we might want to play around with those questions and ask the right questions, if there are any right questions, for the study of hip hop and religion. My work is mostly dealing with theory and method and trying to expand the range of cultural products as it relates to hip hop, so looking at film, looking at dance, listening to music, looking at interviews, trying to expand the range of pop culture.

In light of your project and my project and other people that you know that are working in the field, where do you see conversations about hip hop and religion moving in the future?

That's a really good question. I think the work will become more interdisciplinary. Scholars, especially of religion and theology, are realizing that our message needs to become much more varied in order to really apprehend the full range of hip hop and religion. Future work will, as I mentioned before, get beyond rap lyrics to consider things such as interviews so that is to say we're not just engaging the lyrics of the song, but we're engaging the life world of very real people. These artists are real people that have their own cosmology, their own philosophy of life, their own interests in producing music. We're working with a cultural form that is now over 40 years old and we haven't given any deep thought to theory and method. So getting more ethnographic with it. Engaging real people and engaging lifeworlds for the artist and the audience.

I should have asked you this earlier, but can you talk about religion? What is religion supposed to do?

Well, again I would first answer the question from my own field of religious studies as a scholar of religion. When we talk about religion and what it's supposed to do in the world, there has been this general discourse that is rooted in phenomenology that assumes that religion is something unique or what we call *sui generis*. That there's something about religion that distinguishes it from the economic, the political, the social, the cultural.

In our area of religion in hip hop, the current approach is to separate it from culture so it becomes hip hop *and* religion, or it becomes religion *and* culture. I am persuaded that religion and culture are really both/and. I like to say religion *in* culture. Religion is not something autonomous, a priori, self-evident, or *sui generis*. For me it's a folk category, the way in which people organize around a particular rubric, just like race, just like gender, just like sexuality. We know race to be real but yet not real. That is to say it has real consequences in the world, but race is not something that is biological or in the DNA. It's a human construction, a social construction that people organize around in a particular kind of way. On a personal level, religion is an idea, an activity, a philosophy, perhaps even an ideology that is a human projection that provides a type of communal belonging and meaning for certain groups.

Can humans be trusted to socially construct their own religions and their own Gods?

I would probably answer the question by reframing it. I can see that humans are persuaded by this thing called religion because it is a dominant narrative in our society—in culture. In my own work, I struggle with this idea of religious habitus drawn from [Pierre] Bordieu's work on habitus and thinking about the ways in which, especially when we are talking about various demographics of youth, the way that religion becomes part of the habitus (or one's durable disposition). So that even before the child is born into the world by way of household and familial inheritance they are already born into a particular notion and understanding of what religion is. It becomes inculcated into their own sense of self or sense of being and so it becomes hard to separate expressions or rhetorical claims of religion as representing belief.

Religious habitus produce durable dispositions that structure the individual in ways that are more often than not unconscious to the subject, so that when we're in the field and doing ethnography, to what extent can we trust the subject to really explicate why they do what they do? I understand when I go into the field I am not excavating people's transcendental place, or their intentional searches for coherence and meaning or their confessional claims to belief. Oftentimes the case, especially with youth of color, black youth and Latino youth, is that they'll rhetorically express claims to God because it's an expression of their religious habitus, but when you extricate their cultural practices, their cultural practices will end up deconstructing that very rhetorical claim to religion or to claims to belief in God. There's something about religion that is inherited from family that is part of the heritage and almost chooses the subject before the subject even comes into the world and before the subject can participate in socialization. It's almost like religion chooses them, and then they have to work out their own constructions of meaning.

Would you say that this concept of religious habitus might explain all the contradictions like "I am thanking God for my success in this rap album where all I rap about is murder, mayhem, and misogyny?"

I think two things about that. One: that's absolutely correct. Scholars of religion have to realize that the religious imagination of pop culture is not something that is stable and coherent. It pushes us to reframe and reorient our own methodology. We're not looking for something stable, not looking for confessional claims to belief. And then the second part of that is there's an altered ethic of faith in rap music in particular. What we might see as incoherent or as a contradiction is taken up in a complex way where both things are held in tension. I might say "fuck you" or I might use terminology such as bitches in my rap music, but I can also give thanks to God. That type of contradiction in terms of American religion is just as American as cherry pie. The contradictions, if they "really" are contradictions, we see in rap music especially between the plastic distinctions of sacred and secular and profane just represents the best and worst of American society. The types of contradictions we see in rap music are the kinds of constructions we see when an elected official gets up and says God bless America and they're talking about war at the same time. So I just think it's sort of a representation or reflection of the kinds of contradictions we have with regard to religion in our own society. But I'm not persuaded that the artist sees it as a contradiction. I see it as more of an issue for us scholars that are extricating this work. Because sometimes we look for something stable and coherent we kind of get blown away by the multiplicative contradictions that are held in tension comfortably in rap music.

Do you think there is something inherent about rap music that holds these contradictions in a noncontradictory way?

I don't think there's something inherent in the rap music. I think it's true for all types of cultural practices and forms. There's all kinds of contradictions that are held in tension that sort of puzzle us as scholars that we are not able to get to the bottom of, but again that speaks more to our methodological and theoretical limitations. Our tools are not robust enough to capture that type of contradiction. In fact, in my forthcoming work, I don't even talk about it as a contradiction. I look at this as a flow of human means, interests, and ends.

For example, if Tupac is expressing five different ideas around the concept of God in a rap song, I don't see it as a contradiction. I see it as him trying to accomplish five different things in five different moments. And I used Tupac as an example because Tupac is an artist that really sort of stumped me in my own work. Listening to interviews of him, listening to certain songs of him, he'll go from talking about God out there in a metaphysical sense, to himself as God, to his Five Percent peeps as God, and he's comfortable with all those ideas of God. But at the end of the day, he says I believe in God. Okay, Tupac, but what idea of God are you persuaded by? It seems that he's persuaded by four to five different concepts of God and they function for him in different moments of his life. When he's writing a song like "Ghetto Gospel" for him God's hand is on his head as he writes that rhyme. When he's locked up in jail serving time then God becomes Five Percenters because he adapts to his environment, and he constructs concepts of God that are meaningful for him and to him at particular moments that serve his human interests.

You've already hinted at this, but let's unpack it a little bit more. Tupac, for example, has all these different conceptions of God. Some of them clearly emerge out of his religious habitus in Christianity and some from the Five Percent, but where else do ideas of God come from, if they're not coming from an inherited religiosity?

That's a good question. People's ideas of religion come from the home first and foremost but also dominant institutions in society. I mean religious ideas pervade us all day every day from television commercials to advertisements to political speeches. People constantly negotiate these ideas of religion as they continually emerge within the lifeworld of the subject. Certainly people get their ideas of religion from the kinds of cultural products that they have contact with. Pop culture is a source by which people also get ideas about philosophy, religion, and life in general.

Times are hard. I'm calling it the Greater Depression, but it hasn't caught on yet. What should we expect these ideas about God and religion to do as the economy continues to fluctuate?

As we continue to wrestle with the social, the political, the economic or these very real situations of life and death and hunger, money, and jobs, those experiences draw people closer to religion and God. Scarcity in general is a religion-making sort of situation. When we have scarcity people turn to things they normally perhaps wouldn't turn to when things are okay. So it seems that there is a correlation between just the experience of marginalization and these anxieties that are religion making and religion producing.

What role do you think God will play in hip hop's future?

I think we'll continue to hear more creative and innovative play with the concept of God in rap music, in particular. Theology that engages pop culture hasn't shown the rich variety and the robust terrain of God play in rap music, but it's so there. It's there in video games. What does it mean when someone can play God in a video game? The future of this is that it will be increasingly complex and will increasingly become more contradictory.

Is technology impacting the relationship between rap and religion? If so how?

Yeah, I definitely think technology is impacting rap and religion. When we claim to do empirical work or ethnographic work, we're already assuming this kind of positivism that's face-to-face, but rap music is mediated technologically in a way that pushes that face-to-face empirical encounter out of the way. And so these things being virtually mediated means that our tools will have to become more robust, as I've been mentioning, especially our ethnographic tools, now that we're having to excavate sound and expressions and lyrics and sentiments and people's ideas virtually. It's definitely an underexplored area and a site that needs more excavation, and then we need to ask those really tough methodological questions around how do we explore this, how do we excavate it, or what do we do with voices when they are technologically mediated? That will be a huge challenge for us scholars doing work around rap and religion in the future.

Are you a fan of hip hop?

Absolutely.

What do you listen to?

I'm pretty obsessed with Eminem actually. I still have my old-school artists that I am very attached to—Tupac, say for example, but I'm pretty obsessed with Eminem. What I find really interesting about his work is just the rawness that you get in his music and that type of existential wrestling and angst that you find in his music. I know folks more generally have looked at DMX in order to explore that existential kind of angst but I think it's also evident in Eminem's work. I love Eminem, the old-school artists, some of the new stuff that is coming out, Nicki Minaj and some of those other more controversial kinds of songs, but I think that Eminem in particular I'm pretty obsessed with. I think for me he's the number one MC.

Wow. Okay, it's on record.

Maybe we don't want to put that in there. I might lose some cred for that.

And do you claim a religious affiliation? If so, what?

No, I don't claim any affiliation. I play with Buddhism, but I think of myself more or less as a humanist.

Rapper Survey Data

The following lists of religious rappers, devil-worshipping rappers, rappers who believe in Jesus, and rappers who rap about God were derived from 175 undergraduates who participated in the 2011 Rap and Religion Survey discussed in chapter 6.

Religious Rappers

The numbers denote the frequency with which students referenced religious rappers. The list includes only rappers with more than two votes.

1. Kanye West 69
2. Tupac Shakur 63
3. Jay-Z 38
4. Lil Wayne 32
5. Nas 26
6. Common 21
7. Notorious B.I.G. 18
8. Eminem 16
9. DMX 12
10. Drake 12
11. Lupe Fiasco 12
12. Sean "Diddy" Combs 10
13. T.I. 10
14. Rev Run 8
15. Snoop Dogg 8
16. Talib Kweli 8
17. The Game 7
18. Ice Cube 7

19. LeCrae 7

20. Mase 7

21. Mos Def 7

22. Run DMC 7

23. Bone Thugs-N-Harmony 5

24. Ludacris 5

25. Matisyahu 5

26. A Tribe Called Quest 4

27. Lauryn Hill 4

28. LL Cool J 4

29. Wale 4

30. 50 Cent 3

31. J. Cole 3

32. Nicki Minaj 3

Devil-Worshipping Rappers

The numbers denote the frequency with which students referenced devil-worshipping rappers. The list includes only rappers with more than two votes.

1. Jay-Z 24

2. Kanye West 14

3. Odd Future Wolf Gang Kill Them All (Tyler the Creator) 8

4. Three 6 Mafia 7

5. Eminem 5

6. Lil Wayne 3

Rappers Who Rap about or Compare Themselves to Jesus

The numbers denote the frequency with which students referenced rappers who rap about or compare themselves to Jesus. The list includes only rappers with more than two votes.

1. Kanye West 84

2. Jay-Z 30

3. Wayne 15

4. Tupac 9

5. Nas 8

6. Eminem 4

Rappers Who Rap about God

The numbers denote the frequency with which students referenced rappers who rap about God. The list includes only rappers with more than two votes.

1. Kanye West 59
2. Tupac Shakur 54
3. Jay-Z 37
4. Lil Wayne 26
5. Nas 20
6. Eminem 15
7. Notorious B.I.G. 12
8. Drake 10
9. Common 8
10. DMX 8
11. 50 Cent 7
12. Sean "Diddy" Combs 6
13. Snoop Dogg 6
14. The Game 6
15. Ice Cube 6
16. Rev Run 6
17. LeCrae 5
18. T.I. 5
19. Ludacris 4
20. Mase 4
21. Mos Def 4
22. Guru 3
23. Ja Rule 3
24. Lauryn Hill 3
25. Lupe Fiasco 3
26. Nicki Minaj 3

Notes

Introduction

1. William J. Wilson, *When Work Disappears: The World of the New Urban Poor* (New York: Knopf, 1996), 49.

2. Michelle Alexander, *The New Jim Crow: Mass Incarceration in the Age of Colorblindness* (New York: The New Press, 2010), 175.

3. A3P News Team, "The 'Unspoken National Crisis': Black Teenage Unemployment Nears 50 Percent," *American Third Position*, http://american3rdposition.com/?p=1945.

4. Elijah Anderson, *Code of the Street: Decency, Violence, and the Moral Life of the Inner City* (New York: Norton, 1999), 33.

5. Michael Eric Dyson, *Open Mike: Reflections on Philosophy, Race, Sex, Culture and Religion* (New York: Basic *Civitas* Books, 2003), 309.

6. Jon Michael Spencer, "Philosophical Prolegomena to Theomusicological Thematizing of the Nonsacred," in *The Theology of American Popular Music* (Durham, NC: Duke University Press, 1989), 9–10.

7. Monica R. Miller and Ezekiel J. Dixon-Roman, "Habits of the Heart: Youth Religious Participation as Progress, Peril, or Change?" *The Annals of the American Academy of Political and Social Science* 637, no. 78 (2011): 94.

8. Marc Lamont Hill, "The Barbershop Notebooks: I Bling Because I'm Happy," in *Pop Matters*, http://www.popmatters.com/columns/hill/050805.shtml.

9. Josef Sorett, "Believe Me, This Pimp Game Is Very Religious: Toward a Religious History of Hip Hop," *Culture and Religion* 10, no. 1 (2009): 16.

Chapter 1

1. Mason Betha and Karen Hunter, *Revelations: There's a Light after the Lime* (New York: Atria Books, 2001), 74–75.

2. Music critics credit Snoop with being one of the first rappers to actually be indicted for the violent activities he rapped about. Death Row Records successfully flipped Snoop's legal woes into a peerless marketing strategy. He titillated those voyeurs who salivated over the blurred lines between reality and fiction. *Doggystyle* (1993), the record Snoop was completing when the drive-by occurred, was "the

first debut album to enter the charts at number one." Stephen Thomas Erlewine, "Snoop Dogg," in *All Music Guide to Hip-Hop*, eds. V. Bogdanov, C. Woodstra, S. T. Erlewine, and J. Bush (San Francisco: Backbeat Books, 2003), 443–45.

3. Michel Marriott, "Death, Hip-Hop Turns to Dirges," *New York Times*, October 13, 1996.

4. No rapper has recorded the female voice of God.

5. Heidi Siegmund Cuda, "Gods and Monsters," *Vibe*, October 2001, 96.

Chapter 2

1. Jason D. Haugen, " 'Unladylike Divas': Language, Gender, and Female Gangsta Rappers," *Popular Music and Society* 26, no. 4 (2003): 433.

2. Elaine B. Pinderhughes, "African American Marriage in the 20th Century," *Family Process* 41, no. 2 (2002): 273.

3. Trina and Josh are no longer in a relationship.

4. Kelly Brown Douglas, *What's Faith Got to Do with It?: Black Bodies/Christian Souls* (Maryknoll, NY: Orbis Books, 2005), 51.

5. Marvin M. Ellison, *Erotic Justice: A Liberating Ethic of Sexuality* (Louisville, KY: Westminster John Knox Press, 1996), 6.

6. Victoria W. Wolcott, *Remaking Respectability: African American Women in Interwar Detroit* (Chapel Hill: University of North Carolina Press, 2001), 8.

7. Kelly Brown Douglas, *Sexuality and the Black Church: A Womanist Perspective* (Maryknoll, NY: Orbis Books, 1999), 84–85.

8. Monifa Young, "High on the Hill," *Essence*, June 1998, 76.

9. Ibid.

10. Joan Morgan, "They Call Me Ms. Hill," *Essence*, February 2006, 158.

11. Men have released tracks exclusively dedicated to a female God. See the discussion on Andre 3000's "God Interlude" in chapter 1 as well as Common's "Faithful" and Charles Hamilton's "Conversations with God" in chapter 5.

12. bell hooks, *Reel to Real: Race, Sex, and Class at the Movies* (New York: Routledge, 1996), 83.

Chapter 3

1. Kanye West, "Jesus Walks Trilogy: Making of the Video," in *The College Dropout Video Anthology*, DVD (Roc-A-Fella Records, 2005).

2. The Cartoon Network aired *Freaknik: The Musical* during their Adult Swim programming on March 7, 2010. Florida rapper T-Pain stars as the ghost of Freaknik. Freaknik was a popular, primarily African American, spring break destination in Atlanta. By 1994, the small picnic originally organized for black college students who could not afford to return home had burgeoned into 200,000 revelers who became increasingly difficult to control. Because of traffic jams, (threats of)

violence, and the general manhandling of women attendees, city officials effectively banned Freaknik by imposing major restrictions on the massive street party in 1999. As a 1980s baby, T-Pain noted in interviews that he was always too young to attend Freaknik, but welcomed the opportunity to reintroduce its celebratory nature.

3. Trap Jesus's tattoos are inspired by Lil Wayne's with the following exceptions: the tattoos on Lil Wayne's eyelids read "Fear God," and Lil Wayne has an additional teardrop under his right eye.

4. Snoop's deal with the devil is discussed in more detail in chapter 4.

5. Although often referred to as Jesus Christ, as if Jesus were a first name and Christ the surname, there is a difference between Jesus and Christ. Jesus is the historical figure admired by many people because he was persecuted for advocating unpopular beliefs and hated by other people for representing those beliefs. Christ is a theological concept emphasizing Jesus Christ as the fully divine, fully human incarnation of God and long-awaited liberator of God's chosen people. The Christ event—death, burial, resurrection, ascension, and promised return—is central to the tenets of Christianity. According to the biblical narrative, Jesus Christ was rebuked for declaring himself the Son of God and daring to perform miracles. Jesus Christ eventually allowed himself to be judged and crucified on a cross for blasphemy. Fulfilling prophecy, on the third day Jesus Christ arose from the dead. He appeared to his disciples and soon thereafter ascended to heaven, but only after he promised to return for those who believe in him. Because of the common conflation of Jesus and Christ and because I am not making theological claims on behalf of the rappers, I do not distinguish between Jesus and Christ.

6. Michael Eric Dyson, *Open Mike: Reflections on Philosophy, Race, Sex, Culture and Religion* (New York: Basic *Civitas* Books, 2003), 286.

7. Lola Ogunnaike, "West World," *Rolling Stone*, February 9, 2006, 44.

8. Frederik Louring (Poster), "Kanye West Gets Emotional During Interview." http://youtu.be/Vdl4aCey1O0.

9. Evan Serpick, "Nas' 'Greatest Hits': A Track-by-Track Journey with the Pride of Queens," *Rolling Stone*, http://www.rollingstone.com/music/news/nas-greatest-hits-a-track-by-track-journey-with-the-pride-of-queens-20071106.

10. Michael Eric Dyson, *Holler If You Hear Me: Searching for Tupac Shakur* (New York: Basic *Civitas* Books, 2001), 263.

11. Ibid., 258.

Chapter 4

1. Bill Harris, "Robert Johnson: Trick the Devil," in *The National Black Drama Anthology*, ed. Woodie King Jr. (New York: Applause Books, 1995), 13.

2. Henry Louis Gates, *The Signifying Monkey: A Theory of Afro-American Literary Criticism* (New York: Oxford University Press, 1988), 5.

3. The Islamic Shaitan or Iblis from the Qur'an is similar to the Christian devil. Both emerge from dichotomous worldviews that pit God against Satan. Some enslaved Africans were Muslim, but this chapter focuses on how the Christian devil was integrated into African Diaspora trickster traditions.

4. T. J. Wray and Gregory Mobley, *The Birth of Satan: Tracing the Devil's Biblical Roots* (New York: Palgrave Macmillan, 2005), 58.

5. Chapter 3 interpreted the conflation of a bloody black Jesus and a white devil in one body as mimicking the white oppression of vulnerable black bodies.

6. Wray and Mobley, *The Birth of Satan*, 111.

7. Rap genius, "Jay-Z—Lucifer Lyrics and Meaning," http://rapgenius.com/24770.

8. Jay-Z clarifies that Lucifer is "never directly identified as the devil in the Bible, just a fallen angel. I don't believe in the devil myself, or at least not the guy with horns and a pitchfork. But I do believe we all have the potential for evil inside of us, which is very real." Jay-Z, *Decoded* (New York: Spiegel and Grau, 2010), 287.

9. Shake, "Ludacris: War of God Was about . . . ," *Hip Hop DX*, http://www.hiphopdx.com/index/news/id.4289/title.ludacris-war-of-god-was-about.

10. Samuel Butler, *The Note-books of Samuel Butler* (New York: Dutton, 1917), 217.

11. Wray and Mobley, *The Birth of Satan*, 69.

12. Snoop Dogg and David Seay, *The Doggfather: The Times, Trials, and Hardcore Truths of Snoop Dogg* (New York: Morrow, 1999), 201.

13. MTV Networks, "Kanye West: The 'Runaway' Interview," http://www.mtv.com/videos/movies/589705/why-this-film-why-now-why-this-album.jhtml #id=1650374.

14. For more on the decline of the middle class in the United States see Arianna Huffington, *Third World America: How Our Politicians Are Abandoning the Middle Class and Betraying the American Dream* (New York: Crown, 2010).

15. Joshua Gunn, personal communication, September 17, 2010.

16. Thomas Connor, "Getting to the Heart of Hip-Hop," *Chicago Sun-Times*, February 24, 2011, http://www.suntimes.com/entertainment/3392919-421/bambaataa-hip-hop-music-says.html.

17. Travis Gosa, personal communication, November 15, 2010.

Chapter 5

1. Kelly Brown Douglas, *What's Faith Got to Do with It?: Black Bodies/Christian Soul* (Maryknoll, NY: Orbis Books, 2005), 49.

2. bell hooks, *Feminist Theory: From Margin to Center* (Cambridge, MA: South End Press, 2000), 5.

3. Paulo Friere, *Pedagogy of the Oppressed* (New York: Herder and Herder, 1970), 55.

4. Douglas, *What's Faith Got to Do with It?*, 49.

5. Ice Cube references the Birmingham, Alabama, 16th Street Baptist Church that was bombed by white supremacists in 1963. The African American church was a central meeting place for the Civil Rights Movement. The explosion killed four young girls and injured many others.

6. Juan Floyd-Thomas, "The Evolution of African American Islam and Contemporary Hip-Hop," in *Noise and Spirit: The Religious and Spiritual Sensibilities of Rap Music*, ed. Anthony B. Pinn (New York: New York University Press, 2003), 60–61.

7. H. Samy Alim, *Roc The Mic Right: The Language of Hip Hop Culture* (New York: Routledge, 2006), 34.

8. Imani Perry, " 'It Ain't Hard to Tell': A Story of Lyrical Transcendence," in *Born to Use Mics: Reading Nas's Illmatic*, eds. Michael Eric Dyson and Sohail Daulatzai (New York: Basic *Civitas* Books, 2008), 195.

9. William David Spencer, *Dread Jesus* (London: Society for Promoting Christian Knowledge, 1999), 92.

10. Jeff Weiss, "A Reinvigorated Busta Rhymes Skirts Controversy, Talks New Album," *Los Angeles Times*, February 27, 2009, http://latimesblogs.latimes.com/music_blog/2009/02/a-re-invigorate.html.

11. Noel Leo Erskine, "Rap, Reggae, and Religion: Sounds of Cultural Dissonance," in *Noise and Spirit: The Religious and Spiritual Sensibilities of Rap Music*, ed. Anthony B. Pinn (New York: New York University Press, 2003), 78.

12. MTV Networks, "The Vice Guide to Based Music: Lil B," *The Vice Guide to Everything*, http://www.mtv.com/videos/?id=1655266.

13. Byron Hurt, *Beyond Beats and Rhymes*, DVD (God Bless the Child Productions, 2006).

Chapter 6

1. For more on habitus, see Pierre Bourdieu, *The Logic of Practice* (Stanford, CA: Stanford University Press, 1990). For more on religious habitus, see Appendix A: God Talks with Dr. Monica Miller.

2. Andrew Newberg and Mark Robert Waldman, *How God Changes Your Brain: Breakthrough Findings from a Leading Neuroscientist* (New York: Ballantine Books, 2009), 95.

3. Of course, my students represent a slightly biased subject pool because I am responsible for teaching them how to think critically about popular culture.

4. Paul Forese and Christopher Bader, *America's Four Gods: What We Say about God and What That Says about Us* (Oxford: Oxford University Press, 2010), 44.

5. Mark Lewis Taylor, "Bringing Noise, Conjuring Spirit: Rap as Spiritual Practice," in *Noise and Spirit: The Religious and Spiritual Sensibilities of Rap Music*, ed. Anthony B. Pinn (New York: New York University Press, 2003), 119.

6. Christopher Bader, Kevin Dougherty, Paul Forese, Byron Johnson, F. Carson Mencken, Jerry Z. Park, and Rodney Stark, *American Piety in the 21st Century: New Insights to the Depth and Complexity of Religion in the US: Select Findings from the Baylor Religion Survey* (Waco, TX: Baylor University Press, 2006), 4, 12.

7. Christian Smith with Melinda Lundquist Denton, *Soul Searching: The Religious and Spiritual Lives of American Teenagers* (Oxford: Oxford University Press, 2005), 41.

8. Forese and Bader, *America's Four Gods*, 42.

9. Bader et al., *American Piety in the 21st Century*, 9.

10. Gary Trust and Keith Caulfield, "Lil Wayne Scores 12 Simultaneous Singles on Hot 100," Billboard.biz, http://www.billboard.biz/bbbiz/industry/record-labels/lil-wayne-scores-11-simultaneous-singles-1005344112.story.

11. Bernard Chris Dorsey, personal communication, October 17, 2011.

Conclusion

1. Jay-Z, *Decoded* (New York: Spiegel and Grau, 2010), 276.

2. Ibid., 287.

3. Charlie Rose, "An Hour with Jay-Z from the Brooklyn Museum," http://www.charlierose.com/view/interview/11337.

4. Jay-Z, *Decoded*, 145.

5. Ibid., 56.

6. Ibid., 279.

Selected Bibliography

Alexander, Michelle. *The New Jim Crow: Mass Incarceration in the Age of Color-blindness*. New York: The New Press, 2010.

Alim, H. Samy. *Roc the Mic Right: The Language of Hip Hop Culture*. New York: Routledge, 2006.

Anderson, Elijah. *Code of the Street: Decency, Violence, and the Moral Life of the Inner City*. New York: Norton, 1999.

Bader, Christopher, Kevin Dougherty, Paul Forese, Byron Johnson, F. Carson Mencken, Jerry Z. Park, and Rodney Stark. *American Piety in the 21st Century: New Insights to the Depth and Complexity of Religion in the US: Select Findings from The Baylor Religion Survey*. Waco, TX: Baylor University Press, 2006.

Betha, Mason, and Karen Hunter. *Revelations: There's a Light after the Lime*. New York: Atria Books, 2001.

Bourdieu, Pierre. *The Logic of Practice*. Stanford, CA: Stanford University Press, 1990.

Connor, Thomas. "Getting to the Heart of Hip Hop." *Chicago Sun Times*, February 24, 2011.

Cuda, Heidi Siegmund. "Gods and Monsters." *Vibe*, October 2001.

Dogg, Snoop, and Davin Seay. *The Doggfather: The Times, Trials, and Hardcore Truths of Snoop Dogg*. New York: Morrow, 1999.

Douglas, Kelly Brown. *Sexuality and the Black Church: A Womanist Perspective*. Maryknoll, NY: Orbis Books, 1999.

Douglas, Kelly Brown. *What's Faith Got to Do with It?: Black Bodies/Christian Souls*. Maryknoll, NY: Orbis Books, 2005.

Dyson, Michael Eric. *Holler If You Hear Me: Searching for Tupac Shakur*. New York: Basic Civitas Books, 2001.

Dyson, Michael Eric. *Open Mike: Reflections on Philosophy, Race, Sex, Culture and Religion*. New York: Basic Civitas Books, 2003.

Ellison, Marvin M. *Erotic Justice: A Liberating Ethic of Sexuality*. Louisville, KY: Westminster John Knox Press, 1996.

Erlewine, Stephen Thomas. "Snoop Dogg." In *All Music Guide to Hip-Hop*, edited by V. Bogdanov, C. Woodstra, S. T. Erlewine, and J. Bush, 443–45. San Francisco: Backbeat Books, 2003.

Erskine, Noel Leo. "Rap, Reggae, and Religion: Sounds of Cultural Dissonance." In *Noise and Spirit: The Religious and Spiritual Sensibilities of Rap Music*, edited by Anthony B. Pinn, 71–84. New York: New York University Press, 2003.

Floyd-Thomas, Juan. "The Evolution of African American Islam and Contemporary Hip-Hop." In *Noise and Spirit: The Religious and Spiritual Sensibilities of Rap Music*, edited by Anthony B. Pinn, 49–70. New York: New York University Press, 2003.

Forese, Paul, and Christopher Bader. *America's Four Gods: What We Say about God and What That Says about Us*. Oxford: Oxford University Press, 2010.

Friere, Paulo. *Pedagogy of the Oppressed*. New York: Herder and Herder, 1970.

Gates, Henry Louis. *The Signifying Monkey: A Theory of Afro-American Literary Criticism*. New York: Oxford University Press, 1988.

Harris, Bill. "Robert Johnson: Trick the Devil." In *The National Black Drama Anthology*, edited by Woodie King Jr., 4–45. New York: Applause Books, 1995.

Haugen, Jason D. " 'Unladylike Divas': Language, Gender, and Female Gangsta Rappers." *Popular Music and Society* 26, no. 4 (2003): 429–44.

hooks, bell. *Feminist Theory: From Margin to Center*. Cambridge, MA: South End Press, 2000.

hooks, bell. *Reel to Real: Race, Sex, and Class at the Movies*. New York: Routledge, 1996.

Huffington, Arianna. *Third World America: How Our Politicians Are Abandoning the Middle Class and Betraying the American Dream*. New York: Crown, 2010.

Hurt, Byron. *Beyond Beats and Rhymes*. DVD. God Bless the Child Productions, 2006.

Jay-Z. *Decoded*. New York: Spiegel and Grau, 2010.

Marriott, Michel. "Death, Hip-Hop Turns to Dirges." *New York Times*, October 13, 1996.

Miller, Monica R., and Ezekiel J. Dixon-Roman. "Habits of the Heart: Youth Religious Participation as Progress, Peril, or Change?" *The Annals of the American Academy of Political and Social Science* 637, no. 78 (2011): 78–98.

Morgan, Joan. "They Call Me Ms. Hill." *Essence*, February 2006.

Newberg, Andrew, and Mark Robert Waldman. *How God Changes Your Brain: Breakthrough Findings from a Leading Neuroscientist*. New York: Ballantine Books, 2009.

Ogunnaike, Lola. "West World." *Rolling Stone*, February 9, 2006.

Perry, Imani. " 'It Ain't Hard to Tell': A Story of Lyrical Transcendence." In *Born to Use Mics: Reading Nas's Illmatic*, edited by Michael Eric Dyson and Sohail Daulatzai, 195–209. New York: Basic Civitas Books, 2008.

Pinderhughes, Elaine B. "African American Marriage in the 20th Century." *Family Process* 42, no. 2 (2002): 269–82.

Smith, Christian, with Melinda Lundquist Denton. *Soul Searching: The Religious and Spiritual Lives of American Teenagers.* Oxford: Oxford University Press, 2005.

Sorett, Josef. "Believe Me, This Pimp Game Is Very Religious: Toward a Religious History of Hip Hop." *Culture and Religion* 10, no. 1 (2009): 11–22.

Spencer, Jon Michael. "Philosophical Prolegomena to Theomusicological Thematizing of the Nonsacred." In *The Theology of American Popular Music*, 1–49. Durham, NC: Duke University Press, 1989.

Spencer, William David. *Dread Jesus.* London: Society for Promoting Christian Knowledge, 1999.

Taylor, Mark Lewis. "Bringing Noise, Conjuring Spirit: Rap as Spiritual Practice." In *Noise and Spirit: The Religious and Spiritual Sensibilities of Rap Music*, edited by Anthony B. Pinn, 107–30. New York: New York University Press, 2003.

West, Kanye. "Jesus Walks Trilogy: Making of the Video." In *The College Dropout Video Anthology*. DVD. Roc-A-Fella Records, 2005.

Wilson, William J. *When Work Disappears: The World of the New Urban Poor.* New York: Knopf, 1996.

Wolcott, Victoria W. *Remaking Respectability: African American Women in Interwar Detroit.* Chapel Hill: University of North Carolina Press, 2001.

Wray, T. J., and Gregory Mobley. *The Birth of Satan: Tracing the Devil's Biblical Roots.* New York: Palgrave Macmillan, 2005.

Young, Monifa. "High on the Hill." *Essence,* June 1998.

Selected Discography

50 Cent. "Many Men." *Get Rich or Die Tryin'*. Shady/Aftermath/Interscope Records, 2003.

Arrested Development. "Tennessee." *3 Years, 5 Months, and 2 Days in the Life Of . . .* Chrysalis, 1992.

Big Punisher. "Boomerang." *Capital Punishment*. Loud Records, 1998.

Bone Thugs-N-Harmony. "Tha Crossroads." *E 1999 Eternal*. Ruthless, 1995.

Brand Nubian. "Ain't No Mystery." *In God We Trust*. Elektra Entertainment, 1993.

Busta Rhymes. "Arab Money Remix Part 1." *Back on My B.S.* Universal Motown, 2009.

Busta Rhymes. "Make it Clap." *It Ain't Safe No More*. J Records, 2002.

Common. "Faithful." *Be*. Geffen Records, 2005.

Common featuring Cee Lo. "G.O.D. (Gaining One's Definition)." *One Day It'll All Make Sense*. Relativity Records, 1997.

The Coup. "Me and Jesus the Pimp in a '79 Granada Last Night." *Steal This Album*. Dogday Records, 1998.

Diddy, Dirty Money. "Angels." *Last Train to Paris*. Bad Boy/Interscope Records, 2010.

DMX. "Angel." *. . . And Then There Was X*. UMG Records, 1999.

DMX. "Ready to Meet Him." *Flesh of My Flesh, Blood of My Blood*. RAL/Def Jam Records, 1998.

DMX. "The Convo." *It's Dark and Hell Is Hot*. Rush Associated Labels, 1998.

DMX. "The Omen." *Flesh of My Flesh, Blood of My Blood*. Def Jam Records, 1998.

DMX. "The Prayer VI." *Year of the Dog . . . Again*. Sony BMG Music Entertainment, 2006.

E-40. "Things'll Never Change." *Tha Hall of Game*. Jive Records, 1996.

Eminem. "Cleanin' Out My Closet." *The Eminem Show*. Aftermath/Shady/Interscope Records, 2002.

Eminem. "My Darling." *Relapse: Refill*. Aftermath/Shady/Interscope Records, 2009.

Eve. "Be Me." *Scorpion*. Interscope Records, 2001

Eve. "Life Is So Hard." *Scorpion*. Interscope Records, 2001.

Fabolous. "Not Give a Fuck." *Street Dreams*. Elektra Entertainment, 2003.

Foxy Brown. "Broken Silence." *Broken Silence*. UMG Records, 2001.

The Game. "The Documentary." *The Documentary*. Aftermath/G Unit/ Interscope Records, 2005.

Geto Boys. "Mind Playing Tricks on Me." *We Can't Be Stopped*. Rap-A-Lot Records, 1991.

Ghostface Killah. "Wildflower." *Ironman*. Sony Music Entertainment, 1996.

Ice Cube. "Cave Bitch." *Lethal Injection*. Priority Records, 1993.

Ice Cube. "The Nigga Trap." *Laugh Now Cry Later*. Lench Mob Records, 2006.

Ice Cube. "When I Get to Heaven." *Lethal Injection*. Priority Records, 1993.

Immortal Technique. "Creation and Destruction." *Revolutionary, Vol. 1*. Viper Records, 2001.

Immortal Technique. "Dance with the Devil." *Revolutionary, Vol. 1*. Viper Records, 2001.

J. Cole. "Dead Presidents." *The Warm Up*. Roc Nation, 2009.

J. Cole featuring Omen. "Enchanted." *Friday Night Lights*. Roc Nation, 2010.

Ja Rule. "Father Forgive Me." *The Mirror*. Motown Records, 2007.

Ja Rule. "One of Us." *Rule 3:36*. Def Jam Records, 2000.

Jay-Z. "Breathe Easy (Lyrical Exercise)." *The Blueprint*. Roc-A-Fella Records, 2001.

Jay-Z. "D'Evils." *Reasonable Doubt*. Roc-A-Fella Records, 1996

Jay-Z. "Empire State of Mind." *The Blueprint 3*. Roc Nation, 2009.

Jay-Z. "Lucifer." *The Black Album*. Roc-A-Fella Records, 2003

Jay-Z. "Pray." *American Gangster*. Roc-A-Fella Records, 2007.

Jay-Z. "Public Service Announcement." *The Black Album*. Roc-A-Fella Records, 2003.

Jay-Z. "U Don't Know." *The Blueprint*. Roc-A-Fella Records, 2001.

Jean Grae. "Take Me." *The Bootleg of the Bootleg EP*. Babygrande Records, 2003.

Jeru the Damaja. "Ya Playn' Yourself." *Wrath of the Math*. UMG Records, 1996.

Joe Budden. "Blood on the Wall." *Padded Room*. Amalgam Digital, 2009.

Joe Budden. "Pray for Me." *Padded Room*. Amalgam Digital, 2009.

Joe Budden. "Ventilation." *Mood Muzik 3: We Got The Remix*. Amalgam Digital, 2008.

Kanye West. "Devil in a New Dress." *My Beautiful Dark Twisted Fantasy*. Roc-A-Fella Records, 2010.

Kanye West. "Diamonds from Sierra Leone." *Late Registration*. Roca-A-Fella Records, 2005.

Kanye West. "Jesus Walks." *The College Dropout*. Roc-A-Fella Records, 2004.

Khia. "When I Meet My King." *Thug Misses*. Indieblu Music, 2002.

The Lady of Rage. "Confessions." *Necessary Roughness*. Death Row Records, 1997.

The Lady of Rage. "Get with Da Wikedness (Flow Like That Remix)." *Necessary Roughness*. Death Row Records, 1997.

The Lady of Rage. "Some Shit." *Necessary Roughness*. Death Row Records, 1997.

Lauryn Hill featuring Mary J. Blige. "I Used to Love Him." *The Miseducation of Lauryn Hill*. Ruffhouse Records, 1998.

Lil B. "I'm God." *6 Kiss*. Permanent Marks, 2009.

Lil' Kim. "Heavenly Father." *La Bella Mafia*. Atlantic Records, 2003.

Lil' Kim. "Single Black Female." *The Notorious Kim*. Undeas Records, 2000.

Lil Wayne. "On Fire." *Rebirth*. Cash Money Records, 2010.

Ludacris. "War with God." *Release Therapy*. DTP Records, 2006.

Lupe Fiasco. "Pressure." *Lupe Fiasco's Food & Liquor*. Atlantic Records, 2006.

Mase. "24 Hours to Live." *Harlem World*. Bad Boy Records, 1997.

MC Hammer. "Pray." *Please Hammer, Don't Hurt 'Em*. Capital Records, 1990.

Monie Love. "Mo Monie." *In a Word or 2*. Warner Brothers Entertainment, 1993.

Nas. "God Love Us." *Nastradamus*. Sony Music Entertainment, 1999.

Nas. "Got U'r Self A . . ." *Stillmatic*. Sony Music Entertainment, 2001.

Nas. "Halftime." *Illmatic*. Sony Music Entertainment, 1994.

Nas. "Hate Me Now." *I Am . . . The Autobiography*. Columbia, 1999.

Nas. "The Makings of a Perfect Bitch." *Street's Disciple*. Sony BMG Music Entertainment, 2004.

Nicki Minaj. "Can Anybody Hear Me?" *Beam Me Up Scotty*. Young Money Entertainment, 2009.

Notorious B.I.G. "Hypnotize." *Life after Death*. Bad Boy Records, 1997.

Notorious B.I.G. featuring Jay-Z. "I Love the Dough." *Life after Death*. Bad Boy Records, 1997.

Outkast. "God (Interlude)." *Speakerboxxx/The Love Below*. Arista Records, 2003.

Puff Daddy & the Family. "Victory." *No Way Out*. Bad Boy Records, 1997.

Queen Latifah. "I Can't Understand." *Black Reign*. UMG Records, 1993.

Queen Latifah. "Wrath of My Madness." *All Hail the Queen*. Tommy Boy/ Warner Bros. Records, 1989.

Rah Digga. "Tight." *Dirty Harriet*. Elektra Entertainment, 2000.

Rakim. "Mystery (Who Is God?)." *The 18th Letter*. Universal Records, 1997.

Ras Kass. "Interview with a Vampire." *Rassassination*. Priority Records, 1998.

Rick Ross featuring Jay-Z. "Free Mason." *Teflon Don*. The Island Def Jam Music, 2010.

Remy Ma. "Shesus Khryst." *Shesus Khryst*. Draft Records, 2007.

The Roots. "Dear God 2.0." *How I Got Over*. The Island Def Jam Music, 2010.

Salt 'n' Pepa. "Do Me Right." *Brand New*. Polygram Records, 1997.

Snoop Dogg. "Murder Was the Case." *Murder Was the Case*. Death Row Records, 1994.

Tech N9ne. "She-Devil." *Absolute Power*. Strange Music/ MSC Entertainment, 2002.

T.I. "Live in the Sky." *King*. Grand Hustle/Atlantic Records, 2006.

T.I. "Prayin' for Help." *Urban Legend*. Atlantic Records, 2004.

T.I. "What Happened?" *I'm Serious*. Arista Records, 2001.

Tiye Phoenix. "Bless Me." *Half Woman Half Amazin'*. Babygrande, 2009.

Tiye Phoenix. "Half Woman Half Amazin'." *Half Woman Half Amazin'*. Babygrande Records, 2009.

Tiye Phoenix. "Killin' Everybody." *Half Woman Half Amazin'*. Babygrande Records, 2009.

A Tribe Called Quest. "8 Million Stories." *Midnight Marauders*. Jive Records, 1993.

Tupac Shakur. "Blasphemy." *The Don Killuminati: The 7 Day Theory*. Death Row Records, 1996.

Tupac Shakur. "Fuck the World." *Me against the World*. Jive Records, 1995.

Tupac Shakur. "Hail Mary." *The Don Killuminati: The 7 Day Theory*. Death Row Records, 1996.

Tupac Shakur. "Letter 2 My Unborn." *Until the End of Time*. Amaru Entertainment, 2001.

Tupac Shakur. "Nothing to Lose." *R U Still Down? Remember Me*. Amaru Entertainment, 1997.

Tupac Shakur, Outlawz. "Black Jesuz." *Still I Rise*. Interscope Records, 1999.

Usher featuring Jay-Z. "Hot Tottie." *Raymond v Raymond (Deluxe Edition)*. LaFace Records, 2010.

Wu-Tang Clan. "Sunlight." *8 Diagrams*. Motown/Universal, 2007.

Young Money. "Every Girl in the World." *We Are Young Money*. Cash Money Records, 2009.

Index

About the Author

EBONY A. UTLEY, PhD, is an expert in popular culture, race, and romantic relationships. Dr. Utley's research explores the tension between power and pleasure in popular culture, examines how Americans talk about race and racism, asks probing questions about marriage and infidelity, analyzes hip hop's manifestations of love, and explains the similarities between rap and religion. In addition to radio, print, and online appearances, Dr. Utley lectures at universities across the country and is an assistant professor of communication studies at California State University, Long Beach. She resides on the web at theutleyexperience.com.